Brenda MacDonald is a new author. She is a wife, mother and grandmother. She is also a business partner in their family business. Brenda has lived in the Edmonton area and on Vancouver Island. She has been married for over fifty years. Over those years, Brenda has endured tragedy and illness and has remained a survivor. She is committed to living a life of happiness, and contentment. Her autobiography is truly inspiring and is a good read.

I dedicate this book to my eternal loves in life:

My husband, ANGUS

My son, IAN

My granddaughter, QUINN

Brenda MacDonald

My Rhythm in Life with Hic-Cups

Sandi
Warm Wishes
Brenda
July 17/22

AUSTIN MACAULEY PUBLISHERS™

LONDON • CAMBRIDGE • NEW YORK • SHARJAH

Ordering Information:
Quantity sales: special discounts are available on quantity purchases by corporations, associations, and others. For details, contact the publisher at the address below.

Publisher's Cataloging-in-Publication data
MacDonald, Brenda
My Rhythm in Life with Hic-Cups

ISBN 9781645753346 (Paperback)
ISBN 9781645753353 (Hardback)
ISBN 9781645753360 (ePub e-book)

Library of Congress Control Number: 2020914385

www.austinmacauley.com/us

First Published (2020)
Austin Macauley Publishers LLC
40 Wall Street, 28th Floor
New York, NY 10005
USA

mail-usa@austinmacauley.com
+1 (646) 5125767

Writing my autobiography was a pleasure for me. I truly enjoyed the process and because it's done in chronological order for the most part, I had the opportunity to grow again and relive my life, with appreciation. Having said that, I guess I'm sending myself a thank you for sticking to my commitment and seeing it through to the end.

I would also like to thank Angus for his undying support and his proof reading of my every word. He has known me fifty-four years of my seventy, so we had a lot of fun reliving events, some tears too.

A huge thank you goes out to my friend, Dianne Zushman, for her encouragement and her willingness to read my book, ten pages at a time.

My sisters-in-law, Marion and Maggie, who enjoyed our reading sessions together, a heartfelt thank you for listening and encouraging me along the way. Also, I would like to thank the family and friends who have read snippets of the book so far and for their encouraging feedback.

A special thank you and appreciation to Susan Luchanski for her commitment to reading the book and for answering my two-page questionnaire, where she answered some pretty tough questions and those answers gave me a good idea of where my book would take me.

Every single person mentioned in my life's story has shaped me into who I am today. Those people from my past and the people in my present will always remain in my memories with sincere appreciation and love.

Author's Note

The 'Eternal Rhythm of Life' symbol is hundreds of years old. It can mean many things. Mother, father, son. Past, present, future. Earth, wind, fire. One definition says it stands for a goddess in her forms; maiden, mother, crone. To me it means what it says, eternal rhythm of life and we are all very much included in that rhythm.

If after reading my autobiography, you find an error in something I have written or in a date of when it occurred, please consider this as purely accidental.

Introduction

I wanted you to read these few pages before you begin my autobiography, so you can get to know me. I have wanted to write about my life for a long time now. It's mine to share and every part has been told in truth, to the best of my knowledge and includes some of my most memorable moments.

I really feel that everyone has a few stories to tell. I am suggesting that 'you' write your stories down, start now, don't wait, because time goes by all too quickly and before you know it, you will be gone forever, and there will be nobody 'Who Will Care' who you were, how you lived, what events took place in your world, and how those events shaped you. If we don't document our stories in some way, for family and others in our life, then how are we, as a society, ever going to improve? Pick up the good stuff and learn from the bad stuff. Make your own legacy; start collecting your thoughts on how you can touch others, with the surprisingly never dull person that you have become. Bind them and pass them on! Why not?

Thinking of myself isn't really how I evolved. We were taught to always think of others first and I have done that very thing. Not boasting, it's the truth. There were so many others in my early life, which you will read about, that there was no time to give any thought to one's self. I still consider others first, for an example, on my birthday, I'll ask Angus, my husband, and Ian, our son, "Where would you guys like to have dinner?" Really! Which makes me think, would you call that considering others first *or* just being considerate of others? Anyway, you put it, that's me.

I know there are thousands of people, who have been through tons more than I. My family looks out for me, I really don't want for anything, although I've never been one to pamper myself because I don't feel the need. I'm loved by my family, liked by my friends, and even smiled at by strangers passing by, so what else does one really need? I'm content.

I have read that writing your autobiography can be difficult, *no*, on the contrary for me. I've gained a special bond with myself. I'm happy to be involved with this creation; it's kind of a strange feeling to be thinking of myself. I'm also pleased that you have decided to read about my life and hope you gain something from the experiences I have shared.

I'm an everyday person, one that you rub shoulders with while shopping or sitting in the waiting room at the doctor's office. I'm very sentimental, which means I have an emotional attitude, one that is influenced by feelings and that I'm affected by emotion. I've never thought of that, but it's so true. In my younger years, when my Nanny would come to visit, I would cry, when she left the room and she was only going to the bathroom—funny! My family would always say, "Don't tell Brenda, she'll cry!" It's true; it sure doesn't take much to get the tears flowing.

I always greet family and friends with a hug, that's my way. I can't stay too long picking out a greeting card for an occasion because I start welling up and get that 'emotional attitude.' I, sometimes, get overwhelmed while grocery shopping, especially when I'm by myself. I feel very fortunate in life and the feelings just come. I'm also very bad with the news. I can't even tell you how many times I've literally come to tears, watching and listening about other people's misfortunes in life. My husband is so used to it that he just waits until it passes and then we carry on. I'm not a pushover either, I'm not defeated easily and I'm very strong in thought, not easily influenced or convinced. I need some time to process what's being said or done. I have personal standards to I live by, I do believe in treating people the way I like to be treated. An example of how I think; like for some 37-40 years, when I made our lunches for work, I would be standing at the kitchen counter and I'd be thinking of how many other women were doing the exact same thing as I was—not particularly liking it—but doing it because they loved their families, too! Somehow, that thought process made the job easier for me. I don't care if my husband, son, or my granddaughter controls the TV remote, I only care that I'm with them, it really doesn't matter to me, that's how I think.

I love to play golf every chance I get. I'm not good, broke a hundred a couple of times, but I love being out there, it's the safest, most peaceful place to be. The eye candy is awesome and the people you meet are usually pretty damn nice. I'm from a camping family and love it, too, although many would say a motor-home is not camping, but my sleeping, in a tent, on an air mattress that leaks during the night, sorry, those days are gone! I love to read, almost anything that is interesting, of course, accompanied with a cup of tea, lovely! I really enjoy having family and friends over for a meal; it gives me a chance to make something new and to catch up. You will find out many more 'things' about me as you read your way through this book. I hope the stories will find you glued to the pages, so you won't want to put it down. I hope you like me for who I am. I hope you are truly inspired by my simple, hopefully, uncomplicated way of explaining my life, as it has unfolded. I also hope that you, too, will share your life with all of us one day! Please, enjoy!

Chapter One: The Early Years, 1949-1960

It's very important to me that you know where, when, and how I evolved. We and I mean baby boomers, growing up in the 50s and 60s had it the best of all others and I'll tell you why. My family lived in a 'war-time' house neighborhood. All of the families had Dad's and/or Mom's that served in the Second World War. These neighborhoods were very similar in design, usually with two elementary schools, pretty much in the center, complete with parks that had swings, slides, a wading pool, sand box, and a shack that held all the necessities for crafting. A Junior High school and or a High school were usually within walking distance, no school buses required. The communities were constructed for the servicemen and their families, after returning from the war. I'm pretty sure I read that about a million of these houses were constructed overall. I do believe there were requirements to applying for and being accepted for a house. You had to have been enlisted, married, and have, at least, two children.

Well, my parents were married on April 26 of 1943, while my Dad was still in the Canadian Navy. They lost their premature first born, a girl they named Karen, at a few days old in 1945. Then, in 1946 and again in 1947, they adopted two girls. Now, they qualified for a wartime house. I was born in February of 1949, so I was two and a bit, when they finally got possession in l951. Mom had one more daughter in 1952 and that was it, four girls.

The neighborhood was new, there weren't any sidewalks yet, and there was mud everywhere. I was told that my Dad carried us kids, one at a time, from the corner, a block away through the clay gumbo to the house. Funny thing is, everybody else was doing the same thing. There were about twenty houses to a block and at least, two kids to every house, but then again, we had four, our neighbors, on one side, had four and on the other side of us, they also had four, so in three houses, there were twelve kids. I'm sure there were, at least, fifty kids to a block and, now, times that by some two hundred houses in a district, that's a lot of kids.

All of us kids had a great time, in every season, too! There was always someone to play with; the ease of life and freedom was there for our enjoyment. We walked to and from school with our friends, we played outside until dark, there were unspoken rules you lived by. You listened and behaved properly. We had fun; we jumped rope, double-dutch, played marbles, especially, in the spring of the year. We were allowed to walk to the corner store where we would spend our allowances, usually on Saturdays. We played outside a lot; even in the winter, we skated and played around the rink with other kids.

The toy industry must have been booming where we were, because we had so much to keep us busy. There were yoyos, with which, we tried to do tricks like 'walk the dog,' 'around the world,' 'rock the baby.' My eldest sister, Vivian, was really good at doing tricks, but not me. I just couldn't get the yoyo to co-operate. We could see the baseball diamond from our front yard, so when we saw four or five kids gathering, gloves in hand, we headed over there, with our stuff. My Dad worked for the school board as a caretaker and he would 'borrow' a few items from the school, like balls, bats, and lost and found gloves, stuff like that. The scrub game was on. Then, there were roller skates, we didn't have any, but if you asked nicely from someone you knew, they would lend you theirs. Man, you had to guard the key with your life, because the key is what adjusted the size of the skate to your foot. I'm talking fifties now, but later on, in the early to mid-sixties, the gals serving at the A&W's back then, wore roller skates—great times.

The park, across the street, was always a hum. In the summer, there were young adults, usually two, that were employed by the City for the months of July and August. When you saw the shack door open, you knew they were getting things ready. A schedule was set up and posted to the door. There were a variety of activities to participate in. There was lots of coloring and crafting for kids, from let's say four to nine years old. All the supplies were put in the center of the table and you created from there. I remember the young girls at our park were really nice, helpful, and were good with all of us. To open our park for the summer, we had a parade. My Mom came up with the idea of me being a bride and a friend of mine, Susan Martin, her younger brother, Stan, could be the groom. I wore a flower girl dress, my sister had, from a wedding she was in, complete with a veil, who knows where that came from. Stan showed up with his tricycle and wearing a suit. Yes, a suit... What a scream we were. Mom tied some tin cans trailing behind the bike, I stood on the back and a cardboard sign was mounted on the front that read, you guessed it, 'Just Married!' Such fun, so innocent, so carefree, it's really nice to remember events like that. My Dad made us kids a pair of stilts, we had fun with those things, and my Mom was pretty good, too! Usually in the cool of the evening, we played games like 'Anti-Anti-I-Over,' where you would throw a ball from one side of the house up and over the roof of the house and the person on the other side would try to catch it, and then yell, "Anti-Anti-I-Over," on the return throw. We played that until Dad had enough of the pounding on the roof and it was 'suggested' that we go play something else. Then, there was Simon Says, Red Light, and, of course, Hide and Seek. Always energized by life, keeping busy, feeling safe, being looked after, and cared for. How fortunate we all were back then.

When it was time to come in, Mom would stand on the front porch and sing our names in unison and in order of age, too, as loud as she could, failing that, she would blink the porch light on and off several times, to get our attention, "Wow, what a hoot as I think of it now." There were, at least, twenty other mothers doing the same thing, too funny!

On rainy days, and we didn't them very often, we were kept just as busy inside. There were board games like Parcheesi, Chinese Checkers, Snakes and Ladders, and Jacks, they were all fun. Mom would wax the living room hardwood floor and tell us to go get our pillows. We would run and jump on the pillow, sliding across the floor and polishing it at the same time. The pillowcases went in the wash and Mom had a shiny floor.

Bath night, usually on Sunday's, started after supper dishes were done. There was no lollygagging around and there were usually two others in the tub with you, too! Mom would come in and wash our hair; she had this flexible plastic circle about twelve inches round and four inches wide, with a hole in the center. I think she got it from the Fuller Brush man. You slip your head through the hole, lie back in the tub, then your face and eyes were protected from the soap getting in. If 'no more tears' was around, we didn't have it! If we had mosquito bites, she would dry us off really good, then dab them with pink calamine lotion, using a cotton ball. You stood there bare ass naked waiting for the lotion to dry, then on went your PJs, a quick brush of the hair, and teeth, then out the bathroom you went, with instructions, "Go say goodnight to your Dad," so we did and off to bed, we went.

One of the earliest recollections I have, as a child, is standing in the back yard at the war-time house and seeing three baby buggies lined up along one side of the house. One in front of the other, complete with mosquito nets, tucked in place, and sheltered from the early morning sun. The babies had already been fed, bathed, and were sound asleep, completely unaware of who had put them there. I was five years old and on my way to school, across the street. As I stood there, waiting for my Mom to tell me when it was time to leave, I wasn't thinking of how caring and efficient my Mom was, I just knew *she* was the one who had put them there.

The babies had come to Mom and Dad from birth, as orphans. They didn't have a mother or father, nobody to care for them, except for good folks, like my parents. They became foster parents for the Province of Alberta. At first, they took in newborns and kept them, until they were adopted into families of their own. Once I remember, we had a little boy by the name of Leslie and my Dad fell in love with him. They tried to adopt him but it wasn't allowed, because my parents were not catholic and the boy was. Leslie was adapted out to an American couple. I know my Dad missed Leslie very much. As the years went by, they had a lot of children that came to stay, some stayed a week, some longer, and some that were placed with us were physically or mentally handicapped, so they were the ones that out lasted all the others. We had some pretty funny 'things' that happened over the years.

Like one day, coming home from school at lunchtime and seeing a little girl about eight years old, my age at the time. We were introduced her name was Lyn Newman. She was very quiet and seemed shy. My Dad was home, too, as he had a gastric stomach at the time and it was suggested that he eat his evening meal mid-day. So, we all sat down, Mom proceeded to dish out chicken stew, and after Lyn finished her first plate, Mom asked, "Would you like some more?" "Yes," is all she said, so Mom filled the plate again and was thinking to herself, *The poor thing must be really hungry*, when, all of a sudden, Lyn threw up with such a force, it flew across the table top and landed on my Dad's plate! Not funny! My Dad was disgusted, the kids were in shock and Lyn, being mentally handicapped, didn't know when her tummy was full. That little girl, who was not expected to even communicate, fooled everyone and learned to be a productive member of society. She stayed in our family home for over twenty years.

That same little girl ate twenty-four frozen butter tarts that my Mom had made for Christmas, one year. Surprising, but she never got sick, all my Mom found were the crumbs in the bottom of the freezer! Now, that's funny!

I was very fortunate to have lived in the same neighborhood, from the time my Dad carried me into the house at two years old, until I left on the day I was married at nineteen and seven months. In Edmonton, Alberta, Canada, we all experienced a sense of community and there were a lot of city events that went on annually and all of us looked forward to them. From the Santa Claus parade in November to the Kiwanis Apple Day the following October, there was always something going on. We had the Edmonton Exhibition in July and we all got free entrance tickets that were handed out on the last day of the school year. We would walk the mile to get there and were given specific instructions on what was expected of us, like stay together, wait for one another, the oldest person in the group was in charge of the money. We would spend all day there; enjoying the rides and candy apples. We didn't go to the sideshows, there was the hairy lady, the man who swallowed a sword, the fattest person alive, the smallest people on the planet, and, of course, the lady, whose body was completely covered with tattoos.

We had five and dime stores downtown, one was the Metropolitan and the other store was Kresge's. We got a dollar each, back then, to buy Christmas presents. I remember buying my Nanny, my Mom's Mom a few bottles of colored toilet water. They were small, about two inches high, they were glass, in the shape of a teddy bear, a dog or cat, an elephant and the liquid was colored red, blue, green or yellow, each sold for ten cents. We would go on the bus in pairs or more and save a nickel for a bag of popcorn from the 'Nut House,' which was a store that was right where we caught the bus to go home. Such fun!

Before we had a refrigerator, I don't remember this but as the story goes, we had an iceman, who delivered ice once a week. The ice was cut from the North Saskatchewan River that separated the north side of the city from the south side. It was stored somewhere around the city. Our iceman had come this one time and the ice slipped off his shoulder somehow and hit the wall beside the ice box, fridge. When my Dad got home, Mom explained what had happened and that we had to fix the wall. Well, my Dad walked up to the ice-box and just slid it over to cover the hole in the wall, fixed! We all had a good laugh about that one, over the years.

We had a bread man, too, who came a couple times a week. Usually, all the goodies were gone by the time he got to our house but, once in a while, we had a package of donuts. Our milkman was Old Roy; he drove a covered wagon, pulled by a horse. The reins came through a hole in the front panel and most of the time Roy would stand up and pull on the reins for the horse to stop. He would step out with a six- pack of milk in a metal slotted carrier with a handle. He would collect the empties that held the proper amount of money, already placed inside the bottles, from the front porch and replace with full ones. If he had enough milk to carry on to the next house, he would signal the horse with a whistle and the horse would move forward and stop directly in front of the neighbor's house and wait for him. I can't remember when the horse wagon was pulled off the milk run, but we missed it.

My Mom was an awesome person, really, I know we all are, but she was one in a million. By the time I was in grade four or five, we had us four girls and there were usually five others that were Wards of the Government that lived with us. So, she had nine kids to feed every day and I never once heard her complain. We helped when we were old enough to do dishes, sweep the floors, and make our own beds. She always did the cooking, cleaning, and laundry. My Dad helped, he would bring home this green crystal cleaner, that really stunk, and he would scrub all the floors, from time to time. With nine kids and two adults, there was a birthday every month. Mom would always make a cake and put nickels, dimes, and just one quarter in between the layers. That quarter was for the birthday person; of course, she would mark the spot beforehand, surprise! On our birthdays, we were always asked what we would like for supper. My favorite was mock duck, which isn't a duck at all, it's a flattened out round steak that is stuffed with dressing, rolled and tied, then baked in the oven, and you slice it like a jellyroll. For dessert, I always asked for Boston cream pie, and it's not a pie, it's actually a cake with vanilla pudding in the center and has a thin chocolate icing, yum! It's kind of funny that I have never made that meal for myself and I've been cooking for almost fifty years. Some things are just too special in your mind to actually want to repeat.

Then, there were those special days, during the year, like the Christmas season. We had presents on top of presents; the living room ceiling was decorated with red and green twisted crape paper that was strung from one corner diagonally to the other corner, which made an X. In the center, a bunch of white sparkly bells hung with red ribbons. Of course, there was a tree, decorated to the nines. We had some awesome decorations, like bubble lights, they were great. Mom got out her special candy dishes and we had homemade shortbread, butter, and mincemeat tarts. Our Christmas day was awesome, too. We always waited for my Nanny and Grandpa Foley to arrive at 9:00 am to 'unfold the tree,' as we called it. We all had to be up, bed made, dressed, have breakfast, and be sitting in the living room, waiting for them to arrive. Dad would be the one to hand out the presents. There were so many of us, we were seated all over the floor. As the day progressed, my Aunts, Uncles, and cousins would arrive, the turkey smelling up the house. Good times, good memories to hold onto and pass along.

Mom made pink cake with pink icing and put those red cinnamon hearts dotted all over for Valentine's Day. We all got a package of valentine cards to give out to our friends at school. The night before, we would sit at the kitchen table and fill them out. Mom would help us to spell their names correctly and we would each have a pile ready to go in the morning.

Sometime in March, we had a day called Pancake Tuesday. Mom made pancakes for us, for all three meals that day. We loved it; it was special and something different.

I remember one Easter. Mom took us on the bus downtown to meet my Nanny. She bought each of us an outfit to wear on Easter Sunday. My dress was pink with sparkly gold stripes, white socks, and shiny black shoes with a pink hat. That outing was very special to all of us, and a very nice thing for my Nanny to do.

On Easter Sunday morning, the kitchen table was, as if by magic, covered with Easter baskets, one for each of us. We didn't have an Easter egg hunt, because the snow was still on the ground. I think there might have been a few candies to find in the living room. We always, always got new toys at Easter, too! Double-Dutch, skipping ropes, and Indian rubber balls to play seven up or one, two, three, alary. You bounced the ball continuously on the sidewalk and counted 1, 2, 3, alary, 4, 5, 6, alary, 7, 8, 9, alary, 10 alary, catch me. When you said alary, you would bring your leg up and over the ball. We also got marbles, new chalk to play hopscotch and jacks. We had one person skipping ropes, too. We played a singing game, as you were skipping on the spot, you would call out…salt, vinegar, mustard, pepper and on pepper, you would get that rope going around and around very fast, once you missed and got tripped up, you lost your turn, and gave the rope to the next person.

It was fun to get the toys at Easter; they set you up for all kinds of outdoor fun. Hula Hoops, we had fun with and usually had competitions to see how many times we could keep it twirling around our waists. We had sidewalk races and while you ran, you would avoid the cracks that separated the concrete slabs, which were about two feet square, all the time yelling, "Step on a crack, you break your mother's back." Really, what fun we had, running, jumping, and playing, without a care in the world.

On Canada Day, July 1st, we got a few fireworks. They were okay but because they were dangerous, it was always the eldest who got to light them with supervision, of course. One year, disaster struck the City and a baby was killed with a firecracker thrown into the stroller that was parked outside a convenience store. The Mom went into the store to pick up a few things and when she came out, the buggy was on fire, and the baby could not be saved. That was it, the City put a ban on them and we never had them again. The Canada Day long weekend marked the end of the school year and summer holidays began. Yahoo!

Some years, we had a vegetable garden in the back yard, we also had alyssums planted on each side of the sidewalk, alternating white with purple, they smelled so good. My Dad had a special garden spot, about a foot wide and ran the length of the garage. He only planted radishes. He would come home from work and grab a bunch, wash them with the hose outside, and eat them with salt. We would do the same with carrots, but, sometimes, we would just rub them on the grass, good enough. Every yard had a rhubarb plant; we would sit on the back porch with a glass of sugar and dip the freshly picked rhubarb in and eat away.

During the summer months, we were always up to stuff and kept busy all the time. We spent time at 'the lake,' which was Alberta Beach on Lac Ste. Anne Lake, more about this later.

In September, we headed back to school, which was exciting and meant we all had to get back into a schedule of eating on time, going to bed on time, and, generally, finding the rhythm we had before summer break. October was gathering fall leaves, for school reports, down by the river and, of course, Halloween. We had Halloween parties at school where you dressed up and took a special treat our Mom had made. My Mom never trusted masks, she said they were either too loose or too tight, so she would heat a cork on the gas stove and, one by one, we would line up and get our faces painted black. That way our hands were free and we didn't have to fiddle around with the mask, as we ran from house to house hollering, "Halloween apples." A traditional supper of hot dogs and homemade French fries started soon after we got home from school. We were allowed to head out just before dark, about four thirty. Pillowcases were used back then, because you could get more in them. When we returned home, all the goodies were spilled onto a sheet in the living room, and everything was divided into groups and stored in ice cream buckets. Not everybody went out, because they were either too young or too physically or mentally handicapped, but that had nothing to do with sharing, everybody got the same. I'm sure we were eating Halloween candy coming close to Christmas time.

In the cool of October, the City had a Kiwanis Apple Day downtown and there were clowns all dressed up and carrying wooden baskets of fresh B.C. apples, which were sold on the street corners for donation prices. We got a nickel and our bus fare, to go. It was fun, cool, and crisp; you knew winter wasn't far off. The anticipation of the Santa Claus parade was very exciting and it seemed November, to me, was the longest month of the year. The snow and cold came all too soon for the adults, but for us kids, it meant new things to do. There was skating, playing around the rink, which lucky for us, was right across the street. We went tobogganing down by the river and had so much fun, returning home, somewhat frozen and ready for something to eat. Keep in mind that our Mom and most other Mom's did not drive in those days. If you couldn't get to what you wanted to participate in, either by walking or taking the bus, you couldn't go, simple as that.

So, Christmas came again and our family was settled into a kind of harmonious state. My family will laugh at that, because there wasn't anything harmonious about our family. My meaning is; like there were events and happenings that took place, around the same times every month of every year, and it seemed to me, nobody tired of them.

Elementary school, grades one through six, were filled to the brim with activity. Montrose Elementary was a Protestant school that I attended from 1954-1960. There was also a Catholic school, St. Clare's that was two blocks away. There was a mix of kids that I played with, my protestant friends at school and my catholic friends away from school. It sounds kind of religious, but that's the way it was for us kids, it didn't mean anything, other than we went to different schools and they went to church on Sundays. We all got along, played together, the parents had no problems that I ever heard about, no conflicts.

I did okay at school, my efforts were always good enough to pass on to the next grade. I liked math the best, except problem solving, didn't do well at that. We had a good time at school, we paid attention, when we were supposed to, and had fun in the schoolyard, at recess time. We played tag a lot, had fun on the monkey bars, too. In winter, if it was too cold, we went to the gym and ran around playing catch me if you can, otherwise, we were outside having snowball fights, girls against the boys. Taking in all that fresh air, stinging cheeks, soaking wet mittens, and cold feet, what fun!

I went home for lunch, except when Mom had a doctor's appointment or something else where she wouldn't be home, which wasn't very often. On those days, we ate our lunch at school from a lunch box that usually had a picture of the latest television stars on it, like Roy Rogers and Dale Evans. They were a married couple in real life and they stared in a cowboy show.

I enjoyed my elementary school years, participated in the school events and the occasional play that we presented to our parents and other family members, if they could make it. In grade six, I had an exchange teacher from New Zealand. He was a great math teacher and he taught us a lot about New Zealand and the Maori people, who live there. We made their traditional dance costumes and learned a Maori song, which our class acted out and sang at one of the school concerts. It was fun!

Our household was unusual to most, but for us, it was normal. My parents did a great job being foster parents and also a great job being our parents, too! As a child, you don't realize how much they do to keep everything going and with nine kids, there is always something going on.

Eventually, the comings and goings of kids settled down and there were the same four or five that were with us for years. There was Patsy and Chuck, who were sister and brother, then Lyn, David, and Teddy. My Mom had the house pretty much ticking like a clock. Organizing became second nature to her. She would have all of us up, dressed, fed, and ready for school *on time* every day. My Dad was gone to work, before any of us got up.

In the winter months, we had hot cereal with toast. We had Empress peanut butter, honey, and jam. They were sold in a two-pound metal container with a lid. Well, because of all the dipping and spreading going on, it was too hard to keep the jam out of the peanut butter and the peanut butter out of the honey, so Mom came up with a solution. She mixed them together by putting half a tin of peanut butter with half a tin of jam and then half a tin of peanut butter with half a tin of honey. Whipped the mixture up in the electric mix master and presto…no more mess! That was such a great idea. Mom thought of things that made chores easier.

Some of the lunches we had were hot soup, a sandwich, and possibly, a piece of fruit, although we didn't have the variety there is today. We had apples, oranges, and only bananas, if they were on sale. My favorite soup Mom made, was cream of potato. I really liked it with lots of pepper, yum!

Our suppers were always good. Mom made meat, potatoes, and vegetables. If she creamed the carrots or cabbage, we liked that. Dessert could be Jello tapioca pudding with those rare bananas sliced up or rice crispy or chocolate puffed wheat squares, homemade cookies, pies, or cake. She also made cake donuts, now and again. We always knew when she made donuts, because the holes were on a plate in the middle of the kitchen table, when we got home from school for a treat. Ice cream was sold in a square cardboard brick, as we called it. She would pull the card board brick completely apart to open it and then slice the ice cream, because that process didn't take as long as dishing out individual scoops to nine kids, smart, ah? In the summer time, we had a whole watermelon sliced up, we ate that outside and it disappeared fast. We had to eat in shifts, because our kitchen table only sat six at a time and we had eleven, including Mom and Dad. We made it work. When TV tables came along, they really helped.

We didn't all have chores, but the ones who could handle them, did. I don't know how many times I lost the skin off my left thumb while peeling potatoes. After supper, dishes were done right away, we usually took turns washing, drying, putting away, clearing off the table, wiping down the stove, and sweeping the kitchen floor, there wasn't a dishwasher or an easy sweep electric broom, we were it. As soon as the chores were done, it was homework, if you had some and then free time till bed.

I have to share this story it's really funny! Picture this… It's a very cold winter morning. We are all busy, eating breakfast and getting ourselves ready for school. The kids that went to school across the street, we left. Then, Mom gets the other kids that are picked up by the school bus in front of the house, ready to go. With lunch pails in hand, they head out to wait for the bus. Well, a couple of hours or even more go by and Mom's working around the house, usual stuff, clearing up from breakfast, up and down the stairs checking beds, laundry, in the bathroom cleaning up, we only had one, and, generally, tiding up. The telephone rings, it's our neighbor Mrs. Paquette. She wonders why the kids are standing outside; she heard on the radio that all school buses were cancelled this morning! Really, Mom can't get outside fast enough…to get them inside. I can just see her, all five foot nothing, marching out there, waving her arms around and all the while mumbling unmentionables.

She was mad at herself, along with being embarrassed, but then again, you have to remember these kids are mentally handicapped and probably, would have stood there till they froze to the ground. We laughed about that incident, but let's face it; she was busy, too busy to be looking out the window…funny!

Doctors used to come to the house, you know, and not all that long ago, as far as years go. It's the early fifties, I'm four and it's a beautiful spring day. My cousins are visiting from a couple of blocks away. Trudy and Clifford Foley, whose parents are Mom's brother, Jack, and his wife, Dora's. So, there is us four, the cousins, and I'm pretty sure there were a couple of babies, too. We are all playing around the house, in and out having fun, and enjoying ourselves, when we are stopped for lunch. Mom notices that Trudy is flushed and generally not feeling well. She encourages her to take it easy. Mid-afternoon arrives and Trudy isn't getting any better, she is showing signs of a rash, Mom suspects Chicken Pox. After contacting the doctor's office and informs them of her situation and how many kids are involved, the doctor will come, meanwhile, nobody in and nobody out.

Dad gets home from work about five, the doors are locked he can't get in. Mom meets him at the door and tells him the doctor is on his way that she has called Jack and Dora, he is welcomed to go wait with them, until the doctor arrives and checks the kids.

Yes, it's the Pox, instructions are given and quarantine papers are made ready by the doctor and taped to the front door of the house.

For ten days, Mom is tending to eight kids. Not all would get the pox, but for the ones that do, it's a lot of work. Calamine lotion is used to help with the itching and Mom made an oatmeal paste to apply at bedtime. Dad ends up staying with his brother, Jim, and his family, who live about six blocks away. He comes to the house to get grocery lists and then delivers them by leaving them on the front porch. After he is clear, Mom slides the contents into the house. Uncle Jack and Auntie Dora would come and say good night to their kids. The kids would stand at the living room window and be so excited to see their parents, kisses, upon kisses were blown to one another, and hugs were exchanged in thin air!

I can't even imagine how exhausted Mom must have been. She did what she had to do and never complained, even laughed about the situation, as she would repeat it over the years. I was only four and the part I remember the most is, when Uncle Jack was standing at the living room window, acting the fool for his kids, so they would not be too upset and go to bed, easier for Mom.

It seemed to be common practice, back then, that when one child came down with something, all the kids were put in a room of the house to play, in hopes they would all get *it* at the same time, and so it was with us, we all had the mumps and measles together, within a couple of days of one another anyway… I wonder what the physicians would say about that practice today.

We didn't have babysitter's, usually my eldest sister, Vivian, watched us. Mom and Dad went bowling a couple of times a week. They bowled from nine to eleven in the evening. We had specific instructions of what not to do or use, when they were away, so we knew, under no circumstances, were we to put on the stove. Well, we did, Vivian made burnt sugar in the cast iron frying pan. It smelled up the house, so we opened up the front and back doors and ran through the house, fanning the air with tea towels. We got caught, got in trouble, but I can't remember the punishment. The burnt sugar was very good, but we didn't make it again.

I clearly remember one beautiful sunny day, we were playing outside and my youngest sister, Sandra, came screaming around the corner of the house. She ran up the back-porch stairs, into the house, and then ran down the stairs to the basement, where she hid under her bed.

"Well, what the hell is that all about?" It was the very first time she saw a black person and it scared her. It took Mom a while, to talk her out from under the bed. A few months later, for Christmas, Sandra got a black doll and all was well.

I couldn't have been more than six, when an all-out search was launched in the City for a missing little girl. Her name was Dianne Mason. The kids went out, combing the neighborhood for her. We looked, our parents looked, everybody in the City looked for her, but she was never found. That incident, for us, was very shocking, as our family had four girls. Dianne went missing not too far from the riverbank in the Highlands area, which was about six blocks from us. Because the incident was so close to us, it stays with you and ordinary things in your life change. We all don't know, if she fell into the river and was swept away or if she was taken and murdered or, perhaps, even taken and raised by another family out of Province or out of the country even, but the safety of our community was compromised. Our parents were always very careful of where we were and with whom, but after that, it seemed we had to be a lot more precise about our comings and goings. Back in the fifties, things like this never happened. I never forgot her, never forgot her name, and over the years, have thought of her and her family.

During the summer months, us kids, along with the neighbor kids, who were the Paquette family, we all walked to Borden Park, from 59 Street and 119 Avenue, where we lived to the park on 74 Street and 112 Avenue, which was a fair distance, about two miles. We would start really early, around seven thirty, packing our bathing suits, towels, a brown bag lunch, along with a quarter, which was our admittance. We had a dime to buy a nickel bag of hot popcorn and a Pep-chew chocolate bar from the concession. We had so much fun, gone all day, swimming, laying on the wooden bleachers, getting baked, then jumping in the cool water on a hot summer day. The pool was packed with kids, my future husband, unbeknownst to me at the time, was probably there, too, as this was his neighborhood. Once we had enough of the pool, we would have our bag lunch in the park, along with so many others enjoying the day. Walking home was fun, too, laughing and joking around, just being kids. It was a wonderful day and we had no problem hitting the pillow, after a day like that.

When we were old enough, about twelve or so, us kids in the neighborhood got a summer job at Zaychuk's Berry Farm, located in north Edmonton. We would get up early and walk, again about a mile, take our lunch with us, and pick berries. We picked raspberries for three cents a basket and there were twelve baskets to a flat.

The first couple of days, we were eating more than we were putting in the baskets, but soon learned that it was better to get the money than a bellyache.

I was mentioning earlier about 'the lake.' I think it's a good time to tell you about that special place that has never left my mind. Today, I'm still talking about 'the lake.'

We always referred to my Nanny and Grandpa Foley's cabin at Alberta Beach on Lac Ste. Anne Lake, as 'going to the lake.' Every summer, our family went for, at least, two or three weeks. The excitement for me was almost too much. I had a hard time falling asleep for days, before we were to leave. It was usually in August, probably, because the weather was pretty much guaranteed to be good.

The preparation for my Mom was I'm sure, less than enjoyable, but she was so organized that 'things' just came together. My Dad had the hardest part, putting everything in the trunk and strapping stuff on top of the roof. Those were the days of no seat belts and we all had to squeeze in. Picture this; Dad at the wheel, a kid sitting next to him, my Mom on the passenger side with our dog Puff at her feet. Then, however more there were at the time, two sat on the floor, facing one another with legs bent at the knees, while the rest sat on the back seat, one forward on the seat and the next one back on the seat. In kind of a zigzag fashion, we made it work. Funny!

That poor car! Must have had a pretty good motor to haul all of us and all that stuff on an hour and a half drive. We were all pretty good, had to be, there wasn't any choice. Once we left the main highway and headed down the seven-mile gravel road, us kids knew we were almost there. One more turn at the corner and we finally arrived.

Oh my! Seeing my Nanny's smiling face, when she opened up that wooden gate for the car to drive in, was so special to me and even more special now. I can still see her smiling; I can see my Grandpa coming out of the shed, wiping his hands on a soiled cloth. I see the yard, the beautiful full trees swaying in the breeze, the smell was unbelievable, and the whole place was moving.

On the left, was a small vegetable garden, where my Grandpa loved to grow his lettuce and dip it in vinegar and sugar, I have that bowl sitting in my kitchen on a shelf, with other treasures. To the right is the outhouse, a one-hole toilet with a sign above the door '4 U to P,' which was made by Grandpa. Inside to make your toilet visit more pleasant, there were pictures from the Star Weekly of beautiful young women posing in see through negligees, the pictures were not offensive, they were just there. On that same side of the yard, just in front of the outhouse was a large bush, then, in front of that, was a fish table, and my Grandpa's shed. One step up and through the open door, you were treated to that 'smell.' The oiled, wooden floor, the kerosene we used for our lanterns at night. His paints all lined up at the back of the workbench. There was so much in that small shed, his tools hung neatly on the walls, and the oars for the boat he made were standing up in one corner. There was a box on the floor that held our sand pails and shovels to make castles and memories, down at the beach. There were inner tire tubes to float on and canvas hammocks we would string up between the four trees in the front yard. We didn't go in there, unless you asked Grandpa, it was his special place. He made the most amazing things for the cabin and the yard.

On the left of the cabin, passed the garden, was a bed swing. It was about six feet long and three feet wide, complete with a canvas back, mattress that lay on top of the metal slotted bottom, a roof, and it swung between two huge poplar trees. It sat four and you could fit two lying down, one on each end facing one another. There was a permanent hole in the dirt at the front, where the adults would push the swing using their feet. I can still see my paternal Grandpa McQuade, head down, hands folded on his lap, and pushing the swing. That swing was his favorite spot, when he came to visit with my

Grandma McQuade; usually, they came and stayed for a weekend each year. As you headed to the front yard, like I said, everything was moving. My Grandpa and Nanny had a terrific sense of fantasy, which was colorful and exciting for kids. There were small windmills placed in holders, leaning out from tree limbs, made of metal, and each pedal on the windmill was painted a different color, bright yellow, red, blue, green, orange, white. He also made his own wooden fan chairs and they, too, were painted the same bright colors. He made whirligigs, the one I remember was a cowboy on a bucking bronco.

As you pass in front of the cabin, flowers graced each side of the two steps that lead to the front door. The flowerbeds were bordered with rocks, painted rocks. Along the other side, ferns were planted, they, too, were bordered with colored rocks. Which brings us to the back of the cabin, where Grandpa had made a huge rain barrel. It was on the left of the back door. We used that water for any number of things, from doing dishes to having sponge baths; it had a tap on it, so we could get the water out. He also made a wash-basin; it sat in the kitchen sink. There wasn't any plumbing, so we had to carry that washbasin outside and spill the water on the ferns.

On the right side of the back door, there was a hole in the ground, not very big, about two feet square, lined with galvanized metal, with a lid. It served as our refrigerator; it held the butter, milk, cheese, and eggs. There was a screen door at the entrance, the ones with about a three-inch wooden bar running across the center. Us kids would push that door open and let it go; it would slam shut with a hell of a bang. The adults were always saying, "Watch that damn door." Funny!

Once inside, it was wonderful. There were pendants hanging all over the walls, from every place in the world. Friends had brought them back from trips they had taken. There were also small souvenirs that hung on the walls, wherever they would fit. One had a couple of bees in flight, shown on a black background and the bees were buzzing around; it went like this,

"The bee is such a busy soul,
She has no time for birth control
Perhaps that's why in times like these,
You meet so many sons of bees."

And another one that I liked read,

"It starts when you sink in his arms
And ends with your arms in the sink"

26

Pictured was a young couple in each other's arms, a very romantic embrace, and the other picture shows the same women doing dishes in a sink full of bubbles! Funny.

There was a fireplace and Grandpa burned coal, usually towards the end of August, when the nights were chilly, no other heat. They had a gas stove for cooking, the old-time ones, on legs about two, two and half feet high, and sometimes, in the early morning, they would put on the stove to heat up the cabin.

There were two beds that folded up against the wall and were covered by a curtain, when not in use. They had a leg that folded out on each end, so when you pulled the bed down, you manually pulled each leg out, so it rested on the floor. They were the first Murphy Beds that we know today, ours were simple and they worked just fine. Nanny and Grandpa slept in separate beds, one on each side of the front enclosed porch at the front of the cabin. Grandpa was one of the first to rise in the morning and when Nanny woke up, he would bring her tea and toast in bed, along with the newspaper. My cousin, Wayne, from my Mom's sister, Evelyn, and her husband, Bob, made model airplanes and they hung from the ceiling.

A popular comic strip, back then, was called 'Bringing up Father.' The main characters were Jiggs and Maggie, with their son, Sonny. Grandpa made very colorful wooden doorstops, shaped and painted exactly like in the comics and stood about 2 feet tall. He made birdhouses from willow; they looked like a little cabin with a front step and two screened windows, one on each side of the bird hole. I still have a survivor. What a talent he was, he could do just about anything. A small corner table in the kitchen was used for the water pail and the dipper that hung off the side of it. The kids would go to the Beach pump, a few blocks away, every day to fill it up.

Some of the things we did at the lake will never be lost, as I'm writing them down and passing them on to our son, Ian, and his daughter, Quinn. Those days were so special and the nice thing is, my husband Angus, because we met when I was sixteen years old, he was at the cabin, and we share in those memories, he was part of them, too!

In the early days, us kids had so much fun, playing down at the beach for hours. The lake was pretty safe because every so many feet, there were sand bars; even so, we were only allowed to go out so far, that was it. During the week, when the lake wasn't so busy with weekenders, we would get on our bathing suits and Mom would send us down to the lake with a towel and a bar of soap. We would walk out in the lake to shoulder deep water and scrub ourselves clean. Never ever thinking that was so bad for the lake; didn't enter into our heads or my Mom's either.

Us kids would nag at my Dad and Grandpa to go fishing with them. As soon as they started to assemble their fishing poles and fishing boxes, we were on to them. I remember this one time when a few of us kids went. The boat held six people. My Dad was at the back with the motor, Grandpa at the front, and four kids on two bench seats in the center. With life jackets on, oars and fishing gear in the boat, Dad and Grandpa holding up each end, away we went, walking single file, about two blocks to the beachfront. We got going and Dad headed straight to Rocky Island, which was an island in the middle of the lake and named appropriately, as all that was on the island were rocks. We didn't know it, but we were about to be dropped off! They left us there, deserted but safe, we had nowhere to go. After that three- or four-hour experience, we never asked again! Lesson leaned—I think!

There was a fish and chip shop at the corner and when they fired up for the day, usually around eleven in the morning, we enjoyed the aroma that floated towards the cabin, freshly fried chips, it was almost irresistible. Sometimes, my Nanny would buy each of us our own order of French fries. A couple of us kids would go and pick them up, sprinkling with white vinegar and salt, scrumptious. We loved that, sitting outside in the front yard, swinging, and watching the cars and people go by.

Late one summer night, while asleep, a fire broke out at the fish and chip shop. The whole place was a blaze and the family lost a child, a boy, who was a twin. So sad, the lake village was stunned in disbelief. The family rebuilt as a confectionary and grocery store after that. Could be that members from that same family might still own the grocery store; it's there on the same corner today.

Fireflies, we had them. We were usually in bed by the time they came out, but, occasionally, we would get a jar and run around the yard, trying to catch them. I preferred watching them fly; they were really quite bright against the big dark trees.

Looking for four leafed clovers in the yard was always good for a couple of hours of fun. Nanny was really good at it; she had books full of them. Each leaf was taped on a page, with the date underneath of when she or someone else had found it. I would give my eyeteeth, for just one of those books, but they are gone—so sad.

The adults would go down to the Alberta Beach Hotel for a couple of cold beers on a Saturday night. The kids would sit around the dinner table, playing card games or board games. We had very strict rules, for when they were gone. The lit lanterns were placed in the center of the table, not to be moved. If you had to go to the bathroom, you were to go in pairs, using a flashlight. Going past the big bush, just in front of the outhouse, it was scary in the dark, but we made it there and back, without too much fuss. Being girls, there was always a scream or two, necessary or not.

Sometimes, we would gather a bowl of rose hips, during the day. Then, at night, we would wrap them individually with foil and use a thick needle and thread to pull them together to make necklaces and bracelets, which reminds me, I have to share this one.

My Nanny was quite fashion conscious, with a very limited amount of money to award such luxury, but that didn't stop her from looking her best. Years ago, there was less than costume jewelry, like these plastic beads that snapped together to make a necklace or bracelet. Well, Nanny would cover them with nail polish, in just the right color to match an outfit. Really, no kidding! I can't even begin to think of how many layers of nail polish were on those beads!

Nanny and Grandpa were wonderful people. Nanny was always smiling and truly, a happy person. My Grandpa worked wonders with his hands and was a quiet guy. They never bought a home for themselves, they always rented. I don't know why that was, but they had the cabin and loved it. There were a lot of friends that would stop by for a visit, and they were always welcomed. Nanny and Grandpa were the best and I will miss them, always.

We used to walk downtown to the big pier, which was a tourist attraction in the old, old days, like 1915 or so, they used to have a train that ran from Edmonton to Alberta Beach on the weekends. Nanny and Grandpa would say that it was very loud, going out on a Friday night, but on Sunday, coming home, the whole train was very, very quiet.

We all loved going to 'the lake' and even as adults, we loved it, too, probably more, just for the memories. From the poplar tree smell to the fresh air after a summer rain, all I have to do is close my eyes and I'm there and that will always be with me. How can I possibly say thank you…? I can't…they're gone!

Getting our first television set was an event. I'm pretty sure it was 1954. We had seen TVs through the window of a TV and Radio shop, about six blocks or so away from our house on 118 Avenue and 65 Street. Lots of kids coming and going from school, each day, would stop and watch, but not for too long, because the owner would come out and chase us away.

We came home from school at lunchtime and the TV was sitting in the corner of the living room; black and white picture on a 19" screen, surrounded by a wooden cabinet, and a set of rabbit ears sat on the top, they were for reception. There were only two channels and they ran till seven at night. After the evening news, that was it for the day. As time went on and it became more popular, there were more shows, more advertising, and the television was only turned off, when you went to bed.

Through the early years, there were a lot of good entertaining shows. A local favorite was Popcorn Playhouse, where kids sat on tiered benches and were interviewed by the host. The birthday girl or boy had a cake and all were given a piece. Each kid was asked a question or two, like their name, what was their favorite game to play, what did they like to do at school, stuff like that. The show was so popular it was very hard to get tickets. Muskeg was a talking moose head that was mounted on a wall. You pulled a string that was hanging from his chin and he would ramble a riddle at you, funny! You either loved or hated that show, but watched it anyway.

Then, of course, we had the Saturday morning cartoons, Mickey Mouse, Tom and Jerry, Yogi Bear and Boo, Boo at Yellowstone Park, I liked Nancy, which appeared in the comics first and then a cartoon on TV, there was Little Lulu, Bugs Bunny, Sylvester and Tweedy, the Road Runner and Wile E. Coyote, so many that Saturday mornings were pretty much booked up. After Mom had had enough of us lollygagging around, the TV went off and we were to, "Get outside and blow the stink off", was her way of saying, "I need some peace and quiet for a while." So, off we would go, and it would take no time at all and we would be busy doing something outside.

I'm thinking that pretty much winds up my early years, till about 1960—grade six.

I'm a happy kid.

Chapter Two: Adolescence, 1960-1966

Passing into grade seven, my Junior High School was Highlands. It's now about a hundred-year-old building, very stately looking, red brick, and a two-story structure where I attended grades seven through nine, from 1960-1964. Suppose to be three years, but I had to repeat grade nine. Because I started when I was five, it wasn't so bad, the kids that started at six years old, just caught up to me!

So, I was eleven in grade seven and fifteen at the end of my second year of grade nine. Wow! A lot happens to a kid between those years.

The school was across the avenue at the corner of our block, which meant an easy walk to and from school, each day. It was a much bigger building than my elementary school, so, of course, you felt more grown up. We now had a homeroom, where we went to start the day. Attendance was taken, but we didn't salute the flag like we did before. At first, I kind of missed that.

There was a weekly schedule given to us and now we went to other rooms, for different subjects and teachers, too! We had a buzzer that went off, after each class, and we had two minutes to get to the next class, at which time you were to be in your seat with your book opened to the lesson at hand. It was in Grade seven that we learned about the menstrual cycle, in health class. I was stunned, never heard of such a thing, and it worried me a lot, because you never knew when it was going to happen, especially, the first time. I told my Mom what I had learned and she said that at eleven I was still pretty young to start, but probably, in a couple of years' time. Well, I was sure relieved to hear that.

It's kind of hard to explain, but growing up can happen pretty darn fast. Lee and Lynn Paquette, my friends from next door, who attended St. Clare's School, had heard about the cycle, before we talked about it. Lee was older by a couple years and she had already started. She explained to Lynn and I that we might get a few stomach cramps and that would be our warning. I had older sisters of my own, but I can't remember talking about it with them, maybe, I was embarrassed or maybe, I just wanted to forget about it, until it happened.

As the school year progressed, there was more schoolwork to do, more books to read, more homework to do and more exams to study for, and a lot more kids, too! We didn't have letter grades on our report cards anymore, you were given a number grade, there seemed to be so many little changes that we all had to get familiar with.

We had sock hops, dances in the gym, where you wore socks, so you wouldn't damage the shiny wood floor. During grades seven and eight, I pretty much stuck to myself, did my work and the years seemed to unfold all by themselves. I had a couple of girlfriends at school and, of course, there was always my best friend, Lynn, even though we went to different schools, we were always good friends, she was my bridesmaid, when I married.

There were a lot of changes and I was unsure of it all. There were kids from all the other protestant schools in the district. We had between thirty to thirty-three students in each class, just the same as elementary school, but because the school was much larger, it felt impersonal and I didn't have the same contact with the same kids; change took some getting used to.

For me, grades seven and eight seemed to pass by really quickly. My marks were okay, always passing into the next grade. I seemed to have gotten my rhythm and I was eager to start my senior year in Junior High School. Nothing exceptional happened during that year, except I started smoking, seemed like everybody was smoking, the only problem I had was, I didn't have the money to smoke, so I baby-sat a lot that summer. I went, with friends of my Mom and Dad's, to a farm in Saskatchewan for ten days. I looked after their twins, who were about two years old and an older girl about four. I had a lot of fun with their family and came home with some cash. There was nowhere to spend my money on the farm, so it worked out perfect for me. When I got home, there was bad news.

It happened like this, there were so many kids in the Junior High Schools in the Province of Alberta that year that the 'powers that be' had to do something, because there weren't enough High Schools to accommodate the up and coming students. So, in their wisdom, they decided that all the kids in the Province would be put on a graph and the lower ten percent, no matter what their marks were, failed.

The letter arrived sometime in July, explaining the whole thing. I was hurt and didn't take it very well. Mom and Dad were sympathetic and it was offered that I could go to another school to repeat the grade if I wanted to. I thought about it, but decided to return to Highlands. I was okay with that and determined not to fail again.

During that summer, we went on a camping trip, for a couple of weeks, to the neighboring Province of British Columbia. Mom got sitters for a couple of the kids. So, after all the arranging, packing, and organizing, we headed off, playpen in tow, on the roof of the car, along with other camping apparatus. I like that word; it means 'the technical equipment needed for a particular activity'. It must have been quite a site for the other campers, looking on, as we pulled into the campsite. Oh! I forgot to mention Freddie and Gladys Marshall, close friends of Mom and Dad's, they were right behind us in their car full of kids and, of course, they had their own apparatus, as needed for their activities! Funny.

We met them at the CFRN TV Station on the highway, which was close to the city limits. Dad's signal light goes on, he pulls over. Freddie is already standing at the rear of his car, trunk open. Dad mumbles something like, back in a minute and gets out. They greet each other with a handshake and then Freddie proceeds to get two glasses out from a box in the trunk, along with a bottle of whiskey. He pours two stiff drinks and hands one to Dad, they clink glasses and down she goes! Really, I'm thinking it must have been a salute to a good trip coming up! Either that or a sedative for the trip coming up! Funny.

Okay, try hard to see this picture. Two vehicles arrive at the same time, one following the other. We are assigned neighboring campsites. When the car doors open, out pours six kids from one car and five from the other car. There are six out of the eleven that you would describe as normal, the others are either mentally challenged, physically handicapped, or are of another race that is totally different from the adults. Too funny! Freddie and Gladys looked after Wards of the Government, too. She had a couple of babies with them, about eight or nine months old. Like I said before, this was all normal for us.

I'm talking seasoned campers here and it doesn't take these four adults long to get it all together and set up. They were so good at it. Almost in unison, putting up their tent trailers, the kids' tents, digging out the propane stoves, lanterns, sleeping bags, air mattresses that needed to be filled, pillows came out, the same ones we had been sitting on all day. The playpen and a couple of baby strollers came off the roof of the cars and were put to use, as the two babies were plunked down, one at a time, fed a bowl of mush and laid to rest in the shade, bottles in hand. In no time flat, they were sound asleep. We had a 'Box' that held everything from dishes, salt, pepper, cutlery, tablecloth, a whole array of stuff. The cooler needed fresh ice, so the kids were sent to the shack that was near the front entrance gate to get a couple of bags. We kept ourselves busy and away from them. It took them about an hour or so, not bad.

We came back from running around, to see two very impressive campsites. Parents finally taking a breather, actually sitting and enjoying a late afternoon drink and gabbing away with one another. Then, the women would get the food prep going and before you could blink, the potato salad, buns, wieners, Kool-Aid, and just about anything you wanted, as a kid, was right in front of you. By the time we ate, helped clean up, sat around the fire a while, we were so ready for bed. We would make the rounds of saying goodnight, into our tent, snuggling in the sleeping bags and giggling the whole time—what fun we all had—never forget it—wonderful, absolutely wonderful!

That summer, my growing up days began, big time. My body had begun to develop. It wasn't any real surprise that the dreaded period was coming. I don't know how the words 'menstrual cycle' got replaced by the word 'period,' but ouch and ouch again!

We got home from our trip and I had had a few hours in the car with stomach cramps. I didn't mention it to Mom, because she was very busy unpacking, so I just bided my time, until I could talk to her. It was very difficult to get her alone, as you can imagine, but patience paid off and after supper, I asked if I could talk to her in her bedroom.

She was great, she told Dad we would be back in a while, and we were going to the store. So, off we went, just the two of us, walking a block to the drug store on the corner. She bought me my own box of pads, a belt to fasten them, and a box of Midol pills. I really felt special and I think that's how she wanted me to feel. On the walk home, we talked about the period, what I could expect, how long they would last, my cramps, the Midol pills. When we got home, we went into the bathroom and she showed me how to attach the pad to the belt, then left, as I put lesson to use. When morning arrived, so did the sight of my period, the cramps had eased off and I didn't feel too bad at all. Wow! This could be okay.

It was getting close to school starting again, so Mom took a couple of us shopping for a few things. I got my first bra, didn't really fill it completely, but my swollen head made up for it. I felt great!

September of 1963 and I'm fourteen in grade nine, again. Can't say that I was all that excited, but that's the way it had to be, so carry on. It didn't take long and I was feeling okay with repeating, my classes seemed more interesting and there were a few new teachers, too. My homeroom teacher was Mr. Dawson, he also taught math. He had a nice manner and smiled at us kids, made you feel comfortable. One day I will never forget, we were in class and an announcement came over the PA system for all of us to return to our home room, as I recall, it was about ten minutes to twelve. We got seated and Mr. Dawson came in, stood at the front of the classroom, clearly upset, and told us that President Kennedy had just been assassinated in Dallas, Texas. It was November 22nd a Friday. We were told classes were dismissed until Monday.

We all just sat there stunned. Mr. Dawson had tears in his eyes and I felt really bad for him; having to tell us such awful news.

When I got home, Mom had the TV on and it was all we heard and saw, too! I couldn't believe they would show that on TV. Somehow, my growing up days had peaked, as I was now considered mature enough to watch a man get shot in the head, in public, while his wife held him in her arms. Man, I cried, everybody cried, how sad we all where. The next few days in the media were crazy, radio, television, people talking, the phone ringing off the wall, friends calling to talk about it. I was really glad when Monday came, to get my mind off of the whole thing. Then, coming home from school, the funeral was on and the site of that little boy saluting his father set us all off again, what a horrible, horrible time. It was now understood that along with all the joys that television brought us, there was going to be the tragedies as well.

There were so many good, clean entertaining shows with funny, funny actors and actresses. Can't possibly mention them all, but here are a few that we enjoyed. Art Linkletter and his show 'Kids Say the Darndest Things' Absolutely priceless, that man was a marvel with kids. The Red Skelton show, what a talented, funny man, who made us all laugh till our stomachs hurt. There was I Love Lucy, with Lucille Ball, Desi Arnaz, Vivian Vance, and William Frawley, hilarious. The Westerns, like Gunsmoke, and The Rifleman with Chuck Connors, and Johnny Crawford, who plays his son. I had a real crush on him. There was Davy Crockett with Fess Parker and Buddy Ebsen, I remember every word of that intro song, along with Zorro, The Lone Ranger and Tonto, also Hawkeye and Chingachgook, his sidekick, in The Last of the Mohicans. The Mickey Mouse Club, I don't know anybody who can't remember the opening lyrics to that show, wholesome looking kids in a variety show, so good. Roy Rogers and Dale Evens, too! When he got in a fistfight, his hat never came off! I could go on and on, there were so many with good story lines and they also taught us good values at the same time.

I can't leave this subject without mentioning The Ed Sullivan Show, The Carol Burnett Show, and American Bandstand with Dick Clark. Andy Williams and Perry Como, Dinah Shore and Dean Martin, Jackie Gleason with his fist shaking in the air, threatening his wife 'to the moon, Alice, to the moon!" Bonanza, if we were bathed and in our PJs, we could stay up till ten and watch the show, on a Sunday night, all of us lying like logs, across the living room floor, heads propped up in our hands. If you get a chance, look them all up and enjoy, they were so good.

Kind of went on a replay there, I'm back on track now, it's November of 1963. Really enjoying my second trip, around grade nine, feeling relaxed, actually tried out for and was accepted on the school basketball team.

Participated in the track and field events, running was my thing. I enjoyed the hundred-yard dash and the 240-relay race. We did well at the city competitions, too! My confidence was getting there, my bra was fitting better, and my periods were not as emotionally upsetting as they had been. I was so getting used to the rhythm of everyday, and the acceptance I was feeling.

As that year progressed, I was worried about the Provincial Exams coming up, so I buckled down and studied, after writing them, I thought I'd done okay. When the results were received in July, I was relieved to have graduated and was moving on to High School.

Meanwhile, during that summer break, I managed to stay busy. I babysat around the neighborhood and saved my money for clothes to start school. I was smoking and sneaking the odd one from Mom's purse that always hung on the kitchen door handle. Unbeknownst to me, my sisters were sneaking, too! So, when Mom went to get a cigarette and the whole package was practically empty, she quit. Said she couldn't afford to be supplying the whole house with smokes. Everyone smoked back then, there wasn't the knowledge that there is today. I did quit, when I turned thirty-three, twenty years of smoking was enough.

My good friend, Lynn Paquette, and I went shopping for clothes. Mom had gotten me an account at a little shop downtown called 'Sweet Sixteen' the credit limit was fifty dollars. We had fun, the two of us giggling away, trying on different outfits. We went to Woolworth's store, to the lunch counter for a bite to eat, feeling pretty grown up.

It seemed like it took forever for my first day of high school to arrive. I remember I wore a navy-blue dress with blue polka dots on white sleeves, with a scarf around the neck to match the sleeves. I wore 1'½" navy blue heels to set it all off. I do have a picture.

Feeling really nervous, I walked to Eastglen Composite High, with my sister, Vivian, she was in grade twelve, her last year. The previous year, one of her best friends committed suicide. We were devastated, especially, Viv. I went to the funeral with her, it was so sad. Judy was very well liked and it seemed the whole school was there. When death touches you so close, the feelings you hold are so profound, they don't leave you, time heals, but you never forget. Over the years, I have given thought to Judy and her family. She must have been very troubled inside, but didn't show it on the outside.

As Viv and I walked the mile or so to Eastglen, she filled me in on what to expect. All the homeroom classes were posted on the outside of the school wall. We found my name and room number, she walked me there and we agreed to meet outside, when we were dismissed. Viv was the one who took my nervousness away and made me feel comfortable, thanks, Viv.

In grade nine, we had to fill out forms for high school in relation to the mandatory subjects and also the electives you were going to take. It was easy to follow, as the subjects were posted in our homeroom, so you just found your name for each subject, wrote down the room number, and time the class started, then, filled out a weekly schedule and carried on. All that worry of not knowing if you could figure it all out, and when the time comes it's not nearly as hard as you thought it was going to be.

High school was much bigger and a lot of the kids were unfamiliar to me, but I didn't mind, because I was unfamiliar to them. In October sometime, I went to see a Roy Orbison concert I was invited by Eddie Melenko. I remembered seeing Eddie at the sock hops, at Highlands, the previous year, he could really dance well. I was so excited, couldn't sleep, what to wear, Roy Orbison, my favorite singer.

Eddie's Dad was driving the car, so we sat in the back. Very little was said, this was my first real date and I was tongue-tied. I still play his music, sing along, have my cry, and then turn him off, till the next time.

Eddie's Dad drove us home. We didn't hold hands or anything. When we got to the back door, I thanked him for taking me, said that I really enjoyed it, and then I gave him a slight kiss on the cheek and said good night. My first date was over.

Saturday's at my house were really fun, all through the years. It was the day, when there were no schedules, no time lines that had to be met. In my younger years, it was the day to play with friends in the neighborhood, go to the corner store, and maybe spend all of your 25-cent allowance at one time. Penny candy was very popular, because you could choose any number of candies. They were in open boxes laid out at the bottom of the chocolate bar choices, which were displayed on tiered shelving. With a small brown candy bag in hand, you chose which ones you wanted. We had licorice babies, butterscotch buttons, marshmallow cones, candy cigarettes, suckers shaped like a horse shoe, candy wafers, marshmallow peanuts, strawberries and bananas, sugar coated mint leaves, jujubes, licorice cigars, pipes, and more. For a nickel, you got fifteen candies, and that lasted awhile. We had these five cent chocolate bars called Pep-chew, they were about four or five inches long, thin with chocolate coating on the outside, with chewy mint toffee on the inside, what a bargain, kept you busy, they were very popular.

In my teen years, I bowled for a few years, five pin. Dad would drive us every Saturday morning. It was fun being part of a team and meeting up with different kids from the city. I even won a few trophies. When we got home, we would put on the record player, sing along to the top ten of the month, and eat mushroom soup sandwiches, toasted under the broiler. Us kids would dance in the living room to Chubby Checker's 'The Twist'. It was a great time. If memory serves me well, I think Mom went downtown, while we were in school and bought the small records, called 45's for one dollar each.

I still feel Saturday is 'the best day of the week,' when I awake, sleeping next to my grand-daughter, who is eight, while I'm writing this, I always ask her, "What day is it today?" and she answers, without hesitation, "Its Saturday, Grandma, best day of the week."

In February 1965, I turn sixteen, I am enjoying grade 10. With spring, comes really nice weather that year and everybody is biting the bullet to get outside in the fresh air. I'm visiting a girlfriend, Laura Have. She lives about six houses down from us. It's a Saturday, April 24th. We are sitting in the kitchen, having a cup of tea and a smoke, when there is a knock at the front door, "Come on in."

A guy, whom I've never seen before, walks in, and stands in the kitchen doorway. Laura introduces us, "Angus MacDonald, he is a friend of Laura's brother, Chris." *Nice,*

I'm sitting here with curlers in my hair! Yikes! We chit chat about nothing really, he asks if I play ball and I answer yes. So I go home, take out the damn curlers, change my clothes, grab my glove, and run back before he has a chance to leave. We started playing catch and before we knew it, the sun had gone down and we couldn't see the ball anymore. Angus asks if I want to go to the A&W?

"I'll just run home and tell my Mom where I'm going," but really I'm thinking, I have to ask permission to go, and go in a car, alone with a guy that I just met a few hours ago. So, I come crashing through the back door, fully out of breath, all excited, and ask Mom if I can go. She says yes, but don't be too long. She says to take a couple quarters off the shelf above the sink for a root beer.

We leave Laura's a little past dusk, the A&W is just across the avenue from Borden Park, about two miles away. We pull in, Angus backs into a spot, with his arm stretched out along the back of the seat, he taps his hand in a motion for me to slide over and sit next to him and I do. He must have known that I was very nervous, so he bends down and gives me a little kiss on the lips, followed by a really nice reassuring smile. Like without saying a word, he tells me it's okay, I'm safe. This was just the first of many, many, many little kisses and reassuring smiles I will receive from Angus over the years. We talk, I learn that he has gone to St. Clare's School, the catholic school about two blocks from my elementary school, but because he lives about ten blocks away, in the opposite direction from my house, I never saw him. We know a lot of the same kids, we laugh, and talk and laugh some more, we are natural together, I feel it right away. He drives me home, park outside the house, a few more kisses, and I float into the house. It's not too late, so I call up the stairs to tell Mom and Dad I'm home and locking the back door. Mom asks, "What was the name of the fellow you were with?"

"Agnes MacDonald," I reply.

"It can't be Agnes, it must be Angus!"

"Yes, that's it Angus MacDonald! Good night."

I can't sleep, I'm restless, and my mind is going a mile a minute. What a nice guy, I really like him, and I'm hoping he likes me back.

Come morning, I awake to a beautiful spring day. My first thought is, *I wonder if I'll see Angus today?* I did. Early evening, his car is parked in front of Have's again, so I grab my glove and head there. We see each other and he smiles. I hold my glove in the air, he grabs a glove from the front hall and out we go. We don't play catch as long, but head to the A&W again, pretty much repeating the day before, except when we get back home, he parks between my house and Have's, where we settle into a necking session I never experienced before, but liked very much. We continue to see each other almost every evening that week and weekend.

On Monday, May 3rd, Angus calls and wants to pick me up.

"Yes, come on over."

It's kind of late to go anywhere, being it is a school night, so we just sit out in front of the house and as we are yacking back and forth, he pulls out a blue jewelry box from his jacket pocket. OMG! It's a ring, the cutest black Alaskan diamond you ever saw, shaped in a heart. We are going steady. Much later, Angus tells me that the ring had cost him a whole week's wages, so he was broke for a while. Funny!

I have had that ring for over fifty years now and I have worn it every day, since the day Angus gave it to me. It has been rebuilt three times, as the claws wear down, but the stone remains just as beautiful today. The stone is a Hematite, found in Alaska, and was very popular in the 1950's and 1960's. A lot of girls had the long narrow Marquise shaped ring. I have never seen another heart shaped one. Once I saw a woman with a necklace, but never a ring. I have gotten so many nice complements over the years from friends, co-workers, grocery clerks, bank tellers, all admiring the shape, a heart means so much. I'm going to give it to my one and only Grandchild, Quinn, on her sixteenth birthday, because I was sixteen when I got it and besides, I want to see her enjoy it.

So, we have known each other for ten days. I'm beaming from ear to ear, so excited, never went steady before… So, he does like me back! Mom and Dad are okay with me going steady, they like Angus and turns out that my Dad knows Angus's Uncle Rod, who is a policeman in Edmonton. Dad's and their daughter's boyfriends can be a very touchy situation.

The school year progresses, I'm doing okay. The forms come around to fill out subjects for grade eleven. I'm in a two-year clerical course, but I would like to take accounting as an elective, but I'm not allowed, not high enough marks in English to take bookkeeping, really! I'm good at math, but that doesn't count, sure hope things have changed since then. Writing exams marks the end of the school year, which is always stressful, so I study and feel confident I will get all of my credits and advance into grade eleven.

Laura and I get a summer job at a laundry cleaning plant, it was called Capital Cleaners. We go on the bus, laugh and giggle all day long, we had a blast. I learned very quickly what a hard day's work was all about. It was not easy; the company did commercial laundry, mostly for hotels and motels. Towels, sheets, pillow cases, and bed spreads. After washing, the linens were manually fed through a very large mangle. It's a machine that rolls the fed linen through heavy rollers to dry and iron them at the same time. The one we worked on was about fifteen feet square, and noisy, with lots of rollers that carried the linens and towels up and over several times, before landing on the folding line. As they fell from the last roller, you folded as quickly as possible, as the linens were fed along the whole width of the machine and arrived within seconds of one another. It was ridiculously hot to say the least, but come Friday we were handed a brown envelope with fifty bucks cash inside, totally worth it!

Angus and I enjoy being together, we had so much fun that summer. We went for drives; we were regulars at the A&W on 112 Avenue and 72 Street, where a lot of our school friends would go, too. There was a band called the A&W Lords, who, on the weekends, would play on the roof. All of us would be out of our cars and dancing till 2 a.m. My Dad bought me a cigarette roller that made one cigarette at a time. I didn't like the tobacco in my mouth, so I bought a cigarette holder, the kind the movie stars were using, except mine was shorter, about 4 inches long. Friends would come to the window of the car and ask me to roll them a smoke. I charged a nickel, so it didn't take long for me to earn forty-five cents, which was the price of a box of 'tailor made' cigarettes, as we called them. What fun we all had! We drove to 'the lake' and he met Nanny and Grandpa. He loved them instantly and really thought they were special folks. Loved being at the cabin and called it whimsical. We spent many days out there, going to dances, swimming in the rain. He met a lot of family members and family friends, who would stop by for a visit.

I, in turn, met Angus's immediate family and liked them all, too! He has three sisters and one brother. Angus is the oldest and in order of birth, next comes Marion, then Margaret, Allan, and Catherine. I also met his Uncle's, Aunties and cousins and their family friends, over the years, too! I will fill you in on our families and special friends a little later, right now, I'm sixteen and my rhythm in life is good, really good.

We go to dances on the weekends, one in particular, called 'Stardust,' not too far from my house, they were at Highlands Community Hall, downstairs every Saturday night, all summer long. Angus can really dance well, very agile, light on his feet. Which brings me to a description of him. He's tall, an even six feet, slim but not skinny, athletic, plays hockey very well, keeps up with the latest fashions, has an engaging natural smile, wavy dark brown hair, soft hands, and strong arms. He likes cars and music a lot. He is easy to laugh, is liked by his friends, is respectful, attentive, has a very nice manner, carries himself well, and has a presence wherever we go. He is very proud of his Scottish heritage. I'm a lucky girl.

The summer has flown by and grade eleven is almost here. I made some money for school clothes, so my girlfriend, Lynn, who was away for the summer working in Jasper National Park, at the lodge, also doing laundry, we made a date to go shopping. We had a lot of catching up to do. We take the bus downtown and have a really good girl's day. I buy three or four outfits that I can mix and match, Lynn, too, so we are both happy. We go for lunch and gab it up! When I take a breath, she talks, when she takes a breath, I talk, too funny! Lynn and I are very close, we have lived beside each other for years and we have grown up together. She knows Angus from their school days and she is genuinely happy that I'm with him. To me, that's the meaning of a true friend, when you can be separated from each other for a long time and when you do get together, the conversation picks up just like you've never been apart. Easy and free flowing, relaxed and spontaneous, nothing left unsaid.

I'm thinking that grade eleven just might be my last year in school; as I did, initially, take an offered two-year clerical course. School is on and once again, I settle into my schedule. Angus is working full time in the auto-body trade and really likes it. We see each other once or twice during the week and are almost inseparable on weekends. Before I know it, it's Christmas again. I decide to get Angus a toolbox for a gift. Dad drives me to Simpson Sears; they have a Craftsman brand toolbox, nice looking, it's grey with red trim. Mom and Dad agree to put the box on their account, I will pay them back in time. Christmas morning comes, Nanny, Grandpa, Angus, my sister, Viv, and her husband, Roland, all arrive at pretty much the same time. Angus likes the toolbox. Unbeknownst to me, almost everyone in the auto-body trade and other trade professionals, have a Snap-on toolbox, all red and chrome. Angus never did tell me that he was the only guy with a Craftsman. In every shop he worked at, his Craftsman went too. It wasn't until years later that he bought himself a nice two-piece Snap-on toolbox and brought the old Craftsman home, where it still is useful to him, after some fifty years.

In January, the start of 1966 brings our family a beautiful baby girl. Viv and her then husband, Roland, become parents. Mom looks after Tamara, while they are at work and we all have a great time with her. She is a delight for Mom and Dad, their first Grandchild.

Funny how some things stay with you over time, it's not that you think about them, but occasionally, in conversation, something is said that triggers a memory similar to yours. In February I turn seventeen, it's a school night. Angus comes over with a gift for me. It's a pair of black bell-bottom slacks and a sleeveless yellow shell top, both were very popular at the time. They fit and look good, too!

As the year carries on, spring is so welcomed, because we had a very cold winter. I earn a little money by watching the kids, while Mom and Dad go out during the week, try to get my studying and school work done and I'm doing okay.

Angus likes eating sunflower seeds, he calls them spits, because you crack them in your mouth, then spit the shells out. Well, come spring, we are sitting on the back porch and eating spits. When Angus leaves, Dad gets me outside sweeping up the shells, because you never know, one of the kids might pick one up and choke. For the same reason, we didn't have fish very often, too funny!

Oh! I forgot to mention this. When Angus and I first met, we had known each other about five days, he's over to take me out and it's the first time he has been to my house. He is waiting on the stairs at the back door and Teddy, one of the kids, who was around five, was back there, too, and he got a whiff of the polish on Angus's cowboy boots, so he's on his hands and knees taking a good sniff. Well, Angus didn't know what to do, say something, jerk his foot away, what! The funny thing is, I didn't tell Angus that I lived with mentally handicapped kids. Really, I never gave it a thought, didn't even cross my mind to mention it. We have laughed about that over the years and he told me much later that he was thinking, "Maybe, he met me on a 'good' day!" Funny!

I'm in school five days a week, while Angus is at work. We see each other usually once during the week and enjoy each other's company very much. We have been together for a year, pretty much everything we do, we do together. We have found our own rhythm.

One evening, towards the end of the school year, I tell Angus that the whole school is going to play hooky after attendance is taken, just before the start of afternoon classes. So, on that chosen Friday, the bell rings to start the afternoon and all hell breaks loose. Literally hundreds of kids are scrambling to get out of the school, as fast as they can. I grab my books, run down the stairs, charge at the double doors, and see Angus's car right out in front. I jump in next to him and, at least, six of my friends are right behind me. A few jump into the back and a few are standing on the running boards and hanging on for dear life. At the time Angus had a 1940 Ford Coupe, we had so much fun in that car. We are all yelling, "Go, go, hurry, we got to get out of here," teachers are running after the cars, as, one by one, they pull away from the curb. Angus drives pretty slow; so, nobody falls off and he heads for the A&W, about six blocks away. Really, what a bunch of rebels we were, making memories, I remember that afternoon and probably a whole whack of kids after fifty years, still remember it, too! It was fun. Exams in a couple of weeks and that's it for grade eleven. Results arrive in July and I'm good, made all my credits and have passed the two-year clerical course. If I don't find a career related job, during the summer, then it's off to grade twelve.

For the life of me, I can't remember how I found out but the Provincial Government had initiated a typing exam, where a person could go to the Administration Building downtown on 109 Street and 99 Avenue, practice typing and take an exam, which was scheduled for three days a week, at preset times, during the day. So, why not, it could lead to a clerical position. I went, practiced typing for about an hour before the exam. The accepted result was forty words a minute with three or less mistakes. We all handed in our typed papers with our personal information filled out, name, address, phone number, education, etc. They would contact us.

The summer of 1966 was really a lot of fun. My parents didn't pressure me into getting a summer job, as I had the possibility of getting on with the Provincial Government, so I was taking it easy. Made a few bucks babysitting and that kept me in smokes. Angus and I really enjoy going to dances on the weekends. We go out to Alberta Beach, where the cabin is, they have a dance hall and it's really packed with kids, some we know, and it's a lot of fun. House parties were okay, we went, but when one of us winked at the other, we were out of there. 'Wouldn't It Be Nice' by the Beach Boys was released and secretly, it was my song. I really related to it, because I knew Angus was the guy, he was the one for me. I never let on that my train of thought was leading to a future with him, because I'm seventeen and he's eighteen, really young. We are good together, we get along, we like each other's families, we enjoy doing the same things, and we laugh a lot. We have been going steady for fifteen months.

I had filled out the appropriate forms for grade twelve classes. School is about to start and I haven't heard from the government, so it's off to school I go. About two weeks in I get a call, Mom takes the message, 'If I'm still interested, call and they will set up an interview for a Clerk Typist I position that has become available.' I'm excited, Mom can read my eyes, and I'm going for it. She feels it's only right that I speak to the school counselor first. She wants to make sure that I can go back to school, if I don't like the job. Fair enough. I'll see the counselor tomorrow and call the government from there. I get in to see the counselor first thing the next morning and she is really nice. She looks at my grade ten and eleven classes, my marks, what I'm taking in grade twelve and we decide it's probably a good idea to try for the job, its right up my alley and, *yes*, I can come back and resume classes, if it doesn't work out. I make the call from the counselor's office and they set up an interview for ten o'clock the next morning. It's in the Natural Resources Building on 109 Street and 99th Avenue next to the building I took the typing test.

Well, I'm happy as a clam, thank the counselor very much clean out my locker, and head home. On the walk home, which is about a mile, I feel funny. It's hard to explain, but it feels like someone just took a pair of scissors and cut away these invisible strings that were attached to me. I'm feeling happy, but, at the same time, I feel kind of nervous inside, because it's weird that I should be walking home, mid-morning, and it's okay, really okay!

Maybe, I'm feeling like this, because the last two days events have been about me and only me. I'm being advised but the direction is entirely up to me. Could this be a taste of freedom? This is *big* for me, because of my evolution, which means a gradual development. Our development years at home were very different from most. There had to be structure, organization, and scheduling. There wasn't any real personal time for any of us, we were all in the same boat, you could say. That's just the way it was. It's like when someone else does your thinking for you, of course, for your betterment, then, what do you do? You follow, that's what you do, because everything is being taken care of for you.

Then, the time comes when you have to start thinking, organizing, scheduling, and planning for yourself and I think that's what these last few days have been about, it's my time!

Chapter Three: Young Adulthood, 1966-1976

When I get home, Mom and I sit down for a quiet cup of tea together. I fill her in and she tells me not to get too excited, but that everything sounds good. Then, she hits me with, "Maybe, you should consider going to a gynecologist and start taking birth control pills! You wouldn't want anything to happen when you and Angus are just getting started, would you?"

"No, of course not, do you know of one?"

She gets out the phone book and looks up gynecologists and finds a Dr. Richard Day, who is the son of her own retired gynecologist that she had for years. His office is downtown, not too far from where I would be working. Lucky for me, the doctor can see me tomorrow afternoon. I give the receptionist all of my information and hang up.

Can you believe this mother of mine, she's wonderful. So listen up girls, you never know what a quiet cup of tea with your Mom might bring to the table.

In the morning, I take the bus downtown and walk the remaining few blocks to the Natural Resources Building. It's a five-story structure, completed in 1931, made of concrete, steel and limestone, originally from a quarry in Garson, Manitoba. It's a gorgeous building, inside and out. Two short flights of granite steps and you arrive at the main rotunda. There are marble tiles in the hallways and maple flooring in the offices. It's now called the Bowken Building and still serves as offices for the Alberta Government. When the interior was renovated in 1980, the province decreed that the exterior must not be altered in any way.

I'm walking up the two flights of granite steps and ask the attendant at the huge reception area where I would go for my interview with a Mr. Lawson, in the Homestead Section. He directs me to the third floor, turn right, go to the end of the hallway, the office will be right there, behind the glass doors. As

I'm walking down the hallway, a ladies' washroom is on my right, so I go in. I'm early so I might as well relieve some of my nervousness!

There is a lovely looking lady sitting at a very organized desk, just behind the glass doors, "Good morning," she says, "May I help you?"

"Yes, I'm Brenda McQuade, and I'm here for an interview with Mr. Lawson."

"Have a seat. I'll let him know you are here."

She comes back and waves me over to her. As we walk through the large open floor plan, it is partitioned with pony walls and inside these areas are young women, all sitting at their desks, typing away. Mr. Lawson's office is in the far corner, his door is closed, probably because of all the noise. She taps on the door.

"Come on in," he says.

"Mr. Lawson, this is Brenda McQuade, here for her interview relating to the Clerk Typist position we are wanting to fill."

"Thank you, I'll take it from here."

She closes the door and he motions for me to have a seat. I didn't fill out an application for the position all I did was complete the typing test. So, he begins by asking me a few simple questions, like my education, if I was from Edmonton, did I think I would enjoy typing all day? That was about it, when can I start.

My heart's been skipping a beat since I walked into the building. Very excited, my first real job. Mr. Lawson calls the receptionist in and tells her to go over the general information with me. I thank him very much and leave his office.

We walk through the glass doors and down the hallway, on the right halfway down, she stops at a metal box, mounted on the wall and along one side are separate slots with cards that have the person's name written on the top. It's a punch card, my card will be in a slot the morning I start. You punch in, in the morning and out, when you leave for the day. I work Monday to Friday, 8:00 to 5:00, with an hour for lunch, my pay is $200.00 gross a month, see you next Monday.

I'm ecstatic, can't wait to get home and tell Mom and Dad. It's 11:00 a.m. and the Doctor's appointment isn't until 1:00. What to do until then? I start walking towards Jasper Avenue, which is the main avenue that runs through the heart of downtown Edmonton. That distance is about four blocks away and the Doctor is another two, he is on 111 Street and Jasper Avenue.

I walk slow and let my mind wonder, wonder if I will like the job, wonder if I will be liked by the other employees, wonder if I will like them, wonder if

I should pack a brown bag lunch, all kinds of wondering going on. Angus will be happy for me and I'll call him, when he gets home from work.

I'm early for the appointment, so I'll just have to be seated and wait. The receptionist calls my name and I follow her down a hallway and into an appointed room. Dr. Day walks in, we introduce ourselves. I like him right away. "What can I do for you today, young lady?"

"I'm here to get a prescription for birth control pills," I answer.

"And why do you want birth control pills?" he asks.

"So, I don't get pregnant."

"Okay, I'll give you a prescription for six months, then I want to see how you are doing on them. Ask the pharmacist to go over the instructions with you."

I thank him and away I go.

What a day, I'm two feet off the ground and feeling fine. When I get home, I go over the whole day with Mom, she is glad everything went well. Dad gets home and he knows the building I will be working in, there's not much to say because I haven't started yet. I give Angus a call, and he's excited for me. Its five days away, so I plan a shopping day, and wait for Monday to come.

Back in the day, pant suits for females were just coming into style, skirts and dresses were still considered the norm. For my first day on the job, I wore a maroon colored skirt with a striped maroon, green, and white sleeveless shell top, with a pair of hush puppy everyday shoes in a tan color. I wear a car coat, as it was called, they were cut at thigh length with long sleeves and a snap or zippered front, usually made of wash and wear material, very serviceable. About three years later, an invention called panty hose took over the market. Loved them, they were sold in chicken egg shaped containers, called L'eggs by Haines. For now, its nylons and a garter belt with attached fasteners to hold them up. Yuk! I walk the seven blocks to catch the bus, the #2 Highlands running down 112 Avenue. It took about forty-five minutes and then a ten-minute walk from Jasper Avenue at 109 Street to 99 Avenue, where the building is located. Finding the quickest driving route on Google today, it's approximately seven kilometers and takes roughly twenty minutes.

I really like my job, I really like the girls in the typing pool, there are six of us and I like the men in the homestead section I work for, there are six to eight of them. The gals are pony walled in an area, about ten feet by twelve feet, we each have our own desks, manual typewriters, a Dictaphone with foot pedal and earphones. The typewriters are old, large Underwood's, but they do the job. A loud bell sounds, when you are at the set right margin, it's a *rat-a-tat-tat* all day long. We take a pile of files off of a communal long narrow table, there are about eight or ten piles, each one has a tape with recordings sitting on top of them. The supervisor explains what we do, which is to type out letters to farmers in the province with regards to growing crops, their yields, and, of course, payments for those crops. There is quite a bit of correspondence that goes on between the farmers and the homestead section, as the farmers are encouraged to ask questions regarding any concerns they may have about their farms. We use standard 8½" x 11" white, bond paper, carbon paper to make more than one copy at a time and we had a typewriter eraser for mistakes. A few of the men did not like corrected mistakes, so you had to type the whole thing over, if you made one. You put the tape in the Dictaphone and listened. Good thing we had a pedal, push down, it went forward, push harder, it would go in reverse, so you could replay what you missed. The tape would squeal on the backup and make a clicking noise, when you resumed play i.e., Tim Potvin here, there are ten files in this stack, one letter per file and one carbon copy for each letter. First file is Mr. Harry Wilson, then he continues with, first paragraph. You typed what he said and a guideline to follow what was in the file, so it was pretty basic. After the letter was finished, you typed an envelope and paper clipped it to the letter, moved that file to the bottom and carried on with letter #2. Once all were completed, you took the pile across the hall to the desk of the fellow who made the tape recording. It was always re-wound to the start and sitting on top of the stack. Next, another pile was always waiting on the table. That about describes my very first full-time clerical position. The gals I worked with were great, we all got along and helped each other out. At the end of the day, our desks were clear, everything put away in the desk drawers and a unique feature built into the desk, was a handle that you pulled and the typewriter would disappear in a holding compartment underneath, sort of like a sewing machine table. Of course, the typewriter was securely fastened.

I must say, I really liked that job, there was always work to do, not too much talking going on, as your ears were always plugged with the earphones. The room was bright, we had three windows, two looking out onto 109 Street, which was always busy and one overlooking the side street. I worked in the homestead section from the fall of 1966 to the spring of 1970, approximately three and a half years.

In December of 1966, Angus's family had a tragedy, his Uncle Johnny, one of his Dad's brothers, was killed in an auto accident, while on duty as a police officer. He had just finished a good deed and was on his was back home from Red Deer, some 150 miles from Edson, where he lived, when the accident happened. He served in the Canadian Air Force, during World War II, as a rear gunner on a Lancaster aircraft. I never had a chance to meet him but he was a great guy, family man, loved fishing, and the outdoors, very much respected as the Chief of Police in Edson, Alberta.

In the spring of 1967, my family had a tragedy, too, my cousin, Wayne Nelson, son to my Mom's sister, Evelyn, and her husband, Bob, was killed in an auto accident. Auntie Evelyn was in the car with him, when they were hit head on by a couple of kids going the wrong way on a one-way street. She was in pretty rough shape and was in hospital the day of her son's service. My eldest sister, Viv, was in the same hospital, at the same time, for a separate accident that she was in.

Adversities in life, we can all live without them. Do they really make us stronger? Or do we just learn to live with the events that happen to us over the years?

From my early years, I write about my Uncle Jack and Auntie Dora with cousins Trudy and Clifford. I don't know what year, by now, they are in Germany, both enlisted in the services and they run the Canadian Post Office on the Canadian base over there. I mention my Uncle Jim and Auntie Allie, they had moved to the Vancouver area, quite a few years ago. My Uncle died very suddenly and we were told he had gotten an infection of some sort and didn't make it. He was Dad's only brother. I remember the morning Dad left for his funeral, by train, he looked so sad, standing in the kitchen with a dark brown suit on and a dress hat and carrying a small suitcase. A taxi cab pulled up in front of the house and he was gone, the house was very quiet, it felt strange. Just a flash back, I'm back on track again.

Angus and I are working away. I'm paying $50.00 room and board, teaching me some sense of responsibility. Our everyday and every week are running along just great. Spring turns to fall and fall turns to winter. It's Christmas, before we know it. Nanny and Grandpa Foley and Angus arrive at nine to unfold the tree on Christmas morning. I get a new pair of figure skates from Mom and Dad. All presents, under the tree, are opened and we are looking at each other's gifts. I bought Angus a vice, which he still has. I carried that thing home on the bus, stored it under my seat, it was heavy. Walking home from the bus with that weight, I thought I was going to drop it a few times. I'm on the couch, nestled in with my Nanny, when Angus says, "Brenda, go upstairs where my coat is, and bring me down what's in the pocket."

"Okay."

I take a small wrapped square box from his pocket and run down with it. I start handing it to Angus and he says, "It's for you."

"Oh," I sit down, open it, and it's an engagement ring. That was it, I put the beautiful solitaire diamond, which was mounted in white gold, on my ring finger and we are engaged. Angus did not get on his knees or ask if I would marry him, but I had him and the ring, so I guess he knew the answer. Everybody was excited, we have been going steady for two years and seven months, I'm eighteen and Angus is nineteen. We have to talk about the date, announcement to come later. So, we talk, need to save money for getting married, a honeymoon, dress, suit, clothes etc. etc. etc. It's payday, so I cash my cheque, take out the $50.00 for room and board, my cigarette money, personal expenses, and bus fare for the month. After supper, at his parent's house, we go up to his bedroom and take out our stash, laughing, as we put it all in little piles on the bed. We make a list of stuff we will need and estimate the approximate cost for each category. Like $100.00 for wedding invitations, $50.00 for the priest, $200.00 for a used couch, chair, coffee table, and end tables, $100.00 for used kitchen table with four chairs, $200.00 for household items like tea towels, towels, sheets, used dishes, pots, and pans, etc. Mom and Dad are buying us a bedroom suite and paying for the flowers, the wedding meal, and music. Angus parents are supplying the liquor. Pretty much all set, now, comes the date. Mom suggests September, because summer will be over and people are back from holidays, plus, it's my favorite time of the year. It will give us a bit more time to save as well. We have half a duplex we will be moving into, when we return from our honeymoon. We found out through a friend of Angus's parents that the rent is $95.00 a month, excluding utilities. Angus's sister, Marion, her husband, Dave, and their son Donny, will be moving into the other side.

We pick September 28, 1968, that will still give us plenty of time for a honeymoon, as Angus is registered for his apprenticeship classes that begin mid-October.

In February, I turn nineteen and go shopping for my wedding dress. It's a fun day; Angus's Mom meets my Mom, Lynn Paquette, and me downtown. Lynn is going to be my maid of honor, Angus's sister, Margaret, will be my bridesmaid and my niece, Tamara, at 2 years and 8 months, will be my flower girl. Angus will have Rob Anderson for his best man and Danny Adams for his groomsman. Both have been longtime friends of Angus. Today, we shop for my dress and we all go to a little shop called 'The Bridal Shop.' It's gorgeous inside, with beautiful wedding and bridesmaids' dresses, along with all the accessories. I try on a few dresses, but keep going back to the very first one I tried on. It's lovely, a long align style with a long trailing veil. The shop lets me put it on a lay-a-way plan. I can go there anytime, make payments and try it on, making sure it still fits. Duty done, we head to the Silk Hat for a bite to eat. This restaurant has been around since 1912 and is otherwise known as 'The Hat' on Jasper. They have a teacup reader there, so after our meal, she stops by our table and asks if we would like to have our tealeaves read? Why not, we all had loose tea, so when you are finished the tea, a few grains are left at the bottom of your cup. She sits down, I'm guessing she would be in her 50s at that time and had been reading tealeaves for a long time at The Hat. Lots of woman in Edmonton would go there with the sole purpose of having their tealeaves read. She's dressed in what I would describe as Gypsy Garb, long flowing gown, bandana on her head, holding a full head of curly, curly hair away from her face. Quite a bit of makeup on, bright red lipstick, dangling earrings, with lots of bangles and beads. She took her job very seriously. I know we all had a turn, can't remember anything she said specifically to me, it was a good. She did tell my mother-in-law to be, that, one day, a son of hers would have his name above a door, and several years later, that did come true, as you will read later, coincidence, probably, but who knows. We all had a great day!

I should mention that on my nineteenth birthday, I got a cedar hope chest. It was made by mentally handicapped teens in a woodworking class. Mom is planning a wedding shower, so the chest will come in handy. I still have it, too!

Angus goes to LaFleche Brothers and has his suit made. Really sharp, lovely shade of dark brown, with some fleck in it, white shirt with rows of tiny pleats on each side of the center button down front. His tie is a black band with several pleats, that run east and west, from one side of the collar to the other, it's about four inches wide, really different. His shoes match perfectly with the suit.

On paydays, I manage to buy at least one or two items, like tea towels, dishcloths, and bath towels. Once a month on the first Tuesday, a department store downtown called Woodward's, has a pretty famous sale day. It was called $1.49 day. It was all across the country, loved going, it was great, as they had all kinds of stuff for the kitchen, bathroom, and bedroom, some clothes and living room items, like doilies and ornaments.

Sometime, in May, the girls get together, Lynn, Margaret, and I, we go shopping for bridesmaid dresses. Yellow is my favorite color, so we pick out two lovely, long, butter yellow, align dresses and the girls look really nice. My sister, Viv, will take care of Tamara's dress and it's a lovely combination of yellow with white lace, she looks adorable. The day of the wedding, her auburn to red hair is in ringlets.

It's starting to come together, but there is still a lot to do. A couple blocks away from work, there is a wedding card shop. After going through the guest list with both families, it is decided that we should try and keep to around a hundred people. We order the cards; they are gorgeous, with a set of gold rings in 3D on the front, linked together with fine gold ribbons on a white background and with lovely gold formal writing inside.

I want the girls to have corsages that will be carried down the aisle on top of the white and gold bibles I have bought them as their gifts. After the ceremony, they can pin them on their dresses and will not have to worry about where they laid down their bouquet. The men will have the usual boutonnieres, Mom and Nanny and Mrs. MacDonald will have corsages, too. I'm having yellow roses my favorite and they will go very nice with the girl's dresses.

Rings, I have my engagement ring, which came with a matching wedding band. I want Angus and I to have matching rings that we will put on one another during the ceremony. We go shopping and find a really nice set, gold in the center with white gold on both sides. They match my engagement ring. it is also a combination of yellow and white gold.

It is decided that the Beverly Crest banquet facility is a good place for the reception, complete with a hot plate dinner and a three-piece band.

Angus's family arranges for a piper, Patti MacIntyre, who is a family friend, to pipe us down the aisle, after the ceremony. As it turned out, the priest says no, just outside the church is allowed and that's okay. He will, also, pipe us into the reception hall.

Mom and my sisters host a kitchen shower for me, it's fun; lots of Mom's friends come, as well as neighbors. There is a lot of joking around we all have a great time. I received a lot of lovely gifts, couldn't have been nicer. Then our neighbors, the Paquette family, hosted a lingerie shower. Every present was PJs, stockings, undies, or nightgowns. Didn't have to buy anything of that nature for a long time. At the bridal showers we played these funny games. One was, you had to put on a heavy man's overcoat, a mitten, a man's glove, a hat, and then button the coat up, all the while the clock is ticking. What a blast, we were howling, couldn't breathe. Of course, the one who did it the fastest, won a prize. There was also the tray game, where a lot of small items are placed on a tray, about thirty of them. It's passed around the room for all to see. We are all given a piece of paper and a pencil, the timer is set for three minutes, the tray is removed from the room and you write down as many items as you can recall. The one with the most correct items won a prize. What fun times, loved every minute.

Angus and I take Mom shopping with us to buy some used furniture. We get the usual, a couch, a chair, a coffee table with two end tables. We either bought or were given a pole lamp, which is a pole that runs from floor to ceiling, with three lampshades that point in different directions. We bought a kitchen table with four chairs. The duplex we are renting will have a stove only, so we buy a fridge from one of our parents' friends for $50.00, it works. It's from the fifties, a rounded style GM Frigidaire, really cute. There is a corner freezer inside, probably held an ice cube tray and a package of sausages, funny!

We were given the keys early, so we did have a chance to set everything up a couple of weeks before the wedding. We cleaned the whole place up and hung some curtains, too!

Time is marching along, summer has flown by and September arrives. All of our RSVP's have come back and everyone is coming.

Not so fast, I have to tell you a quick couple of stories about Angus's 'hot rod' days. Together, we buy a 1940 Ford Deluxe Coupe, from a neighbor, the Dewitt's eldest son, Gary. We each pay him $50.00 a month for four months back in 1966 to 1967. During one winter, Angus works on the car, rebuilding the motor, etc., etc. Come spring, it's ready for the road. I walk to St. Claire's Church, where we will be married, to attend mass and meet him outside afterwards. We get into the car he starts her up, but can't seem to keep her running? The motor is so big he had to put some stuff in the trunk. It turns out a gas line tube has come off. Who will get in the trunk to hold it on? Yes, it's me. I climb into the trunk, with my Sunday best on. It's about six blocks to my house where Angus can get a clamp from a buddy on the block. We pull up, my Dad's outside on a ladder, washing windows. You can hear the car coming from blocks away, so when we pull up, Dad automatically turns, has a quick glance and no Brenda. He watches as Angus gets out, walks to the rear of the car, and opens the trunk. Angus helps me out. I'm drunk, from the gas fumes, staggering like crazy. He steers me towards the front gate, opens it and says, "I'll call you later." Can't say I blamed him, as my Dad is very well put together, wearing a summer undershirt with tattoos and muscles popping out all over the place. Angus is wise to just wave and let me do the explaining. I've got a hell of a headache, so I go lay down to sleep it off.

The very next week, same thing, I meet Angus outside after mass, we get in the car, he starts her up and Yikes, this warm black goop squirts from under the dash and hits me right between the legs and I'm wearing a mini skirt. He quickly turns the car off, but it's too late, the skirt is ruined and so are my new shoes, covered in oil. Well, that was just a couple of funny things that happened, which we have laughed about and repeated over the years. Wouldn't change a thing.

We had a lot of fun with that 40. Angus did get it running well and we enjoyed it for a couple of years. We sold it, before we got married. In July, we bought a 1968 Dodge Charger RT, running a 440 Magnum, a blue exterior, black vinyl roof, white interior with bucket seats, and a console in the center. No more sitting next to Angus. Angus's Dad co-signed the loan, because, back then, you had to be twenty-one and Angus was only twenty. We drove out to 'the lake' and took Grandpa and Nanny for a ride. They really enjoyed it! Grandpa sat up front with Angus and Nanny sat in the back with me. Well, we're cruising along pretty good, when Grandpa opens his window and spits his snooze out. I'm sitting directly behind him and get the stuff right in the face. Yuk! That's the last time I sat in the back seat.

We had a receipt book in those days; you tore one off at a time, in sequence, when making a payment. I did this every month for 36 months. My monthly pay cheque covered the car payment, my bus fare, and a strawberry shortcake from Woolworth's, for Angus. We have never been able to find another that was as good. Angus pay cheque covered all other expenses. When the car was paid off, we took the shell of the receipt book, put it in an ashtray, and burnt it. Life's funny, I thought that was the last of car payments for us, too funny!

It's here, the wedding day! As the clock ticks away, you're hoping that all the planning will pay off and we will all have a lovely day. My sister, Viv, has volunteered to be our photographer for the day. The ceremony doesn't start till four, so there is no hurry, everything's arranged, flowers are delivered to Angus house, as well as ours. There are two floral arrangements that will go on each side of the Alter. The girls arrive about two, gowns in tow. Both have gotten their hair done at the beauty parlor, put up with lovely curls hanging down. We have these little yellow butterflies to pin in, really cute. My hair is pixie short, so there's not much to get done! For weeks, us girls made these white and yellow plastic flowers for the wedding car and the head table. After the rehearsal last night, we go to the hall and decorate, get home about midnight, no problem falling asleep.

My something old is a pair of white heels, something new, my dress, something borrowed is a pair of pearl earrings from Lynn, and something blue is my garter.

Viv does a great job taking pictures, some are taken at home, just before we all leave for the church. I ride with Mom and Dad in the back seat. As Dad pulls up to the front of the church, no Angus, so I ask Dad to go for a drive. I need a smoke and, besides, I don't want to be early. Some people are starting to arrive. So, the three of us drive around for a few minutes. The next time Dad comes around, the decorated wedding car is parked in front, empty, so Dad stops. Mom and I get out, head in, and the girls are just off to the side waiting. I can't remember how they got there. Dad has parked the car and joined us to wait, until all have arrived and been seated. I'm nervous, the music starts, and Tamara is coaxed to begin, followed by Margaret and Lynn. I asked Angus to wink at me, so I wouldn't be too nervous, he does and I'm better, although my Dad had bruises where I was hanging onto his arm.

54

With the ceremony over, we are introduced as Mr. and Mrs. Angus MacDonald and head down the aisle. The doors are opened for us and as we step out, a deafening shrill blasts into our ears, from the bagpipes where the piper is standing off to the side, which makes me jump. The confetti is flying everywhere, the people are all mingling on the steps, cars are honking, the sun is shining it's a beautiful day. We don't have much time between the church and the reception, so the wedding party jumps in the just married car and we drive around honking and waving. As we enter the hall, the piper is there to pipe us in. People are starting to arrive and it's a good time. The speeches are great, the meal, delicious. We do the first dance and switch partners with our Mom's, Dad's, and my Grandparents. We also cut the cake and I throw my bouquet to the ladies. A girlfriend of an auto-body technician that worked with Angus, at the time, caught it, and they eventually got married, too.

Angus and I borrow his Dad's car and drive to my house, so I can change. The door is locked, of course, never thought of that. We go next door to the Paquette's and the sitter lets us in to phone the hall. Dad arrives, more than two sheets to the wind, without the key, really! The bathroom window is open, so Angus hoists Dad up and he climbs through. He survives the short fall and heads back to the reception, funny!

When we get back to the hall, everybody gets in a circle, holding hands, and singing, but I can't remember what song. It's getting late, so we ask for a lift to Angus house, where the Charger is parked inside the garage, with the trunk open, just in case I have a last-minute suitcase or something. We pull up, the lights are on in the garage, strange? Angus opens the door and our wedding party is inside, just about to fill the car with bags and bags of puffed wheat cereal. I look in the trunk and Lynn has my suitcases open and is tying my clothes in knots—we laugh, she didn't quite get through the whole suitcase, so that was good. We leave those characters and head out of town to begin our honeymoon.

Destination is British Columbia, our neighboring Province, its beautiful there. We had previously booked a room on the south side of Edmonton, at a motel called 'The Saratoga,' which was located right on the edge of town. We let them know we would be arriving about midnight. Well, we pull up, Angus goes in to register and a *big bang* is all I heard from the car. I can't repeat what he said to the guy, as he slammed the screen door, but it wasn't nice. They gave our room away—really—now what? Instead of south, we head west, as we know there are a few small towns in that direction and with any luck, we will get a room.

We are driving down the highway, yacking away about the day and suddenly, I remembered that I still had my blue garter on. I take it off and tell

Angus that he was supposed to take it off my leg and throw it to all the single guys at the reception. "Their loss," he says and slips it onto the sun visor, where it has stayed put for forty-eight years. Yes, we still have the 68' Charger and the garter! I'm writing this bit in July 2016.

The distance from Edmonton to a very small town named Wildwood is about 75 miles. Picture this; it's like an old movie. We pull up and stop in front of this motel, the 'open' neon sign is flashing in the window. There's the main entrance, and there are a few steps up to a screen door. An elderly man comes, walking down a hallway, towards us, with his thumbs hooked into his suspenders; that are overtop a white summer undershirt, his belly being his most dominant feature. Coughs a couple of times before asking, "How can I help you?" directed at Angus.

"Do you have a room for the night?"

He looks Angus up and down, looks to the side of him and out towards me in the car, snickers to himself and says, "Wait a minute." Comes back to the door with a key, "Follow me." The three of us walk down this old lopsided wooden sidewalk, its pitch black, we follow him and the beam from his flashlight, where he stops at #6.

He opens the door and says, "This will be six bucks."

We walk in, what's not to like, its two o'clock in the morning, we have had a hell of a day, we are tired and "Is there any heat?" Angus asks.

He walks over and ignites one burner on a two-burner stove. "There you go!" slaps the key on the kitchen table, and slumbers back to his office. I'm frigging freezing, we stand there just looking at one another, can see your breath in the place. Angus leaves and moves the car to just outside the door and brings in the suitcase and sundry bag. I head for the bathroom, to freshen up. Now, remember that lingerie shower, where I received all those lace PJs and nightgowns? Well, I also got a one-piece, flowered, flannelette jump suit for lounging around in. Perfect, it covers me from head to toe with a front zipper that stops at the base of my neck. I walk out of the bathroom in this. Angus is sitting by the stove on a kitchen chair, facing me. Words cannot describe the look on his face—I mean really, this is our wedding night! He was probably thinking, "Look at what you have to look forward to for the rest of your *life*!"

We wake up at about eight, nine o'clock. I head for a shower, run the water for a few seconds, and get in. Well, the water is spitting at me through the showerhead and it's *orange*, yes, *orange*. I start screaming, almost hyperventilating. Angus rushes in to see the commotion and bursts out laughing. It turned out, the well water's full of iron. I guess I should have run it for a while longer, before I got in, city girl! Wow, everybody should have a wedding night like ours, so you can talk about it for years to come and laugh each and every time!

We have a couple of weeks to just go and enjoy ourselves, so we are doing just that. This will be the first of many, many trips we will take together. We stop in Cloverdale, British Columbia, where Angus Uncle and Auntie live with their family. I also know this family, as they lived in Edmonton, right next to the DeWitt's on our block. Their son, Bill, had voluntarily signed up for the Vietnam War and was away at the time of our visit. We saw pictures of him and his enlisted buddies. He came home with two purple hearts, not physically hurt, but mentally, we didn't think he was ever the same Bill. What those guys were exposed to, not many were ever the same. When he did return, he settled in Edmonton and lived with his Baba. We got together quite a bit. He only opened up one night, while visiting us and he never spoke of it again. One day, he dropped by Angus parent's house with his van and a canoe strapped to the roof. Said he was headed up north and none of us ever saw him again, he was gone! The family hired a detective and he did find traces of his belongings along a riverbank, but nothing else, no other leads. We still remember Bill he just wanted to experience life.

So, here we are, about ten days into our honeymoon, we are in Kamloops, British Columbia, sitting across from one another, eating breakfast at the motel restaurant. Angus looks up from his plate and I'm trying to hold back tears that seem to roll down my cheeks and end up at the corner of my mouth. Well, what the hell is this? I have never been away from home or family for any length of time, I'm homesick and wearing my emotions on my sleeve.

Why is it that some or I should say most people can control their emotions and I can't? Even when I was teased about crying when I was a child, it did not bother me. My tears, they come for any number of reasons. I have cried for more strangers in my life than I have ever cried for myself. I cry for sad events that are on the news, I cry at movies 'cause I put myself in the movie. I cry at happiness, too! I cry, when Ian buys me that perfect card that says I'm the best Mom, so now he tends to buy me funny ones and that's good. Dr. Oz says you should never apologize for showing your emotions, so I don't, that's just me.

It's kind of hard to explain, the situation is perfect, I'm on my honeymoon, having lots of fun, enjoying the trip, taking in all the sites but, for some reason, I'm homesick. We head home, couldn't be happier. After being away for nearly two weeks, we open the door of the rental and we are excited to be back. The place was pretty much set up, before we left. Our bedroom suite hasn't arrived yet, just the mattresses, but we don't care. During the wedding reception, the wedding party and a few other fellows had delivered our gifts and they were all in the living room, just waiting to be opened. I guess that's the final stage to a wedding, when all the gifts are opened and thank you cards are sent. We did receive some nice things, too.

Angus and I settle into our life, we love it. We have our routine. There are all of the regular things to do that neither of us have done before, because we have gone from living at home, with our parents, to living as a married couple. Like cooking, for one, my house was so busy there was never any time for cooking lessons. I have no idea how Angus survived my cooking, especially the first year, but then again, yes, I do. He used to stop at his Mom's before coming home from work and she would always have something for him. Actually, I didn't know that for a long time. Somehow, one day it slipped out, but I was okay with that. I learned through trial and error, a few phone calls to my Mom helped, too! I have to share this one, it was so stupid that over the years it has turned out to be funny!

One night, after work, Angus goes in for a bath, while I prepare supper. We had a box of English Fish and Chips in the freezer, so I thought that would be good. I quickly read over the instructions, put the oven on, and popped the whole box into the oven. A few minutes later, the kitchen began to fill with blue smoke. I opened the oven door and was hit with a wall of smoke. I quickly retrieved the box and through it into the sink. Wow! What to do? I put the fish and chips on a cookie sheet and then replaced them in the oven to finish cooking. With both the front and back doors open, I ran with a tea towel, flapping it in the air, as many times as I could, before Angus got out of the bathroom. We sat down. Angus took a couple of bites and said, "Doesn't this taste a little like cardboard to you?"

"Yes," I said and confessed my stupidity. I think we settled for a bowl of soup. I'm a pretty good cook now and I enjoy making different receipts. At this point, we have been married for coming up 48 years, so I guess I'm a keeper.

The rental had a washing machine. One Saturday morning, I was doing the laundry and housework, when I heard this *bang, bang, bang* coming from the basement. I opened the door, turned on the light, and saw the washing machine walking across the basement floor, with the chord stretched to its limits. Angus bolted the thing to the floor, too funny!

It's getting chilly outside winter is here. One night, after supper, we are watching TV in the living room, when the furnace kicks in. *Whoosh!* Followed by the sound of plastic flapping in the breeze, as if strung out on a clothesline. It's the living room curtains. As long as they are just hanging, you can't really tell they are plastic, *but* add a gust of air from the furnace and look out! We sat there, looking at one another, while the curtains were flapping about three and a half feet off the floor. Angus came up with a good idea. Sew some weights in the hem; that will work, and get a couple of air deflectors. Both of those did help. Man, have we laughed about that over the years!

We sure didn't have much back then, but life was good, we had each other, steady jobs, and the fridge was full. Angus sister, Marion, and her husband, Dave, along with their first-born son, Donny, were living in the other side of the duplex. We would go over for weekend breakfasts, toasted bacon and tomato sandwiches with mayo, first time I ever had one, they were delicious. We had an empty spare bedroom, so the four of us would go in barefoot and smack a balloon around, trying to keep it from touching the floor, sometimes for the entire evening, we had a blast and mention it from time to time on visits. Like, remember when…!

One weekend night, we babysat Donny and they went to a drive-in movie. He slept over and Dave came in the morning to pick him up. After he left, I started tidying up and Angus went out to wash the car. Angus was only gone a minute, when he came back in and pulled a bottle of wine from a brown paper bag, said he found it propped up at the bottom of the porch steps. We took it over to Marion and Dave's and asked them if they knew anything about it. Just as Angus was going to take a whiff, they started laughing. Dave had peed in it at the drive-in and thought it would be a funny prank—it was, we laughed and a few swear words were exchanged. It didn't take much for us to be entertained. The four of us would get together with our jugs of pennies and play Rummoli. Marion and I would play crib, too. On some Sundays when Dave was available to watch Donny, Marion and I would go to bingo at the local bingo hall, not far from the house. We would meet my Mom, Nanny, and my sister's, Sandra, and Viv, too.

I remember on one of Angus' birthdays, I didn't have any spare money to get him anything, so I stayed home from work and made him a loaf of bread, because he liked homemade bread. I put a bow on top of it and took a picture of him on the back steps. I was very proud of that, as my cooking skills, at the time, were very limited. He said he liked it, but I'm still not convinced.

It was late fall of 1968,' around November, when Angus decided to park the Charger, because of the winter road conditions. We bought a 1951 Dodge Pickup. Of course, being an excellent auto-body refinisher, as well as a body-man, he 'had' to re-do the body and paint. It was such a fun little truck he painted it lime green with candy colored circle overlays on the lower panels, with fat exhaust pipes mounted on either side of the rear cab, like the eighteen wheelers. The windshield defrost didn't work too well, so he mounted a little fan in one corner of the dash, to keep it from fogging up. We had gotten a tent trailer and he painted the shell of it the same as the truck, boy, did we have fun.

We went everywhere with that truck, all the hippies in Jasper National Park and area would give us the peace sign, as we drove by. It even hauled a moose one time. Angus and his Dad went to pick it up and brought it home and his Dad butchered it. The whole animal was used for hamburgers, mixed with a brine they were so good.

Angus got an opportunity to buy a 1964' GMC Pickup from a customer, at the shop, where Angus was working. It was in excellent shape, so we sold the 51'.

We stayed in the duplex from the time we were married in September of 1968 till the spring of 1971, always working hard, trying to save for our own house. Dave had won $3000.00 at a big bingo game and they used the money for a down payment on their first home. We gave notice, and moved to, another house. We rented that house from the spring of 1971 to the spring of 1972 when we finally had saved enough for a down payment for our first home.

We were so excited, a three-bedroom, one story bungalow, with an undeveloped basement. It had a detached double garage on a fairly large corner lot, great. The house was on 122 Avenue and 42 Street it's still there. We took possession March 1, 1972. I had turned 23 in February and Angus would be turning 24 mid-April. First things first, we had to get rid of our old living room furniture to buy new, we kept the kitchen set, it still looked good. A new bedroom suite was in order, so we got that, too! We had new carpets installed in the three bedrooms, with color coordinating drapes and blinds. We really liked this house there was no wasted space.

Back then, feature walls were in style, and there was already a felt designed feature wall in the kitchen/dining room. Angus put a veined mirror feature wall in the living room. All set and ready to tackle the basement, to make a rumpus room, which is a recreation room, complete with a wood burning stove for those cold winter nights and a ping pong table. Angus did a great job, he surrounded the room in tongue and groove 1"x6" cedar, with a T-bar suspended, white tiled ceiling, with built-in pot lights. The feature was a bar, with glass shelving, a bar fridge, four bar stools, and a TV mounted high at one corner of the room, closest to the bar. We put down a really serviceable wear and tear carpet. Now, all we have to do is have a party, so we did. We had our closest friends over and told them to bring another couple with them. Well, we all had a great time lots of food, drink, and dancing till the wee hours of the morning. When my girlfriend, Lynn, left with her soon to be husband, John, he told me, while shaking his index finger at me, "If you guys ever have another party and don't invite me, you are in big trouble," followed by a big bear hug. So, it was a success.

We also did a lot outside, too. Poured a concrete sidewalk up the front to the front porch, around the side of the house and continuing to the garage where we had an area poured for entertaining. We also had an area poured to one side of the back door and put in a permanent self-standing clothes line; the carousel type. We planted trees and had a really nice flower- bed, at the front, with petunias and dusty millers. Two permanent gas lanterns were installed, they were mounted on poles, about five feet tall, black in color, one at the front, lighting up the sidewalk area and one in the back yard, lighting up the BBQ area. We put together a yard shed, but not without 'trying' our patience first.

We had ordered the shed from Eaton's and received a call that we could pick it up at the loading dock. We go, pick the box up, and head home. It's a beautiful spring Saturday. We spread all of the contents out in the yard. My job is to read the instructions, while Angus assembles. Well, two to three hours go by, and it's pretty clear, I can't read and Angus can't assemble either. So frustrated, we call the loading dock and let them know what's going on, which is nothing, so far. "Hold on," the guy says and comes back with, "There's another box here that goes with the one you picked up."

"Okay, we will be right there."

Now, are we going to call it a day, once the second box is brought home and its contents scattered all over the backyard, too? No, of course not, its read, assemble, and work, till it's done. Pretty much getting dark, by the time we are finished. There must have been 1000 screws that Angus screwed in that day, his hands were blistered, but the shed was up. Endurance, there is nothing like it.

Angus built a good neighbor fence and I say Angus, because I didn't do much. I'm the gopher, the holder, the meal maker. It turned out great.

I kind of got carried away with the house stuff, so I have to take you back, just a few years, as there was so much that happened between the time we got the house in 1972, to the time we built the fence in 1978.

With due respect, I have to mention that in 1968 my Dad lost both his parents. His Dad, my paternal Grandfather, passed away first, of heart complications, followed ten months later by his Mom, my paternal Grandmother, of cancer, she suffered terribly and it was a blessing, when her suffering ended. My Mom's Dad, Grandpa Foley, passed away in 1969, while on vacation with Nanny, Mom, Dad, and my niece, Tamara. They had to ship him home on the train. It was a terrible blow to my Nanny, as Grandpa really wasn't ill, when they left. He had been a welder for many years. Back then, they didn't have oxygen supply and his body was clogged, so when they hit the heat down south, by the Grand Canyon area, he couldn't breathe and his body succumbed to the situation he was in, so sad.

In the summer of 1972, we had bought a small truck camper, no more tent trailer. A fellow Angus knew from work, had moved to Victoria, British Columbia. The family was George Vriesen, his wife Jikki and their daughter Sonia. We had been writing back and forth, keeping in touch. We decided to drive there for our vacation in the 64' pickup and camper trailer.

This is quite comical, if you can picture this.

We had been to British Columbia on our honeymoon, but didn't go to the Island. Neither one of us had ever taken a ferry before. We arrive at the ferry terminal and wait for the next available departure. We board, follow the crowd up to the cafeteria level, and wait in line to get our meal. The captain comes on the PA system, shortly after we leave the dock, and announces all the safety issues and informs us that the trip will be approximately one hour and forty minutes. We finally got our lunch and find a table for two. Relaxed and enjoying the beautiful scenery, the ferry seems to slow down considerably, the ships horns blast long and loud, we look out and can see land. *What*, are we landing?

Quickly, we swallow our food and practically run down the steps, arriving on the lower deck, where the truck is parked. Whew! Beat the crowd. Looking at the time, we must have misunderstood the announcement and the trip is only forty minutes. So, we are sitting in the truck, looking around, and *nobody* else is making their way back to their vehicles. Flatlanders, it turns out that the ferry had just gone through a narrow pass and we still had another hour to go, too funny.

We had a lovely trip, the Island is truly beautiful lots to see and do. We stay with George and Jikki and they give us the usual touristy stuff to go and see during the day. We love it, seems the air is fresher here and we sleep so good, windows wide open in the camper. We start thinking this might be the place for us, but there's an election coming up and it looks like the NDP are the strongest contenders, so we will see. Angus has followed politics and says if the NDP get voted in, we are not moving and they do, so we are definitely not going, that's that.

Can't remember when, but come the following summer, we got a motorcycle, a 1973 Honda 750, a real nice bike. We would go through the city to get out and onto the highway, we really enjoyed it, and went on a few highway scoots, so I could get used to it. Come holiday time, we decide to ride to Victoria, stay in motels along the way. Well, I have to tell you, there's a whole lot of difference between going for an hours scoot and riding for hours down the highway.

Anxious to get to Victoria again, we head out early in the morning. I'm still smoking, so we stop, every once in a while, for a smoke break. I'm getting stiff, really stiff, actually my ass is numb. It's been quite a while now and I need to get off. We are entering Kamloops, British Columbia, which has been a 500-mile trip so far today and I'm really antsy. We stop for a red light, I lean forward, and "Get me the f**k off this bike, *now!*" is how I put it. Angus immediately turns and drives into a neighborhood, pulls over, and stops. I can't move, really, my legs don't work. Angus has to literally pull me off the bike and I fall onto the lawn like a sack of potatoes. Back in those days, we never heard of or even had a bottle of water. There was no talk of keeping yourself hydrated, bottled water didn't exist, anyway. Some people were standing at their front living room windows, watching the proceedings. I rested awhile, stretched a bit, and we decided we would stay at the Davy Crockett Motel for the night. Angus felt really bad for not stopping for such a long stretch, so we came up with a plan. When I tapped him on the right side of his helmet, it meant I needed to pee and when I tapped him on the left side that meant I needed a smoke break. He wasn't following the plan! When I tapped him for a smoke break, he didn't pull over, so I learned to only tap the right side, which guaranteed me a pee and a smoke!

When we got around Hope, British Columbia, it started to rain, not your ten-minute shower that we were used to, no, this was rain, a steady downpour, a curtain of water. It pretty much never stopped raining for the two weeks we were on our trip. Our rain gear didn't even dry out over-night, so we had to put it back on damp. Funny thing is, we made that trip two years running, summer of 1973' and 1974', with the same result, rain, rain. We did have fun times. Our friends, George and Jikki, had had their second child, another girl, Suzanne.

It's 1974, I remember it's a Friday, the phone rings, it's Mom, letting me know they took Nanny to the hospital with possible stomach problems. We will go see her tomorrow. After supper, early evening, Viv, is on the phone, explaining that Nanny had a massive heart attack and has died. I'm overwhelmed, my Nanny gone, can't be. She is such a wonderful, high spirited, and full of life woman. She is the kindest soul you would ever meet and I was so thankful to have her in my life. Her death hit me hard, at the time and I didn't think I would ever breath normally again.

I can hear my Nanny and Grandpa's echoed voices in the porch of the cabin at the lake, saying goodnight to each other, then, the lamp goes off, and all is quiet.

We all thought the world of them. What a tribute to one's life, to be remembered with such love and fondness, after all these years, it can't get any better than that.

I have to share this one, because it's funny and we have repeated the story on many occasions, with laughter abound.

We had a couple, living directly across the street. Our living room windows looked directly into one another. They had gotten a snake, a boa constrictor. I don't know how long it took to grow, but when Angus and I were invited to a feeding, it was huge, about seven to nine feet in length. It had a very solid body and was kept in a cage in the basement. They fed it live experimental gophers, which were used by the University of Alberta. Apparently, they will only eat what they kill, so that's why they feed them the live bait. Yuk! Anyways, the thing died that winter from either eating too many experimental animals or old age, but it was dead, nonetheless. They were going to get it stuffed, so they coiled it up and placed it in a plastic garbage bag and put it in the freezer. Well, come spring, they had second thoughts and decided to just get rid of it. They hauled it to the back yard and placed the bag beside the garbage can.

It's garbage day, a *bang, bang, bang* at the back door. Dianne goes to see what's going on. The garbage man is standing on the other side of the screen door, with eyes as big as saucers, gasping for air, and pointing to the garbage. "It's okay," she says, "It's dead." I guess the guy went to pick up the bag and it was very heavy, so he opened it and saw the thawed-out snake, all wet and slimy and it freaked him out, no wonder, too funny!

I really can't remember too much detail about 1975. We were in our own rhythm, working away, improving the house had kept us busy. I was restless and felt I needed a change. Since being employed with the Provincial Government since 1966, I had applied for and had gotten two other positions, both of them, I enjoyed very much. I was now applying for a Clerk Typist III position, which was a step up for me.

I got the job and the change was really good. I was still in the same building, but my duties were a lot more challenging and I liked it. My pay cheques had grown, too, and that was nice. We hadn't really discussed having children, up to this point, and I wonder, now, that that's probably the reason I was so restless, I felt it was time to either have a child or submerse myself into some education to further my career.

Chapter Four: Adulthood, 1976-1992

It's January, Angus and I are trying to get pregnant. In February, I turn 27 and mid-April Angus will be 28. Following is a poem that my sister Sandra, gave us after finding out we were positive.

On the fifth of February, you were told,
There's one in the oven, still a little bit cold

Excited and waiting on the bus to get home,
Couldn't think of nothing, but seeing the little guy roam

Called the Cyclone number, upon admission,
Couldn't wait to tell Angus there'd be an addition

All excited, his working he had to stop,
Shouting and screaming, hey, guys! I'm a Pop

Now comes all the planning and preparing,
One little guy, for you both to be sharing!

Pretty clever, don't you think?

It happened like this. I missed a period and was feeling off, so I booked an appointment to see Dr. Day, who had been my gynecologist, since I was a teenager.

Every year, I would go for my yearly physical and Dr. Day would always ask when Angus and I were going to have a baby. This appointment, after his examination, he says, "You're pregnant." Oh my, I'm very excited and ask him the due date. He tells me that according to his calculations, it's going to be

September 23rd. We have known one another for a long time now, so I ask him, "Where are you going to be when I have the baby?"

Because several of my girlfriends had had their babies and their doctor's where not there for delivery. He glances over at me, picks up a red pen, and prints in very bold letters on the top of the page, 'MUST ATTEND DELIVERY!'

I smile and he smiles back.

I call Angus from a pay phone, to give him the news. We are both very excited! We go over to his parent's house first, to tell them and they are happy for us. Next, we go to my parents. We sit down at the kitchen table and say we have some exciting news "Guess," I say.

"You bought a new house, a new car, you got a new job?"

"No, no, and no, we are going to have a baby."

Well, I, no sooner got that out of my mouth, and all kinds of plans were being discussed, they, too, were very happy for us. Angus and I, never once, got any pressure from our families about having kids. I'm pretty sure they knew that we would know when it was going to be the right time, and now it felt right. Come September, we will be married eight years.

So, I'm three, four months pregnant and couldn't be happier. I'm sticking out my belly and wearing maternity tops, already. The days and months fly by and pretty soon, I'm giving notice at work. It's the end of June, I've worked for the Provincial Government for 10 years now, 1966-1976, and I want a few weeks off, before the baby comes to get things ready.

I have an appointment with Dr. Day, he doesn't like the swelling in my legs and my blood pressure is too high. "You have to rest," he says, I want Angus to take you to your mother's on his way to work and pick you up on his way home, "Sit, with your feet up and relax." So, that's what we do, it's the beginning of September and I'm becoming uncomfortable. Now, I have to see Dr. Day once a week, so he can monitor me. It's toxemia, which is blood poisoning in the system and it's very dangerous for the both of us.

It's, now, three weeks to delivery and I'm at another appointment with Dr. Day, he's not happy, "Thought I told you to rest?"

"I am resting."

"Well, I'll tell you what, you be at the Royal Alex Hospital, just after supper time tonight and we'll make sure you're resting!"

OH! I'm upset, really upset, I call Angus and tell him, he calms me down, and says it's probably for the best. Mom and my sisters have planned a shower. "Not to worry Mom says," we can have it anytime. So, after three days of 24 hours a day resting, he lets me out, on the condition, if I don't feel well, get in ASAP. Mom gets the shower ready and everyone has a great time. I get some really beautiful baby gifts. We didn't know if the baby was a boy or girl, but I was hoping for a boy. I already had his name picked out.

It's about one am, September 23rd, and I awake with stomach cramps. Oh, I guess I should write the times down when the cramps happen. Angus gets up at six, finds me in the kitchen, pen and paper in hand, with the list of times when the cramps start and stop. "Phone your Mom and tell her," he says. She says for Angus to drop me off there. We go in the house, I sit down, Mom comes and takes one look at me and says, "That's a contraction," she phones the hospital and was advised to bring me in. I was thinking, just cause it's my due date, doesn't mean you will have him today.

Angus gets me to the registration desk and leaves for work. I'm admitted and put in a room by myself. I'm not there long, when the door opens and it's Angus, he has come back.

"What are you doing here?" I ask.

"I was at the shop mixing paint and thought I'm having a baby today! What the hell am I doing here? So, I left."

He stays by my side all day, it's not fun, I'm not dilating and in extreme pain, all back, no front pain at all. Dr. Day has cancelled all of his appointments to be with me. I'm doing fine, Dr. Day never leaves the hospital. They are concerned, so they take me out for an x-ray, the babies coming, very slowly. I have a pain monitor hooked up to me and its readings are off the charts. Angus leaves to get a coffee and, of course, while he's in the cafeteria, they take me to the delivery room, and after one final push, "It's a boy," says Dr. Day.

"Is he all there?" I ask.

"Oh yes," he's all here!"

The nurses take him to a side table, where they clean him up, weigh him, and place a band on his wrist. Angus and Mom come in, it's very emotional with hugs and kisses and congratulations. I find out later that Dr. Day went into the waiting room and announced that Angus was the proud father of a baby boy, Angus questioned, "Are you sure," because everybody said I was having a girl. Even when they took me out for x-rays, they wrote the female symbol on my hospital gown. Surprise, it's a boy and we are two feet off the ground. Ian was born at six minutes after four, so the labor was about fifteen hours and its Thursday, September 23rd. I'm starving, but by the time they get me to my room, supper is over, damn! Then, a nurse comes in and offers me an egg salad sandwich and a cup of tea. Delicious!

Angus has entered our 64" GMC pickup in a car show and it has to be at the facility and set up by eight, that same evening. He calls on his brother and my brother-in-law to help him. He's passing out cigars to strangers, having a ball, and they manage to pull it off, all set.

After the truck is done, Angus comes back to the hospital. A couple of Government forms have been left on my table, to be filled out registering Ian's birth. I ask Angus, if I can name him Ian Patrick and he says, "After what you went through, you can name him whatever you like." So, that's it, IAN PATRICK MACDONALD, we are so very happy!

Come Saturday night, after visiting hours, around eleven, Angus shows up at the hospital, trophy in hand. He won the class for his 64' GMC. We still have that trophy and it has Ian's birthdate on the plaque. We still have the 64' and it looks just as nice today, as it did then.

At that time, a person was kept for six or seven days in the hospital. So, on the morning of September 28th, a Tuesday, Dr. Day came to the showers, where I was and hollered, "Do you want to go home today?" "Yes," I reply.

"Okay, away you go, call for an appointment next week." "Thanks, I will."

It's our eighth anniversary, right on the nose. Angus comes to pick us up and we drive to his Mom and Dad's, it's a beautiful fall day, next, we stop at my Mom and Dad's then home. My youngest sister, Sandra, drops by and says, "You sure couldn't have a nicer present than this," she was so right.

At the time of writing, I couldn't remember anything significant that took place in 1975. Duh! I wanted to learn how to drive, which turned out to be a bit of an undertaking. Winter is the best time to learn, get familiar with the snow and the ice on the roads. The process started with Angus taking me out driving. Well, I just about made six blocks, when he tells me to pull over. I'm grinding the gears and not getting the hang of the clutch, which is making the truck jerk ahead each time I shift from one gear into the next. I'm wrecking the truck, so I sign up for lessons. Come the morning of my road test, Angus thinks it might be a good idea, if I wear a skirt!

"Really," he says, "It couldn't hurt." I go for the road test and sure enough, the instructor is a guy, younger than I am and I catch him eyeing my legs, as I'm driving and shifting gears. We get back to the parking lot, where I'm to parallel-park between two orange cones, placed a vehicle distance apart. I did okay, just tapped one cone, it didn't fall over, just wobbled a bit. He said if it was a car, I probably wouldn't have hit it. Good, I get my driver's license. Best thing I ever did, except marry Angus and have Ian.

Okay, back to having Ian. I have to pinch myself every day. I'm a stay at home Mom, with a son of my own. Angus is looking after us, the best Dad a boy could ever have. We waited to have a child and it was worth it, we have a home for him. Our rhythm in life is really good. Angus is away at work, during the day, which leaves Ian and I to work out our days together. I'm pretty structured, which means I like things organized. I take comfort in planning my day, completing tasks as scheduled, so I'm not boiling baby bottles at midnight or vacuuming, during the evening news, you get my gist. Ian is really a good baby; he eats well and sleeps just as good. Sometimes, I have to go in his room and wake him up, so he will sleep through the night. I love being at home, with Ian. The day's fly by, it's Christmas, before we know it. On Fridays, we take Ian to my Mom's. She has offered to babysit, while I drop Angus at work, then carry on with grocery shopping, along with other errands. Usually, I arrive back around one o'clock, where Mom and I have a chance to have a lunch together and, of course, catch up on Ian's progress.

So Christmas Day arrives, Ian is almost three months old. We prop him up at one end of the couch and place a heavy pillow on top of him, so he can see everything that's going on. We spend Christmas morning at my parents, then the afternoon with Angus family, and then back to my parents for dinner. By the end of the day, we feel like rubber bands but have had a good Christmas Day with both sides of the families.

Come spring, Angus decides he wants to park the 1964 GMC and buys a 1967 Chev. Malibu. It's in really good shape, an automatic, a four-door sedan, a family car. So now, we have two parked vehicles, the Dodge Charger and the GMC pickup. Both vehicles are worth saving, so I'm okay with that decision. We will share the Malibu. I'm fine, at home, with Ian and anytime I want the car, it's available for me.

We have a nice couple living next door, Dave and Mary Harris. Unfortunately, Dave passed away very suddenly, leaving Mary a widow. We have become quite close and enjoy taking Ian for a daily walk in his umbrella stroller. He is now 7 to 8 months old and really likes getting out in the fresh air. I hang our laundry outside, eat my lunch outside, weed the flowerbeds, while Ian is napping and thoroughly enjoy myself. Ian and I take days off, where we just play, chase each other around the house, as he is crawling now and we giggle all day! Such fun!

In the summer, we do fun things, like go camping with Angus folks. We all have a great time. Come vacation time for Angus, we decide to drive to Victoria, see George and Jikki, Sonia and Susanne. We stay in motels with Ian, who is just shy of a year old. The girls play with him for hours on end they are now six and four and love the company.

One morning, I was in the kitchenette and saw a huge spider this thing was the biggest spider I had ever seen. I caught it between a drinking glass and a saucer, and placed it on the kitchen table, to show the maid. Hoping to get a positive response from her, once I showed her the good deed, I had done. She just looked at it and said, "There are a lot bigger ones than that," and flushed it down the toilet. That was a good one on me…

Going home was difficult, because we love the Island, so the ferry trip was pretty quiet. Once we landed and got going again, the silence was broken. We were driving along and came to a construction zone, with freshly poured gravel. There was a car coming towards us, going pretty fast, so Angus slowed down and pulled over, just as a rock came flying across the road and struck the windshield, to which Angus responded with a few unpleasant words directed at the driver. Ian, sitting in the back, in his car seat replied, "Bad Vroom, Vroom!"

We couldn't help, but laugh!

Once home again, it feels good, we get back into our regular routine. It's fall again and can't really believe how fast Ian's first year has gone. His birthday falls on a Friday. I get the car for the day, so we go grocery shopping and stop at Mom's for a visit. He's walking now, so you can't take your eyes off him. Mom and I take him to Sears, to have his picture taken in a cute little sailor's suit and his first pair of shoes. I made him his own little birthday cake. In the evening, Angus folks drop by for tea. It's time for cake. I strip Ian down to his diaper, tie a big bib around his neck, and then set him in his high chair. He blows out the one candle and goes at it, squishing the chocolate cake and icing between his fingers and then to his mouth. I don't think he got too much down, which was good. Grandma and Grandpa laughed, and so did we. All done, into the tub, he goes. That was a fun day.

It's now November of 1977. Mom calls and says that Dad has had a really bad headache for a couple of days, hasn't gone to work, which is very rare for him. She had gone upstairs to check on him and he had practically taken a whole bottle of aspirin, trying to get rid of the headache, so she called the ambulance. He was admitted into the Royal Alex Hospital. Mom said, "Don't be surprised, if he doesn't recognize you." Angus watches Ian and I go to see him. Mom was right, I walked into the room and he thought I was Gwen, one of his sisters. He was scheduled for some tests, we would know soon. Turns out, he has a brain aneurysm that has been slowly leaking, causing the headaches. An aneurysm in the brain is a bulging weak area in the wall of the artery that supplies blood to the brain.

He will require surgery, immediately. Because his aneurysm was just leaking and hadn't burst, was a good thing, although the prognosis was not good. He may not make it. He is 55 years old, strong as an ox, but hasn't treated himself well for years. He is a heavy smoker and an alcoholic, besides.

The surgery day for us was a very long day. He is placed in I.C.U, we will have to wait and see how he comes out of it. We are allowed to see him, but he is not awake. Seeing him lying there in that darkened room, surrounded by ice, tubes, and monitors beeping everywhere, a drain tube stuck in the top of his head, covered only with a thin sheet, made you sick. How could he possibly be alive?

A few days later, he is looking a lot better. It will be a while before he is allowed up, but so far, he seems to be doing alright … NOT … Mom goes up every day and she says he's not right, senses that his brain has been affected, somehow, because he's just not right.

Well, another few days pass, he steals the clothes that belong to the man in the bed next to him, takes them from his locker. A nurse goes in the room and she finds Dad sitting up, legs hanging over the side of the bed, the man's pants are about a foot too short, the shirt won't button up, and Dad's already eaten half a box of chocolates that he took off the man's table. It was really funny! Although, I guess, the man didn't think so!

They have to strap him in bed and when he does get up, they walk him for some exercise and then strap him to a chair, where he eats his meals. What to do, the doctor's say it will take time.

It's been a few weeks now, Mom calls about six, one evening, very upset. Dad walked out of the hospital, got in a cab and got Mrs. Paquette from next door to pay for it, as Mom wasn't home at the time. She has called Viv and her boyfriend, Wally, to come. I tell Angus and he watches Ian, while I go over and try to help.

When I arrive, Viv and Mom are on the phone to the Doctor, my Dad's GP. They are stating our case that Dad's just not right in the head, if you know him, you would pick up on it right away. They answer several questions and the Doctor says he will phone the Alberta Hospital, a mental institute, and see if they have a room for him. The Doctor calls back within minutes, yes, they can take him. The Doctor makes us aware that by law, they can only detain Dad for 72 hours and he will go through an assessment procedure.

Dad's upstairs in their bedroom, laying out his wallet, keys for the car, his school keys, he is the head custodian at Eastglen Composite High School, his clothes, shoes, etc. He is getting ready to head back to work in the morning. Well, this is a delicate situation, but if anybody can persuade Dad, it's Viv.

She and Wally get him in Wally's pickup truck, sandwiched between them. On the way, Dad looks right at Viv and says, "I know where you are taking me." When they arrive, an orderly greets Dad, extends his hand to Dad, they shake and the orderly says, "Welcome, Mr. McQuade," and they walk in.

That moment must have been so very difficult for Viv, to watch, and see your Dad, being escorted into a mental institute.

As it turned out, Dad needed a bit more time for his brain cells to recover from surgery and he stayed there for a couple of weeks. I took Mom there to visit, as much as I could. The building was strongly guarded and as you went through one door, it was locked behind you, then through another and it was locked behind you, too.

We were taken to a communal visiting area, where Dad was on one side of the table and Mom and I on the other side. Dad bends over the table towards me and says, "Don't look now, but see that guy over there, he's nuts." Really, at that point, I thought, *let's just hope we can get you out of here*. It was an odd feeling and I have had a few dreams about being locked up and not being able to get free, nightmares, actually.

Dad gets a release from the hospital after being assessed by a team of doctors. I don't think it was a miracle, I think it was the surgical team, his after surgery care and my Dad's will to live that got him through. At the hospital, they had his picture up on their success wall for a long time. The aneurysm had mellowed him quite a bit, he seemed quieter in his demeanor and he lost his sense of smell, altogether. Not too bad for what he went through.

Come spring, he is back at work full-time and seems to be doing just fine. He is no longer drinking and Mom is very relieved. He hasn't even shown any signs towards wanting a drink.

In that spring, I met a very nice young mother and her son, six months younger than our Ian. She and her husband, Art, live just behind us, we share the same alley. We met one beautiful morning, as Ian and I were going on our morning walk. Kathy was outside, playing with Laurence, who was about a year at that time. We had a nice chat over her fence and said we would have to get together for afternoon coffee.

Can't remember how it unfolded but usually, twice a week and sometimes more, we would have an afternoon coffee break together with the boys. We went back and forth, sharing our time at each other's houses. The boys got along great, as did Kathy and I. Angus and Art began chatting to one another as well, which completed the friendship. Ian couldn't pronounce his L's at the beginning, so he called Laurence—Ornance, too funny!

So, I'm back to the fence building. It's the early summer of 1978. In our neck of the woods, projects like this have to wait, until the ground unfreezes, in order to drill out the earth for fence posts. Angus has never built a fence before. As a matter of fact, he has never done any of the great projects he has completed in and around our home, since we moved in, in 1972. He just has a knack for it, he definitely has used his natural abilities to their fullest. He would probably say by a lot of trial and error, but for me, I haven't seen anything that he won't take on and succeed at. Of course, he's intelligent, so he doesn't profess to know everything, so if he is unsure, he will seek advice from those who do know. He's not an electrician, a plumber, or an appliance repairman; he's just so good at what he tackles.

The good neighbor fence is made of 1"x6" cedar planks. It surrounds the back yard, with a gate at the side of the house, just before getting to the back door. We have decided to paint it with a real good quality, colored stain, alternating two white boards with one mid to bright green, really nice. It's now June, we are in the process of painting both sides, which takes a while.

Actually, I'm stalling…because this next part of my life is the worst tragedy ever. I don't know how to approach it, other than to just tell you how it happened.

"Mommy, will see you in just a little while," I say, as I laid Ian down for his afternoon nap. I cover him and caress the side of his little head to comfort him and as I see his eyelid begin to droop, the telephone starts to ring. So I back out of the room and close the door to almost shut. "I'm coming," I whispered, as I hurry down the hallway and grab the wall receiver on the third ring. "Hello," I say.

"Hello, its Mrs. Paquette calling," she begins.

"I know, Mrs. Paquette, I would recognize your voice anywhere, how are you?"

"I'm afraid I have very bad news."

"Oh," I questioned.

"Can you come over to your Mom and Dad's house, right away?"

"Gosh, I've just put Ian down for his nap, can't you just tell me now? Besides, Angus is at work, so I don't have the car,"

"It's your Mom," she says very quietly.

"What's wrong with her?" I respond.

"She's been in an accident."

"What kind of accident?" I ask.

"She's been hit by a car," she replies.

"What hospital is she in?" I question.

"She isn't in the hospital," she says, then there's a long pause… "She didn't make it, she's dead." I shout back, "No, she's not," followed by a slight giggle of disbelief, "no, she's not!"

She apologized for having to tell me that way. We concluded our conversation by me thanking her and asking if she could please tell my Dad that I would be there, just as soon as I could. I hang up, absolutely stunned, couldn't move, and my heart was pounding so hard. I'm shaking and quivering uncontrollably. I start to cry. My brain is racing a mile a minute. I'm scared!

What am I supposed to do?

I have no Mom, I have no Mom, pacing in the kitchen, trying to calm myself, my head is thumping, Call Angus, he'll come and take you to Dad's, yes, that's it, call Angus. I know he can hardly understand me on the phone, as

I try to explain the accident and that my Mom is dead. To say that to him was one of the hardest things I've ever had to do!

After calling our neighbor, Mary, she comes right away. Angus gets home and we head to Dad's. We arrive at my family home, my sisters are already there, it seems so quiet when we walk in; it is too quiet. We are all speaking very softly, each of us not knowing what to do, what to say. Someone puts the kettle on for tea.

The front door bell rings, it's the police. He's the investigating officer and once we are gathered in the living room, he proceeds to explain what happened. She was hit crossing 118 Avenue at 66/67 Street, in a crosswalk, going to her part time job at the public library. She was dragged about 100 feet, under the vehicle, because her clothes were caught. It's a hit and run, they have lots of witnesses, a description of the car, they are looking.

They need a family member to identify the body… Vivian, my eldest sister, volunteers to go, Angus offers to go with her. They leave. I'm very upset. I'm once again, consumed with emotions I can't seem to control. It's too much, it's so wrong. My Dad hasn't even fully recovered, yet!

The next few days are a blur. We manage to pull ourselves together, in order to make the arrangements. It's the long weekend in July 1978. Mom was killed on Thursday, June 29th the service is to be on Tuesday, July 4th.

Mom was to retire on that Friday, after being a foster mother to over fifty kids, in the span of twenty-five years. There were two remaining, a boy about 17 years old, and Lyn, the girl they had taken in approximately 20 years before. Mom had the boy's clothes and personal belongings packed and ready to be picked up. He had an eye disorder and was in the city for treatment, but was going home, after the long weekend. Lyn, who was now 28, was in the hospital, fighting a bladder infection. We contacted the hospital and explained the situation; they were able to keep her there, until after the service.

Life will never be as it was! I was 29 when Mom was killed I'm 67 now. To this day, I miss her. I will always miss her. She was one in a million. Can you just imagine the organizing, the planning, the scheduling, the shopping, the preparing, the housework, the laundry, the lost socks, the meals, and the dishes, every day of the year, for over twenty-five years? There was us four girls, usually five live in orphans, who were physically or mentally challenged to some degree, a husband, a dog, a cat, and sometimes, a bird to care for. How are we going to live without her?

The events that unfolded were as you can imagine, the police keeping in touch, they caught the four guys who were in the car. In the early morning hours, they spotted the car parked in a parking lot at a local motel. They stayed there, out of site, until the four came into view, then they waited to see who

74

would get behind the wheel, and charged him with hit and run, causing death, and leaving the scene of an accident.

In two and half years of court appearances, he got off, nobody could make a positive ID of who was at the wheel, and the other three were not pressured into saying, so I guess the car was just driving itself. So, my Dad got $15,000.00 from the car insurance company and that amount was determined, because she was deemed 'past her prime.' That's the way it went… Am I angry? I'm still unforgiving and that will never change. I'm constantly reminded of awful events in life by the daily news and have come to tears on many, many occasions. Angus and I will be watching the news and a report of a family losing a loved one or some other devastating event that has taken place and he reaches for the Kleenex. Sometimes, we just look at one another and we know how hard it will be for them. Angus is my rock and has always been there for me.

I can't fully explain how my mother's death has affected me. It's deep and profound.

One never knows how you will face adversity, until challenged. I felt alone, really alone, of course, Angus and Ian, my family and friends were there, but *who* the hell was going to care if and when Ian got a new tooth or didn't feel well and I needed her to give me that new mother confidence to care for him. You just know that it's your Mom, who cares the most.

She wasn't old, wasn't sick, and was full of life, looking forward to her retirement, for which, she had worked so hard for. She was totally innocent, when she stepped off that curb to cross the street. Every Mother's Day, her Birthday, the Christmas's without her, the sharing of time together, all gone. Absolutely, every part of my being was damaged. I don't believe in justice, because the punishment never fits the crime. My son will never know her and she loved him dearly. As the years have gone by, I now think of how fortunate I was to have had her as my mother. When I think of her, I smile and have such good memories to hold onto. I can only hope that once I'm gone, the ones remaining will still be smiling at the thought of me, after some forty years and beyond.

The service is a blur. We have a closed coffin, as Mom had to have an autopsy performed to make sure it was the hit and dragging of her body that killed her and not that she had a heart attack and fell into the car.

Lyn is released from the hospital. She will stay with Angus and I, until we can find a new home for her. It's a couple of weeks and we get her into the Good Sheppard Home, in Edmonton. We go take a look; it's a really nice clean, bachelor suite. Lyn likes it, too! We go home and gather up linens, towels, ornaments, etc. We set the little suite up really cute for her.

It turned out really good, we explained that Mom was gone, that she had died, but we never told her how. Lyn was enrolled as a day laborer, putting small manufactured parts into bags, like nuts and bolts, washers, things like that. She earned her keep and she met friends, too. They had special arts and crafts to do. All of the residents ate in a cafeteria. She is liked and treated well by the staff; all is good.

Dad, I can't even imagine how tough it was for him, to go home, after work, to that empty house. Over time, that busy, busy household had changed dramatically. Us girls all grew up, married, and moved. The orphans dwindled down to the remaining two and they were gone within two weeks of Mom's death. You can't be prepared for tragedy, it happens and you are left to pull yourself together or fail miserably, there is no other option.

In July, we have a painting bee at our house, to finish the fence. Angus, Ian, and I are getting away on a trip to Victoria. Everyone from both sides of the family come to help. We do have a good time. The weather is good, food is good, and the fence is finished.

Summer turns to fall and fall to winter and before we know it, it's Christmas. We all make an effort to give Dad as good a Christmas as we can and it goes okay. Our hearts weren't into it. Angus receives a two-week vacation, an all-expense paid trip to Hawaii. His boss has a condo over there and he is time sharing with those employees who have earned the trip.

We talk about it and decide to ask our good friends Art, Kathy, and their son, Laurence, to join us. They will only have to pay for their flights and food. Yes, they can, and they are as excited as we are. It's been a very cold winter and it will be nice to get away and enjoy some warmth.

Dad drives us all to the airport, at a ridiculous time in the morning, but we don't care, the kids are good, so we are good. We take off our winter coats and Dad stretches his arms out to receive them. I give him the return flight information; he will pick us up.

A very long day, as we had a layover in Honolulu, where we changed planes to continue onto the big Island of Hawaii. Those, who were transferring, were shuttled by bus to the terminal. It's hot on the bus, it's +80 degrees and when we left Edmonton, it was -35 degrees. Angus pipes up in the silence and says to Art, "Hey, Art, I'll bet you're the only guy on the bus with long johns on?"

Well, the whole bus burst out laughing and the funny thing is, he also had cowboy boots on. Too funny!

We finally touch down on the Kona Coast, on the big Island of Hawaii. It's not quite dusk. The kids are starting to get restless, as they have been tossed between parents for the last ten hours or so. We all pile into a two-door compact Toyota that belongs to Angus' boss, it has been left parked at the airport. It's decided that we should eat, before we do some grocery shopping. Sizzler, it's a family restaurant. We go in and are met with very friendly smiling faces. The staff goes out of their way for us and get the kids seated in high chairs, at a fairly large round table. A waitress greets us, her name is Lalonie, and she's carrying a large jug of ice-cold beer, sets it down, and says, "You guys look like you could use this!"

The smile on Art's face was priceless.

After being regenerated, we head for the grocery store. Angus and Art grab a buggy of their own, while Kathy and I get one, too. Laurence stays with us and Ian goes with Dad. We head off in different directions, the guy's head straight for the beer section, while Kathy and I head for the food.

It's dark, the Toyota won't take another thing, as we have grocery bags on the floors, front, and back, between our legs. The trunk is jammed with suitcases and baby totes. We retrieve a hand drawn map to the condo from the glove box and set off. The road is narrow and its pitch black, we don't know where we are going and Laurence poops his pants! Now, we have all four windows open, there's no room in the car to change a diaper and no place for a vehicle to pull over.

Art was doing his best with the map, pronouncing the Hawaiian street names, which, in his Dutch accent, is really funny! We all get the giggles; it's been a long day.

Finally arriving was such a relief. A two-story building and ours was on the second floor with exterior steps leading to the front entrance. Angus opens the door and flicks the light switch on. Kathy enters and screams, while holding her mouth and pointing to the wall. Art runs towards a small lizard, who running twice as fast, takes off a cowboy boot and throws it at the thing, which cuts it in half. Wow! We are here.

The guys unload the car, while us girls get the kids cleaned up and ready for bed. The four of us are getting settled in, passing each other in the hallway, leading to the bedrooms. The bathroom was in the center of that hallway. Angus comes up to me and asks where the camera is. I get it and he heads down the hallway, where the bathroom door is open and there stands Art, in front of the sink, in his long johns and cowboy boots, shaving! Too funny, we have the picture!

Come morning, we are happy, the sun is shining, the kids are playing on the deck, and we are just lollygagging with coffees and enjoying our view. We are overlooking the sea, which is just beyond a golf course and swaying palm trees, couldn't have been nicer.

Here are just a few of our memorable moments from that trip.

We were on the west side of the Island, on the outskirts of the City named Kailua. We started quite early, one morning, to drive around the Island. The Island is beautiful we had never been on a tropical island before and were thoroughly enjoying the sites. There are beautiful parks, a Polynesian Cultural Center, views, and access to the beaches all over the Island. We toured the macadamia nut factory, where we stocked up on gifts to bring home, like chocolate covered macadamia nuts, made right there and shipped all over the world, delicious! Watched some surfers on the north side of Hilo, they were good. We had a great day, the round trip took us about eight hours, as we stopped, quite a bit, to stretch and make the kids happy.

We went to the beach almost every day. At first, the boys would run into the water, ankle deep, stop, look down at the waves hitting their little legs, loose balance, and plop down on their bottoms, they were dizzy, and it was funny!

There was a food/beverage truck, painted all different colors, with the side of it open for serving customers. The beer was ice cold and the popsicles for the kids were great. The fellow, who operated the truck, was an Irishman, from Ireland, who apparently went to Hawaii on vacation and never left. He had a surfboard, leaning against the truck, and when he noticed the waves getting higher and higher, he would close up and go surfing. No rules or regulations for that fellow!

Us girls decided it would be nice to go out with our husbands for a quiet evening. So, Angus and I babysat Laurence one evening and then Art and Kathy babysat Ian. Angus and I went to a place called Huggo's. It was very scenic, right on the waterfront, beautiful sunset, too. We were seated at the front of the restaurant, where it was open to the air, built on stilts, so if the waves got rough, you were splashed. As the waves got worse, it was suggested that we move back just a bit, so we wouldn't get soaked. We had a great time, good food, nice and relaxing evening. I looked them up on Google, and Huggo's is still there and considered one of the top ten waterfront restaurants on the Island.

We experienced an earthquake, in the middle of the night. Ian was sleeping on a single cot, beside our bed, and when the shaking woke us up, he sat straight up, crisscrossed his legs, and said, "What the hell was that?"

That was funny coming from a three-year-old. In the morning, we discovered a couple of coffee cups in the cupboard that had swung off their hooks and lay broken on the shelf. Also, in the living room, there was a glass tabletop that had jumped out of its recessed frame and was lying cockeyed on top of the table. Looking outside, there were coconuts and palm leaves scattered about, but no real structural damage that we could see.

On our last day, we stayed at the condo and did the linens up and cleaned house. Angus and Art were on the deck with the boys, enjoying a beer, and watching the golfer's putt, just in front of the condo. Angus decides to pull a fast one on the next group, approaching the green. There was quite a steep hill shot to get the ball up and rolling onto the green, which couldn't be seen by the golfers. Angus goes down to ground level, waits for a ball to come, grabs it, and places it in the hole, then returns to his chair on the deck. So, the golfer and his buddies come up the hill, each looking for his ball. The golfer is scratching his head, can't figure out where his ball could be, when his buddy discovers it in the hole. Well, you never saw the likes of this, the guys hopping around the green, ecstatic, whistling for the beer wagon and can't bloody believe he got the ball in the hole. They carried on for a few minutes, saw the guys sitting on the deck and were asking if they saw the ball go in, to which, they both replied, "No." They let them walk off, the guy's ten feet off the ground and he is probably still talking about the eagle he got in Hawaii.

We load up the Toyota and head for the airport. It has been a great trip, one that will be remembered with very fond memories. We take a Hawaiian Air flight to Honolulu and then transfer to a flight on Ward Air, one of the finest airlines at the time. After running, playing, and having a ball at the beach for two weeks, the boys were hard to contain. Art, Kathy, and Laurence were sitting in the three seats in front of us. The boys were playing peek-a-boo with one another, but the flight is eight to ten hours long, so there's just so much peek-a-booing one can do!

Actually, the boys weren't misbehaving, they were restless, so we tried to keep them busy. After our dinner was served and eaten, Ian finally fell asleep, lying on the seat between Angus and I, with his legs on my lap. A stewardess noticed and offered me a cup of tea, which I accepted, without hesitation. I lowered my tray, where she sat it down for me to enjoy. I reached for the teacup and in one split second, Ian's leg kicked up in his sleep and the tea splashed everywhere, mostly on me, and my new white slacks. Ouch! So much for my relaxing cup of tea, Ian remains asleep!

Touch down is celebrated with applause and we are all glad the flight is over. Dad is there to greet us, although we are cold, he tells us that the weather has been pretty nice, while we have been away. We are home around midnight on a Friday, which will give us the weekend to get settled in.

It's, now the second weekend in March and, surprisingly, come Saturday morning, the sun is up, clear blue skies, it actually feels like spring is in the air. A lot of the snow has melted and Ian can play outside.

A few days go by, Angus is back at work, Ian and I are back into our routine, when a storm hits. A lot of snow falls in a two-day blizzard, wet heavy snow. Yuk! Winter again!

After being in the sun, surf, and sand on a tropical Island, this is hard to take. Angus and I start talking about getting away from the winters and the big city. Raising Ian in a smaller place like Victoria, where we have gone on holidays for the past eight years and where we have heard the winters are a lot nicer than ours.

We have been communicating with George and Jikki over the winter, mostly letters with a couple of phone calls thrown in. George informs Angus that there is lots of work in Victoria and for Angus, finding a job won't be a problem.

That's it, we are moving! It's perfect timing, we will have spring and all summer to get relocated and settled in. We call George and Jikki, to give them the news and Jikki volunteers to get some housing information ready for Angus. He is welcomed to stay with them. A flight is arranged and Angus' Dad drives him to the airport. They discuss the move and Angus says to his Dad, "This will either be the best or the worst move I've ever made."

That same day, through a girlfriend of Viv's, who is a real estate agent, the house is put on the market. It's the Easter long weekend. The 'For Sale' sign goes up on Friday afternoon.

On Saturday morning, I take Ian to Big Boys for a breakfast treat. We get home around eleven and shortly after that, the front door bell rings. A lady, in her sixties, I would guess, is standing on the front porch. I open the door and greet her. She is visiting her daughter, who lives just a few doors down. She is a widow, interested in moving into the city and would I show her the house. "Yes, of course come in". I show her through the house, she likes it. I take her out to the back yard, she likes it, and then I show her the garage. We walk back into the house where Ian is playing in his room. We sit in the kitchen, chatting, while I make a cup of tea. She asks what the house is selling for, I tell her, and she says "Sold." I'm excited, I explain that Angus is in Victoria, looking for a house and is expected home on the holiday Monday. We set a time to meet here on Tuesday evening, with the real estate agent. Wow! The house is sold, that took just about an hour, if that.

Angus is going to call, after his day of house hunting, so I'll wait, because he won't be there to take my call. I telephoned Laurel, the real estate agent and give her the news, along with the lady's name, phone number, and the time of our scheduled meeting on Tuesday evening. Things are moving right along.

Angus calls that evening and I give him the news about the house selling. He says he has looked at twelve houses that day nothing catches his eye, but that he has one more to see tomorrow. The house is owned by an acquaintance of George and Jikki's. There is an out building on the property that will house our Charger and the GMC, sounds promising.

On Sunday, he looks at the property, goes over the house, the price, any conditions that might be relevant. It's a private sale. Angus likes it and tells the owner he will think on it over-night and let him know.

I get the call from Angus, he seems to be quite excited over the whole thing and I tell him if he likes it, then I will, too!

Come Monday morning, Angus decides to buy the acreage. The paperwork was drawn up, witnessed, and a down payment exchanged hands, the possession date is set for June 1st.

So, let's sum this up! We get home from Hawaii on March 9th, storm hits, we talk, put the house up for sale on April 13th, Good Friday, sell it on April 14th. Then, Angus buys a house on April 16th, Easter Monday, it's done! We are actually going to move to British Columbia. We are so excited. I turned thirty in February and Angus will be thirty-one on the 17th of April. He arrives back home on his birthday.

I'm pretty sure we stayed up till the wee hours of the morning. Discussing the move and making a list of things we have to do. We have to call everyone and break the news. Angus parents are happy for us and said they may consider retiring there, come the spring of 1980. That was great to hear. Angus's Dad had just retired from the Edmonton Transit System, after driving a bus for 34 years. My Dad took the news okay, but I really got the feeling he wasn't too keen on the idea. He did spend some time in Victoria, as a sailor, during the Second World War and he always said it was too wet for him. Art, our good friend, was flabbergasted. To this day he says, "All of a sudden, you guys were gone!" LOL.

That's pretty much how it happened, too. The list of 'to dos' kept us busy and as the days dwindled down, the list got shorter and shorter, tattered around the edges, kind of like me. There was a lot of organizing, planning, and scheduling to be done, but I had learned all that from Mom, so I put my skills to work and everything fell into place.

On the May long weekend, Angus has arranged for a couple of friends, with flat deck trailers, to haul the two vehicles to our new home. They loaded them up and left early on the Saturday morning. It was two weeks to our possession date, but the owners said it was okay to bring them and put them in the outbuilding. Angus was riding with Gary in his pickup, hauling the Charger and Gary's friend followed in his pickup, hauling the GMC. They stopped in Clearwater, B.C. for the night. Getting closer to the ferry, Gary decides to pull over at a weigh station. He is curious to see how much it all weighs. Well, the attendant on duty takes a look, then measures the trailer and guess what? It's too wide to continue… What! They have to leave that trailer parked.

So, Angus and Gary hop in the other pick up and the three of them drive to the ferry, take the ferry trip across, which is an hour and forty minutes, deliver one vehicle, that was another thirty minutes from the ferry terminal. Drive back to get on the next available ferry, back to the weigh station, that is approximately an hour away, pick up the second vehicle, back to the ferry, drop off that second vehicle, and head back to the ferry once again, arriving at the weigh station to pick up the truck and trailer that was parked. By the time they headed down the highway home, it was getting pretty late. Wow! All because Gary's trailer was 2½ inches too wide and the agent was an asshole!

Gary's friend has arranged to pick up a load of shingles for his house, so that worked out good. All said and done, they got home late on the holiday Monday, safe and sound. Angus said they actually had a good time, lots of laughs, and a trip to remember.

The last weekend in May, Angus and Art take Ian and Laurence to the park to fly kites. We filled them in on the move, we would keep in touch, and then we said our goodbyes.

The events were happening in a kind of domino's effect, one action that led to another, then another, and another. It was the last week in May, a Monday, the movers came early and before we knew it, our house possessions were in the truck and gone. We had gotten full access to the guest house/garage on our new property, so the movers could unload anytime they arrived.

Angus had taken Ian to his Mom and Dad's for a visit and to pick up his brother, Allan, who was coming with us, as far as Nelson, B.C., where their sister, Marion, her husband, Dave, and their, now, family of three boys had moved to, just a couple of years before.

Our neighbor, Mary, was watching the proceedings from her living room window. When the movers had gone, she came out and asked if I would like to have lunch with her? "Yes, that would be nice." We sat at her kitchen table and discussed the move and our new house. She tells me that she has a brother on the Island up north, when she goes to see him, sometime, she will come to visit.

Angus got home, hooked up our loaded utility trailer to the Malibu. My Dad pulled up to say goodbye, on his lunch break and said once we got settled that he would come for a visit.

I put Ian in his car seat, with a plastic pail filled with his hot wheels collection on the floor. We got in the car, took one last look at the house and we pulled away. The feeling was good, I had no tears to shed, we are headed to a new place to raise our Ian, a place where we have enjoyed going to for the last seven years.

It wasn't early in the day to head out, but we are just looking to get on the other side of Calgary, which is four, four and a half hours away, then we will stop for the night.

We arrived in Nelson on our second day out. We stayed with Margaret, her husband, John, and their son, Johnny, who had recently moved to Nelson from Yellowknife. John is a chef by trade and they had purchased a meat market, along with Dave and another fellow. Allan was hired on. We had a few fun-filled days. Ian was coming up three in September and he had such a good time with his cousins, running on the beach, riding in the boat, swimming, bon fires at night, it was great. Couldn't ask for better hosts.

We leave on Thursday, one sleep over on the road and arrive at the ferry terminal around 10:30. We did get on the next ferry and, before we knew it, we were off-loading and heading for our new home. We were on the familiar Pat Bay Highway that takes you into Victoria, when Angus takes an exit called Wilkinson Road. The road was narrow and really pretty with lots of trees, fields, a couple of hobby farms, and a sprinkling of houses that lined the road.

I wasn't there when Angus bought the house, so when he turned on his left signal light and slowed, I was seeing our new home for the first time. It's huge, I see a wall of glass behind an upper deck, with a carport underneath, then a back carport with a deck above it. There are four entrances, the front door, a side door, a rear door, and rear stairs that led up to the rear deck with a sliding door into the kitchen. There is a grassy area between the house and the combination guest-house/double-garage. At the end of the driveway, the property widens and there are fruit trees and a large garden area. A few feet further, there's a creek that runs the width of the property. It's three quarters of an acre.

We pull in and Angus parks the car by the shed, which is located across from the garage, where the property widens. We unhook the trailer and head over to George and Jikki's, about a fifteen-minute drive. We have an appointment at the bank, so we have to move it. A quick hello, leave Ian with Jikki, and head downtown on a Friday afternoon, it's busy.

We get to the bank with ten minutes to spare. The paperwork for the house has already been set up, ready for us to sign and away we go. We are excited to be here, very excited.

After picking Ian up from Jikki's, we head back to the house, it's now about four thirty. There doesn't seem to be any action going on, we didn't notice that the first time. We park at the end of the driveway and walk back towards the house, where we see a young woman standing on the back deck.

She hollers for us to come up. We are introduced and then she proceeds to explain that they, meaning her, her husband, their two boys, and his parents, who live in the lower level, are not quite ready to move. What! Inwardly I'm shocked, Angus is not; he is totally calm. They haven't got their ducks in a row; it will be July 1st, before we can get in.

What to do, not much, we head back to Jikki's. After quite a discussion, we spend the weekend there. We call Margaret in Nelson, explain the situation, and she invites us to come back and stay with them, no problem. After the weekend, I had calmed down. Angus has a way of doing that for me, he reasons things out and this trip will be good for us. Being with family is the best. Our Ian, what a little trooper, sitting in his car seat, playing with his hot wheels, never caused a fuss. Driving from Edmonton to Nelson, Nelson to the Island, and then back to Nelson. That was a lot of idle time for a three-year-old.

We really do have a good time. Angus sister's Marion and Margaret, with their husbands, Dave and John, along with our nephews, Donny, Danny, Robbie, and Johnny, they were great. We were kept busy every day, from morning till night. The boys are still in school, but come the weekends, the preparations to get eleven of us ready to go, for a day at the beach, was, for me, almost as much fun as being there. It reminded me of my own family years before, when we were all getting ready to go to 'the lake.'

The women would get the food ready and packed in coolers that never saw any down time. Bags were filled with essentials like water, paper plates, cutlery, paper towels, you name *it*, *it* was in there. Bathing suits and towels were gathered up, toys to play with, and, of course, they all had their favorites to bring. Let's not forget about the dogs, food, dishes, and special blankets were made ready. The men would hook up the boats, all gear checked and the picnic stuff stowed away. It was like a wind storm and when the wind calmed, we were all in the vehicles and heading out of town for a fun filled day of exploring, laughter, sunshine, and good food, what else is there?

We kept in touch with George and Jikki, who, in turn, kept in touch with the people who were over staying their welcome in our new house. Everything was looking good on their end and we were given a green light for our new possession date of Sunday, July 1st. The families will be gone on the Saturday and will leave the keys with George and Jikki. Great!

So, we pack up and head for the Island, with one night's sleep over, we arrive at the ferry terminal on Sunday morning.

Our new house is situated in a district called Saanich, which is between the ferry terminal and Victoria, in the countryside; quiet and not too populated.

Can't wait to get everything unpacked and get settled in. The unpacking goes well. George helps Angus with the heavy stuff, while Jikki and her girls help me with the lighter things. The guys get all their hauling in and up the stairs, but it takes another two days to unpack everything else.

Inside the front door and up a flight of stairs, you are in the living room. The upper level is pretty much an open plan, as the living room goes into the dining room and then into the kitchen. There is a bathroom and two bedrooms, works out great. On one side of the lower level, there is a legal suite with a living room, one bedroom, a bathroom, and kitchen and on the other side, there is a laundry room where the hot water tank is and where we put our chest freezer. Funny, there isn't a furnace. The house is heated with electricity.

At first, it was funny, because at bedtime, we would run around the house, locking all the doors and there seemed to be a lot of them, four to be exact. It didn't take us very long to get used to all the new space that we now had.

We need quite a bit for the house, so shopping becomes a regular chore, although it's pleasant, it will be nice to be finished, for a while. We buy drapes for the wall of glass in the living room. I make curtains for Ian's room and also the guesthouse.

We get Ian a little wading pool and set it up under the huge oak tree standing at the side of the house. Angus builds him a sand box with a lid, a place to build roads, and hills for his hot wheels and new Tonka trucks. Ian is given boundaries, because of the creek at the back and the road at the front. Prickly blackberry bushes line one side of the property, and the neighbors have a fence on the other side.

The weather that first summer was really beautiful and because of it, I did very little laundry. Ian was in his bathing suit from morning till bedtime and loved every minute of it.

We decided that Angus should take the rest of the summer off, before looking for work. We made the most of it, too. We would go to the sea and watch the comings and goings of pleasure boats, tugs, and freighters. Take Ian for long walks and let him run. We would possibly stop and visit with our friends George, Jikki, Sonia, and Susanne. We took day trips and explored the Island. That was a great summer, one that we have talked and laughed about often.

The move is complete, we are settled in. It's coming up September and we have enrolled Ian in a pre-school at the little church, just down the road from our house. Angus takes a job at a body shop but really isn't fussy on the place. Every day at lunch, he skims through the classified ads looking for another job.

The old owners have left a field of tomatoes behind, so I make a lot of green tomato relish and give half to Jikki. There are a lot of black berries to pick and eat. I make a concentrate for Ian, he loves the stuff and it tastes great.

Jikki's girls are back in school and Ian goes to pre-school two days a week. This frees us up a little, so she shows me the ropes around grocery shopping and where to get the best deals. We have a good time together and enjoy each other's company, as we always have. I remember she told me if I paid more than 0.25 cents for a roll of toilet tissue, I'd be paying too much.

It's the day before Ian's third birthday, September 22nd, 1979. Angus' Mom and Dad drive down the driveway in their truck and holiday trailer. We knew they were coming, but didn't know the exact day they would arrive.

Just a gentle reminder, it's 1980. There weren't any cell-phones or any other communication available, other than a hardline phone or writing a letter. It definitely wasn't like it is today, that's for sure.

Ian's Grandma and Grandpa are here, just in time for his 3rd birthday. They like the house and property. We have a good time, usually sharing our evening meal together. Angus is at work, during the week, but in the evenings and on the weekends, we show them the Island and they love it. It's now October and the weather is good, so green, hardly any signs of fall, very different from what we know.

This is a funny story. While driving around, Dad spots a barber on West Saanich Road and makes a comment that if they stay any longer, he will have to get his hair trimmed. We pull in and Dad goes in to check the hours of operation. "Yah," he says, "The old fart is open six days a week, so I'll come back during the week." Well, after breakfast one morning, Dad takes Ian with him to get his hair trimmed. They park, go inside and when the fellow comes in from the other room, Ian asks, "Is this the old fart that is going to cut your hair, Grandpa?"

Kids can say the darndest things.

Dad is concerned there might be snow in the mountains and wants to get back to Edmonton, before winter sets in. Mom and Dad stayed just shy of a month, we will miss them. I remember the morning they pulled out, it was a very windy morning and we were thinking that the ferries might not be running, but they didn't come back, so they made it.

Mom and Dad are seriously thinking they will move to the Island, too. We let them know they can stay in the guesthouse. They will let us know, but it won't be until spring, anyway.

Angus continues on with the shop he really dislikes, while Ian and I enjoy being at home. Fall turns to winter and our first Christmas is very different. No snow, no freezing cold weather, there is still a lot of leaves on the trees. It doesn't feel like Christmas at all. We do our own things, like Ian and I bake sugar cookies shaped like bells, stars, and trees. We sprinkle and decorate them. We put up our artificial tree, too, and have fun decorating it, while listening to Christmas music. It rained quite a bit, far more than we were used to and far more than we had expected it to.

Angus has been continually looking for another job and has found a teaching position for the Auto-body trade, being advertised. The position would be at the College, not far from the house. He applies for it and gets an interview. The last question asked was, "Do you think you will like working at the college?"

Angus replies, "Let me ask you guys that same question, 'How do you like working at the college?'"

Smiles and nods all around the table. The telephone call came the next day, and Angus got the instructor's position.

The daily routine changes for the three of us. Angus doesn't leave the house until eight, he's home for lunch for almost an hour, and back again before five. Ian and I just get into something, we turn around and Dad's home. Yes, this is definitely different. The previous instructor hasn't left any pre-made lessons, so Angus has to start from scratch. I stay up with him, at night, going through the material that is required to be taught and before we know it, the course is outlined and made ready to be presented, one chapter at a time. There are scheduled exams and all the students are doing just fine, but Angus isn't, he doesn't like teaching. The final exam has been written and all of the students pass into their second year.

As soon as the course is finished, around the end of January, Angus resigns. I receive a phone call from the head of the college. He wants to inform me that by making the decision to resign, Angus will probably never get rehired again. In response, I tell him that Angus makes his own decisions and he will be fine, thank you.

Spring does come faster than we expect it will, the trees are budding in late February and will soon have beautiful fresh blossoms. The bulb flowers like tulips, daffodils, and the iris are breaking through the earth and will soon be in full flower. In Victoria, the City of Gardens, they have a 'flower count' every year. I can't remember the exact amount of blooms they get, but at the end of the week, the total turns into the millions, so that's a lot of flowers.

Searching the classified ads, Angus spots an auto-body shop for sale. We go for a drive, have a look from the outside and he likes it, the size, structure of the building, and the location appear to be good, too. First thing, Monday morning, Angus calls and talks to the owner and makes an appointment.

After a couple of hours, arriving home, wearing a smile from ear to ear, Angus fills me in on the details. The owner wants to sell the business and lease the building, with an option for us to buy the building in five years' time. We really hash it over and agree that a two-stage deal is good for us. The five years would give us plenty of time to test the water. We have no business degrees, no prior business operating knowledge, or experience and being new to Victoria, we would be flying by the seat of our pants. There are two very strong points in our favor; one, Angus, knows what he is doing, he is an excellent body repairman and an extremely talented refinisher and two, is us. We have a very strong relationship; married for eleven years and we are willing to work hard to make the shop a success.

Angus contacts the owner for a meeting. We sit down and draw up the sale of the business and then the five-year lease. March 1st would be the take-over date, as it is the owner's fiscal year end, whatever that means.

There is not much time, as March 1st is just around the corner. The finances go through without a hitch, but it is quite stressful waiting. The owner is leaving a few pieces of equipment, the office furniture, and the lunchroom table and chairs.

Angus meets the owner early on Saturday, March 1st. The two of them go over business contacts, the estimating sheets, and how to process them, etc. etc. There is a lot to learn. After spending the weekend getting the shop cleaned up and the office somewhat organized, we are open for business. I have picked up some office supplies that I think will be useful.

Angus has asked me to be the receptionist and bookkeeper, on a part time basis. I will work Monday, Wednesday, and Friday. The days off will give me time to keep the house and spend time with Ian. The owner's wife, will teach me how to keep the books, I don't have a clue. I wanted to take accounting/bookkeeping in high school but didn't have an A in English, so that was that.

During all of this, Angus and I go see a couple of daycare places in the area, not too far from the house. "Nope, no way," we are looking for a private sitter. We found a nice single Mom, with a son a little younger than Ian and she lives just a few blocks down from the shop.

It's Monday, March 3rd. We are up extra early and can't wait to get going. I take Ian into the sitters, which he has met the Friday before. He gets settled all is good. A beautiful spring morning, we open the shop at 8:00 a.m. The overhead doors in the shop are open, the spring air is whistling through the place, it's empty. Angus is pacing the shop, looking at the clock, hoping someone will come in. Around 11:30, a guy pulls in, opens his trunk, and pulls out a kitchen hood fan. He walks into the office where I'm sitting behind my desk. He wants to get it painted, they bought new appliances and it doesn't match. Angus can see us through a window that is between the office and the shop. He joins us and the guy asks how much to paint the fan. "Twenty bucks,"

Angus tells him and you can pick it up the same time tomorrow. I thought Angus was going to kiss the guy. That was our first job. It was a couple of days, before we had any collision work to do, but it really didn't take too long for the shop to be busy enough to hire a body-man and for me to start working full-time; so much for the part-time employment. Of course, I didn't mind, although I really missed my time with Ian, but he seemed to enjoy being at the sitters and I enjoyed being at the shop with Angus. Our rhythm in life is good again, we are happy.

So, the body-man did the bodywork, Angus did the estimating, prep and paint, the vehicle clean up, and everything else that needed to be done. I did the ordering of parts, invoicing and calling the customer, when the vehicle was ready for pick up.

To get more work, Angus went around town, introducing himself. Some of the guys would ask, "Where are you from?" which was a very strange feeling. Angus would reply that he was from Alberta and the response would be, "Oh, you're from back east." Now, coming from Alberta, a western Province, we never thought we were easterners. East, in our mind, was any Province east of Manitoba and Manitoba is two provinces over from Alberta. Alberta, actually, is the neighboring Province to British Columbia.

As time went on, we got busier and I found myself getting more confident in taking calls, scheduling work in and out, typing up the final invoices, and paying bills. Keeping the books was a different kettle of fish. I didn't even know what a debit or credit was. Didn't have a clue about record keeping, and balancing the books to the bank statement. The previous owner's wife was really good, any questions I have she helps me out and the first six months I go to their house and she shows me how to reconcile the books. There is a lot to learn, and I get headaches quite frequently, they are from trying to make sense of it all. It took me a good year, before I was okay with what I was doing and didn't have to make any more phone calls for help.

In April, Angus's folks arrive. They stay with us for a while, until they find a house. I take a couple of days off to show them around the different areas and in May, they buy a house in Sidney, a small town, about ten minutes from the ferry terminal and about twenty minutes from our house. They love it there, a brand-new house, in a brand-new neighborhood with neighbors around the same age; it is perfect for their retirement. They go shopping and buy new furniture and really enjoy putting the house together. They are settled in and are truly happy they have made the move. Mom and Dad have traded in their holiday trailer for a motorhome. One weekend, we all go camping up Island and find a lovely spot, along Kennedy River. Absolutely no one else was there.

This is a funny story. Mom and Dad are asleep in the double bed, Ian is sleeping on the couch, and Angus and I are in the upper bed, six inches from the ceiling. Angus starts to squirm, really restless, tossing and turning, Dad's snoring, Mom's making noises like she's not sleeping, clearing her throat, now and again, I'm just lying there, aware of all the sounds. Angus starts scratching his hand, scratching his arm, swatting at his ear, it's pitch black, can't see your hand in front of your face, when, all of a sudden, Angus pops up, hits the light by our head and starts to swear. "What the hell?" I pop up. Mom is awake, while Dad snores on. The motorhome is full of no-see-ums and we are getting bit everywhere. No-see-ums are tiny, little flying bugs that get through your screens and they bite. Mom shakes Dad. "What," he asks, as he squints with the bright light hitting his eyes.

"We got to get the hell out of here, Dad," Angus says.

"Why?" Dad asks, not being bothered by the no-see-ums at all.

"We're getting bit by no-see-ums, Dad, there's hundreds of them."

Slowly, we all get up, close the screen windows, and start getting dressed. It's 3:30 in the morning, when we pull out and head for home. The day before, I went for a dip in the river and end up with a rash all over my body, Angus has several bites that are really swollen and itchy, Mom, too. Ian and Dad are fine. No wonder that there wasn't a soul to be seen and why we were the only ones parked by the river. Wow! That was a lesson learned, camp in designated areas. Not funny, at the time, but we sure have laughed about that trip over the years.

We continue at the shop. Mom and Dad love being here, too. On the weekends, we see them and, usually have them for dinner on Sundays. We see George, Jikki, and the girls on a regular basis and we all enjoy each other's company. We are kept busy and like it that way. The move has been a good one.

My Dad drives out from Edmonton for a visit. He likes our house and seems to be proud of us for going into our own business. I take a couple of days off, so Dad and I take Ian to the lake for a swim and picnic. It's good to see him, his health seems to be okay and he is keeping busy with work. He has remained in our family home, but I'm sure the memories are hard for him from time to time.

Summer turns to fall and fall to winter, once again. We decide it would be great to spend Christmas in Nelson, B.C., where Angus's two sisters live with their families, the same ones we spent some of our time with, while waiting to get into our house. Mom and Dad agree, so the five of us load up and off we go, where its winter there, and Christmas feels like Christmas should feel, for us, anyways. Ian and his cousins have so much fun outside, enjoying the snow and the adults enjoy cooking, baking, and laughter, it's a really nice time.

We got home after New Year's and we are feeling refreshed, energized, and ready for work. It's 1981, Ian will be five, this coming September, and where has the time gone?

Ian's sitter has decided to go back into the work force, so Grandma and Grandpa start looking after him during the weekdays. For me, it's a lot of driving. Angus is dropped at the shop for 8:00am, then Ian and I head out to Sydney, about a half hour drive to Grandma and Grandpa's. I head back to the shop for the day, then after work, if Angus is ready to come with me, we drive out to pick Ian up and then back home. If Angus isn't ready, I pick Ian up and bring him home, make supper and wait for Angus to call. Sometimes, I would put Ian to bed and have to wake him, in order to go pick Angus up at the shop. We pretty much have that routine from March through to September, when Ian will start kindergarten.

This is a cute story. Ian and Grandpa are bicycling one day, when Grandpa pulls over and says to Ian that it's time to head home because he has a pill to take at 3:30 p.m. Ian looks up at him and says, "If you don't take it…are you going to die?" Grandpa just laughed and they kept on cycling. Funny.

It has been so good for Ian to have his Grandparent's care for him. They loved spending time with him and Ian loved it, too!

When there was an event that we wanted to go to off the Island, we would call Grandma and Grandpa, tell them to get their duds together, we were all heading out for the weekend. Boy, did they enjoy that, such good family time, we stayed in Hotels and we ladies got a break from the kitchen.

It's the beginning of September 1981 Ian will be five on the 23rd. On the morning that he is to start kindergarten, he wakes with a terrible looking infection of some kind, on this arm, near his elbow. I'm afraid it might be contagious, so we walk to the school, which is a good three blocks away. I leave Ian out in the hallway, go into the classroom to explain that I have a nurse coming by the house to examine Ian and I will get him to school, just as soon as he's okay. Mr. Lumley, the teacher, comes out of the classroom and introduces himself to Ian and says for him to take care and that he will see him soon. The nurse comes and takes a swab to be tested, meanwhile, make sure to boil his cutlery and dishes, keep his towels and face clothes separate from ours, until she gets back to me. Ian is feeling not too bad, kind of sleepy and looks pale, otherwise, okay. We wait till Wednesday, the nurse calls and we discuss the infected area, which has cleared up quite a bit already. She says there is no need to worry about it being contagious and it probably will be gone in the next few days. I keep Ian home for the week, come Monday, the infection has cleared up and he is ready for school. Funny, they never did tell me what it was, but Ian was left with a scar near his elbow, just as a reminder.

In the first half of the school year, Ian attends a half-day in the mornings and then the class switches, so he goes half days in the afternoons, for the remainder of the year. It's near impossible for Ian to continue with Grandma and Grandpa. There is a notice board in Ian's classroom and that's where I find a stay-at-home Mom, who will look after kids from the school, before and after school hours.

It works out great. Angus and I drop Ian off at their house, before work and she either drives Ian and her son to school or they walk. We pick him up after work, so the situation couldn't be any better for us. We continue on with this routine for years. We become friends with the family and have lots of fun through the years. The boys playing organized hockey, baseball, BMX racing, and the occasional sleep over.

Summer of 1982 Ian has completed kindergarten. We are busy at the shop, but decide it would be a good idea for me to take a couple of weeks off to spend time, at home, with Ian. This will give us all a break and with the shop busy, Angus can stay late and go in, as early as he likes. If there is something pressing, Ian and I can go during the day, for a couple of hours. This works out very well; Ian gets a break from his day-care home and is excited to return there for the rest of the summer days, till grade one begins.

Every year on the long weekend of July, we are all reminded of my Mom's tragic death. It's been four years now and seems like yesterday. Mother's Day is especially difficult, as there is so much media hype. Angus's Mom is a wonderful person and I love her dearly, so I really try to give her a memorable Mother's Day every year. Buying the card becomes very sentimental for me, so standing there in front of all the selections, I end up silently bawling, as I read each one and try to keep myself together. I usually walk around the store, until I'm 'ready' to go through the till.

September rolls around again and Angus and I are, now, thirty-four and thirty-three, married fourteen years and Ian is six. Our rhythm in life is good, really good. Ian is and has been nothing but a joy, from the day he was born. We do everything together.

I have to share this story. It's a good one. We are in the car, driving somewhere and out of the blue Angus asks Ian, who is sitting in the back, "What would we do without Mom?" and without any hesitation, he answers, "Lots," and the three of us burst out laughing.

Grade one comes on very quickly. We have had a great summer and now fall has arrived. We have the same routine as the year before and Ian's day-care home is great. Mom and Dad come over on Sundays for dinner and we all have a good visit. Ian's drawings from school are usually taped all over the fridge and Grandma gets such a kick out of them. Some of them need an explanation as to what's on the paper! Through those first school years, I keep his drawings in scrapbooks. There is one for every year of elementary school, grades kindergarten to grade seven. I looked through a few, just a couple of weeks ago and, *yes*, a lot of them needed interpretation, funny!

Ian has started hockey, what a great time we have with that. The kids are doing pretty good, considering most of them, including Ian, have never even skated before, so there is a lot of falling, sliding, and usually, ten kids go after the puck at the same time, like little magnets, it's funny to watch. At their ages, you either played for the orange team, the blue team, the yellow, or red team. No names were on the jerseys, but there wasn't a parent there that didn't recognize their own kids, funny how that works! That winter passed very quickly.

We tried baseball in the spring, but Ian's not fussy on it. Too slow moving for him, but he did stick it out to the end of the season.

One game, in particular, Ian's out in center field, it's hot. The game is over, Ian walks up to his Dad, who notices a substantial wet spot in the front of his pants. Ian looks up at Angus and says, "It's hot out there, Dad, I'm really sweating." We, of course, say nothing, just take him home. Funny! Another time, Ian's out in right field, the games pretty slow. When Angus looks out to see Ian, he's not there. A few seconds pass and there he is, coming out of the bushes that lined the ballpark, too funny!

With the baseball season over, Ian has completed grade one and summer is upon us, once again. Mom and Dad are into caring for Ian during the summer. They take him camping and Grandpa teaches him the way of the woods, like how to throw an axe at a tree and have it stick and how to start a fire with fire starter, as opposed to using kindling. They let him stay up, as long as he likes, give him a hot toddy in the evenings, when the air cools, made with good scotch, boiling water, and honey. That settles him and he is ready for bed. Grandma and Grandpa were good at teaching him the 'good' words in the Scottish Gaelic language, too. What a very special time for him.

Back home in their neighborhood, Grandpa and Ian would get into all kinds of fun, while Grandma kept the meals coming and couldn't wait for the stories to be told at supper time, the three of them laughing away at the day.

Angus and I would usually work late at the shop. We would have late suppers and fall into bed, after those long days. We loved it, we were busy, building a reputation for turning out good work and we were building quite a customer base, as well.

Mom would call and have us out for supper, usually on Wednesdays and then come Friday, after work, we would pick Ian up for the weekend. Sometimes, on Fridays, we would treat all of us to a chicken dinner at Tommy Tuckers. It was a small franchise that grew too fast and didn't last, but they sure did serve 'a good clean bite,' as Grandpa used to say.

So here comes fall again. Ian will start Grade 2 and will turn seven on September 23rd. Our families routine in life continues the same, with Ian having the same home care family. The families and kids at school seem to be very consistent, which is a good feeling. The area, we are in, is very family orientated and it's also a safe place for all of us to raise our kids. There is a lot to be said for contentment in life. Your head hits the pillow and you're out.

One fall Saturday, the three of us go to the Woolco Shopping Mall. There is a pet shop, a few doors down, and as we are walking past the window, Angus spots some puppies playing with each other in a small fenced off area. We go in to see them. As we are watching, this one puppy comes up to Ian, as if it knows him, tail wagging, all excited. Angus makes an inquiry about the pup, it's a beagle and it's sold.

The beagle is absolutely adorable, it's known as a tri-beagle, because it's three colors; black, white, and brown. We are very interested and ask if they have any information on a breeder, in the City. Turns out, there is a breeder and she lives up Island near Cobblehill, it's about an hour's drive from Victoria. We get her number. Angus and I talk about it, later that evening, when Ian has gone to bed and decide that if Ian wants to get one, we will.

Ian would love to have a dog, the beagle is decided on, so we contact the breeder.

We have a lengthy discussion on the telephone and she invites us to her place to see some beagles. She has a litter that will be born in January. We go to see her on the weekend and it's really fun. She has lots of beagles and they all coming running up to us, as we approach the outside fenced area that she has them in. She gives us a lot of information regarding beagles and the most important one is that they will leave the warmth of their home, any day for a scent, as they are members of the hound family and their hunting instincts have been bred into them for hundreds of years. The pup will have to be on a lead, at all times.

She leaves us, so we can talk about it and we decide that we will take one of the new puppies to be born in January, a female, only. Angus says he will have a run built for her, just outside the back door to the house. When we walk her, she will be on a lead, no problem… The lady takes all of our information, along with a down payment for the puppy, and, hopefully, there will be a female born in the litter. We will get a phone call, a few days after birth, when she is convinced that the puppy will survive.

Our puppy has been born, on January 20, 1984. We get the phone call and the three of us couldn't have been more excited. We can go see her as often as we like and, for us, we like to visit a lot. Once a week we go see her, Ian names her Polly, after her mother, whose name is Polliyanna. She is adorable and can't wait for the eight weeks to pass to bring her home. Those eight weeks will give us plenty of time to get things ready for her and by then, hockey season will be over.

Come mid-March, we get our Polly home. Ian and I take the drive to pick her up, then drive to the shop to see Angus. We are excited and Polly is great, love her to bits. Now, comes the training, something I have never done before. Because we live on the upper floor of the house, we have to tether Polly using a long rope that allows her to go down the stairs to ground level, do her business, and then come back up. It doesn't take her long to figure it out, so the training process was easy. Ian loves having her and teases her relentlessly, all in good fun, of course.

Not soon after we got Polly, I'm in the kitchen and hear an advertisement on the radio for a BMX race being held at a newly constructed BMX track in the Metchosin District, not too far, about a twenty-minute drive. It's a Saturday, the first day of a two-day race event. We load up Ian's street bike, his helmet, our Polly and away we go.

Once there, it's a buzz, the parking lot is full, adults, kids, bikes, kids in racing outfits, and the ages are ranging from three to teens. There is a shack with a registration sign, above an opening on one side. There are two women taking registration fees from the kids and parents lined up. There are even some Dad's in racing outfits. The track is behind the registration shack.

The scene is really busy, and there are a lot of kids on the track practicing. It sure looks like a lot of fun. We watch for a while. There is an adult, who is at the top of the starting hill, where the kids line up, across the width of the track, eight at a time, balancing themselves on their pedals and holding onto their handle bars, when the adult yells out, "Racers ready," and then the gate drops, where the kids have been balancing against. It's quite a bang, then the kids all take off at once and race around the track, which has single, double, and triple jumps to maneuver, along with berms that help them to maintain their speed and can pass their opponents, as they peddle as fast as they can and race to the finish line.

Ian likes it, so we buy him a set of elbow and kneepads, which are compulsory gear, from a fellow, who appears to be 'in the know' about the whole event. Turns out, he owns and operates a bicycle shop on Esquimalt

Road, not too far from our shop. We find out a lot of information in a very short time. There are different racing classes and if Ian wants to race today, he will be entered as a beginner and will race kids in the same class and around the same age. We sign a waiver for the day, Ian needs to get a BMX racing license, if he wants to continue.

Ian is signed up as a 7-year-old beginner. This BMX is really something and it takes a lot of guts to get up there, on that gate, rubbing elbows with your competitors. There is a lot to learn and a lot that is explained to the three of us. Basically, the racers race three separate races, called motos, against the same riders. As they come across the finish line, their positions are written down by the finish line volunteers and are passed on to the registration people in the shack, they tally the riders finishes in each of the three motos and from those results, prepare the main sheets and post them on the shack wall. The motos are run numerically and start with #1 and continue through, to how many motos make up the day of racing.

I'm pretty sure Ian has four other riders on his first day. Angus takes him to the moto line up, while Polly and I wait on the sidelines of the track. Ian's moto number is called, so he heads up to the top of the hill with the other riders. Each rider has been given a lane number 1 through 8, so, once at the gate, the riders maneuver themselves into position. The starter makes sure all riders are in position and ready. He will say, "Riders ready," and the riders will balance themselves on their pedals and handle bars, all the while pushing their weight against the gate. When it dropped, my heart was in my mouth. We did watch a few motos before Ian's, but when it's your kid up there, every move is so vivid and scary, for me anyways. He did really well, came in third, third, and third. He placed third in the main and was presented with a third-place trophy. What a day, we really enjoyed it and Polly was a hit, too! Ian didn't fall, or get injured he's a good rider. Anything that has wheels on it, he has ridden, since forever. Even his walker as a baby, he would run with it down the sidewalk and when he got pretty good, he would lift his feet up and glide. My Dad called it his 'speed buggy.' He's also had a trike, worn out two big wheels, is on his second street bicycle and by the way it's going, I can see a racing bike in the very near future.

It's a two-day event, so we decide to do it all over again the next day. We learn so much from everyone. All of the people involved couldn't have been nicer. We find out that the two-day event was held in order to ready our riders for a Provincial Race weekend in Kamloops, B.C. It will be held on the upcoming Easter weekend and will be a three-day event. Riders will come from all over, some from other Provinces to participate.

Come Monday morning, Angus is down at the bike shop, totally involved with ordering Ian a racing bike. I know it's a Diamond Back frame with different components, added for racing. As the week goes on, Ian has his new bike, racing clothes, proper racing, full face helmet, and Van running shoes.

Keeping in touch with the bike shop owner, he gives us the scoop on previous events and in general, how it all comes together.

During the week, the track is open in the evenings, for practicing. Ian's first race was on his street bike and now, he has a proper BMX race bike. We have decided to attend the Provincial Race weekend in Kamloops, so this practice time is great. We get to the track and, once again, it's a buzz. Ian is excited to try his new bike and heads to the gate. He picks a lane and when the starter lets the gate go, he flies down the hill, like really fast. As the evening passes, he is able to practice his gate starts, from different lane choices, practices getting speed off the berms, and how to pour it on to the finish line. He's getting to know the other BMX racers and is enjoying their company. The whole atmosphere is great. We have got the bug!

It's the Easter long weekend, the shop is closed for four days, and Ian is off school, so away we go. We find a really good dog kennel for our Polly, taking her with all of the commotion that's happening, she is better off. Stan, the kennel owner, likes her a lot. I know she will be fine.

There have been extra ferries put on for the weekend rush, so we catch the six o'clock on Thursday evening. We head up to the buffet for our supper and run into several other BMX families that are going to Kamloops, too! We all have a good crossing; the hour and forty-minute trip goes by in a flash. The kids are excited, as well as the parents.

We received Ian's BMX Association License, just before we left, so he can race. He is still a 7-year-old beginner, at this point, so we are hoping there will be enough in his class, if not, he will be moved up and will race more experienced riders.

We arrive in Kamloops close to midnight. We have booked into the same hotel, as some of the other BMX families. Racing is scheduled for ten the next morning, so it's off to bed. We meet at a local restaurant for breakfast, around seven, the next morning. The kids are excited to be here and the Island will have a good showing for the Provincials. The track is close by and when we arrive, the track is already open for practice. Ian is anxious to try his bike on a different track. The excitement is fun, lots of families, and it's a scramble for the Dad's to get the rider's bikes ready. There are different combinations of gears and sprockets that change the ratio, too complicated for me. Angus and

Ian try out some combinations and after about an hour, they know what they are going to use.

As more people arrive, the registration booth is a hum. The women have a lot to organize, but come close to ten, most of the moto sheets are posted, the men are pre testing the gate, volunteers are taking their assigned spots around the track, as they are very essential in keeping everyone safe. They actually do a lot, they scramble to a spill of bodies on the track, undo bikes that are twisted together, not to mention help the kids with possible injuries. They maintain the track by sweeping, and raking it. They use different colored flags that will notify the starter at the gate to 'hold up' or 'continue on,' as all has been cleared and readied, once again.

A big table is sitting outside of the registration shack and it's covered with trophies that will be awarded at the end of the race day. The riders meeting is called, a short welcoming speech is made, and it's race time. I'm so nervous, but try not to show it. Ian seems ready and Dad is hoping that the chosen gear combinations will be good.

Ian will be racing more experienced riders, but he fits in really well and looks very confident to get going. There is a saying in BMX, which probably holds true for any kind of racing, "When the gate drops, the bull-shit stops," and truer words have never been spoken. I can tell you this, once that gate drops you are on your own, you make it happen with guts, knowledge, strategy, ability, and strength and let's not forget determination, heart, and the love of the sport.

He's got it. Ian does really well and is awarded a second-place trophy at the end of the day. There isn't much time to socialize during the day, as the parents are busy with their kids. There are some families that have three kids racing. As we get to know the parents from the Island, exchanges are made, high fives are given, and Dad's discuss their racing strategies. When its Ian's turn to race, I can't help it, my emotions just take over and I cheer like crazy.

It's been a long, but exciting day. We are ready for something to eat. Back to the hotel, the kids go for a long-awaited swim and some fun time. We awake the next morning, ready to do it all over again. Ian has gained so much confidence, so the second and third days are successful. Ian has won two trophies, coming in first. We head for home with three beautiful trophies and Ian, who has gotten through our first out of town racing event, intact. He has learned how to use his elbows in the corners. No spills, no bruises, and no broken bones—we are happy!

And so it was for the three of us, for the next three years. Ian raced and won his way to become accepted as one of four racers on a Titan Race Team. He graduated through the ranks of beginner, novice, and expert classes. The

Titan Team had customized bikes, made of titanium metal, which is super light and super strong. The appearance is unique, there isn't any paint on the frames, so they look a bit unusual, as they are bare metal. By the time we were finished building Ian's bike, it ran us in the neighborhood of twenty-three to twenty-five hundred dollars.

Quick story: the three of us are on our way home from Bakersfield, California to Victoria on Vancouver Island. It's late. We drive up to the border crossing. The usual questions are asked. Where are you coming from? Why were you there? Then, the officer asks what's that wrapped up in the back? Angus tells him it's Ian's race bike. The officer has a good look at Ian, who is seven, remember, and then tells Angus to pull over. The officer proceeds to ask more questions, like, is it new? No, it's not new. How come there's no serial number? Because it's custom made. What's it worth? The bike is around twenty-five hundred dollars. Do you have your invoices? Yes, at home. Now, we are mad, you can see that the bikes not new, we have Ian's helmet sitting there, along with his racing clothes, but that's not enough to satisfy this officer, so he gives us forty-eight hours to take our invoices into the Customs office in Victoria, so all can be verified. Fine! With that delay, we miss the last ferry and have to spend the night on the mainland, which costs us a lot. Another night in a hotel, Polly has another night at the kennel and most annoying, is the time. We are late to open the shop and Ian is late in getting back to school. I took our bike file with invoices to Customs the next morning and that was that. Next time, we will travel with the file. The season for BMX is coming to an end; it's the fall of 1984.

It's time for hockey. Ian has turned eight. I'm pretty sure this year our shop, Quality Collision, sponsors a house team at our home rink. Angus is one of the coach's, which leaves me to be the runner for fresh brewed coffee for everyone. There's not many, if any, of the Mom's that show up for early morning practice. Most of the families have more than one child, so it's not really fair to get a second child out of bed, just to go see his or her brother practice so early in the morning. I go, because I can't stay away. I love watching Ian and get such a kick out of all the kids, it's fun, practice or not.

Before I get too far into the 1980s, I have to tell you that when we moved into our house on Wilkinson in 1979, we met the neighbors right next to our house, Terry and Phyllis, a younger couple, about ten years our junior. They had just gotten married. The four of us were busy working. Angus and Terry would talk over the fence, while Phyllis and I would get together for tea and she always included me in her Tupperware home parties and I really enjoyed that. Their house was a one level bungalow, really cute with rounded plastered openings between rooms, not cornered like regular houses, if you know what

I mean? It was originally Phyllis' Grandma and Grandpa's house. They had the full acre, at one time, and then divided it, they kept ¼ and we ended up with the ¾ remaining. They stayed there for a couple of years and then moved just up the road from the little church, where Ian went to preschool. In the summer, they would call us up for a swim, as they had a huge above ground pool. We had a blast, lots of fun, and laughs. After some time, they moved again, to a larger property, just down West Saanich Road, where Terry would have room for his automobile projects. After eight years of marriage, they had their first daughter, Christina, in 1987 and then a second daughter, Abby, in 1988. They quit, after those two girls. There will be more about this family as I go along.

Okay, so it's back to the winter of 1984 and hockey takes up a practice a week and a game, possibly two on the weekends. The three of us are really enjoying it and time seems to be going by way too fast. Mom and Dad come to see Ian play, occasionally, as they are hockey fans, too.

Come spring, we take up with BMX again and really get involved with racing, all over the Island, take in special events on the mainland, as well as flying to and from Alberta, Manitoba, and even, California. During spring break, Angus and Ian team up with friends of ours, Rae and Dianne, their son, Johnny, along with four other Victoria riders; ranging in ages from seven to seventeen. It's pretty close to a two-week trip. I stay and manage the shop, which is hard for me to stay away from the racing, but the trip will be great for Angus and Ian. They all have a ball, they race in Alberta and hop all over different cities in British Columbia, too. Angus and Rae look after the six riders, while Dianne makes the nourishing meals. They travel in a rented van and sleep each night in tents, it's a lot of work but the kids love it. They all come home exhausted and full of memories. Stories that they probably have passed on to their own kids by now.

In August, we are going to the BMX World Championships in Whistler, British Columbia it's about a two to three-hour drive, north of Vancouver. Ian is registered as an eight-year-old expert. There are quite a few riders and their families that will be going from the Island. We are booked into a Hotel and our Polly is at the kennels. If you are interested, there is some information on Google about the event. The track is built into the side of a mountain and the first turn is about a hundred-foot drop-down and has an abrupt first corner to the left. Most tracks Ian has raced on, the first corner has gone right. I'm sure this is quite different for a lot of the riders. It was a trek to the top of the hill, where the starting gate was.

What a site from up there, spectacular, mountains abound. I wasn't fussy on the layout of the track at all. It scared me and I wasn't racing. There were racers from all over the world, very skilled and experienced, too. It was a crazy scene, as there were kids of all ages riding their bikes all over the place. They were all excited and talking with one another, a lot of them not speaking English and I found it very loud and, somewhat unruly. I wasn't comfortable at all, nervous for Ian and it was so hard not to show it. We arrived a day ahead, to scout things out. Settled in our room, we went to the Village of Whistler for a look around. I really don't know how many riders, probably, six to eight hundred and for every rider there was, at least, two people came to cheer on their rider, two to four thousand, I'm thinking. Whistler, at that time, was just beginning to get recognized as a worldwide tourist destination. It is home to the world champion skier, Nancy Greene.

We met with a few of the families we know and all was a buzz. The track was very much in conversation and all the action that was going on. There will be three days of racing; first day is qualifying, second day they run all the quarter and semi-finals, and the third day they run the mains, for the wins.

I'm just a nervous wreck, this world's event is big and it means a lot to the riders. I volunteer to work the finish line, as there are signs posted that they need help. It's good for me to keep busy, while Angus tends to Ian. At the finish line, there are five or six people that are given sheets with the moto number printed on the top, followed by numbers one through eight, running vertically down the page, spaced out, so you have room to write the bike's plate number down, as they come through. We are lined up on both sides of the finish line, each person sitting on a chair and each one is lined up, so you can see past them and have a clear view of the track.

Now, you think that might be easy, it's not. There are eight riders coming full speed, going as fast as they can. You have a split second to write as fast as you can and in order, the plate numbers, as you see them, cross the line. As quick as you have finished, the sheets are gathered and taken to the registration shack to be compared with the others and then finalized. Another moto has begun, so you make yourself ready for the next bunch. Maybe, they have cameras now, but not back then. The older boys were the hardest, because they were so close to one another. I hope I did a good job.

Ian didn't take any hardware home in the way of a trophy, but he sure did take a lot of knowledge and experience with him. We are so very proud of him and he never got hurt. There were sure a lot that did, because that first turn left was very dangerous, as I had thought, the first time I saw it.

In September, Ian turns nine and we have an Island Provincial race being held in Campbell River, on the Island. As a new nine-year-old, Ian will have to face a couple of good racers that are on the verge of turning ten. We get some practice time and some races in, in August and September, so when it's time to head for Campbell River, we are ready.

It's an exciting day, the weather is good and the track is in good shape. We are booked into a motel that overlooks the inside passage of the Island, so nice. We arrive in town on the Friday. First thing Saturday morning, we are at the track. The gate is pretty high on this track, which gives the riders a very fast start. The first turn is left, but it's quite far away, far enough that by the time the riders reach it, they are spaced, somewhat, away from one another, so it's not that dangerous to maneuver. Ian comes in third, as I expected, we will just have to see how tomorrow goes.

It's Sunday, final race day and I'm thinking, watching the races and keeping an eye on the first turn. Usually, but not always, when a rider comes out of that first turn in front, he can stay in that position, as long as he stays focused and keeps on pedaling to the finish line. There is a lot of cheering in BMX and I'm the best or the worst, whichever way you look at it. You can often hear the fans yelling, "Pedal. Pedal," as the riders pedal their way around the track.

The final main moto sheets are posted. The race lanes are assigned. There are eight riders. The two riders I'm concerned about have lanes three and four, while Ian has number eight. The number one lane starts as the inside lane, being closest to the starter and number eight lane ends on the outside, furthest from the starter. There is a little time, before they begin, so I call Ian over and we have a little chat. I explain my concerns, explain the competition factors with the two older boys and let him know they will be too busy with trying to beat one another that when Ian gets to that corner first, he will be in a good position to win.

"Rider's Ready," and *bang* goes the gate. Ian flies down that hill like a bullet, totally focused, and looking forward. The two other boys are sneaking peaks at one another and using their elbows to jostle their positions. Ian takes the turn first and never looks back he wins the Island Provincial for his class. The strategy worked and we couldn't be more proud of our Ian. What a way to spend Thanksgiving!

Home, once again, mid-week we take a ride out to Sydney, where Mom and Dad are, for a visit. We drive by an RV dealership, very slowly and like what we see. On the weekend, we go take a look and end up buying a Class C 1985, Travelaire, 23-foot motor home. We are very excited, now we can go camping with Mom and Dad. When we race, we won't have to stay in motels or hotels anymore and best of all, our Polly will be with us.

Life's rhythm is really good. BMX is over for the season. Not! We hear that there will be some winter racing on the mainland. We can go on the first ferry in the morning and be back home in the evening of the same day because the event is only going to be one day. That will work.

I don't think we signed up for hockey that season, as Ian was racing and he, certainly, couldn't do both. At Christmas time, we talk to Mom and Dad about, maybe, taking a trip to Hawaii, around spring break. Sounds great to them, make the arrangements to suit us. It's a two-week trip and joining us is Angus' cousin's wife, Susan, and their daughter, Bonnie, who is about three years older than Ian. They fly from Alberta to Victoria and we all take off together. We have rented a large condo and there is plenty of room for everyone. We rented a larger vehicle to go site seeing; we all have a great time.

Quick, funny story:

We had been out grocery shopping, Mom and I are in the kitchen, putting things away, when, all of a sudden, this thing ran across the floor and scooted under the stove. Well, Mom and I stopped dead in our tracks, "Did you see that, Mom?"

"Yes, what was it?"

"I'm not sure, but I'll phone down to the main gate and ask."

"Hello, main gate."

"Yes, this is Mrs. MacDonald in 103 calling."

"Yes, Ma'am."

"We were in the kitchen, just now, and saw a large bug run across the floor and now it's under the stove."

"That would be a roach, Ma'am."

"As in cock…roach?" was my reply.

"Yes, Ma'am."

"Well, what are we going to do about that?" I ask.

"First thing in the morning, you and your company go out for the day and we will come in and fumigate."

It did sound funny, because, apparently, the way I had sounded out, as in cock *pause* roach, everybody laughed. Angus, actually, stepped on one that evening, heard the back-shell crack, but it wasn't there in the morning! The fumigating team did their thing and we never saw another one.

Oh, yes we did! We were all at a *luau*, a Hawaiian party. We were all seated at long tables with separate long benches. We were eating and had our heads down, when a flying cockroach came flying right for us. It was making a clacking sound, as it flew. It got pretty close to Bonnie, who was sitting next to me. She looked up, saw the thing flying directly towards her, screamed, and fell off the bench! It was comical at the time. We were served a good dinner, the pig was actually cooked in the ground, covered with leaves, along with other side dishes. *Poi* was one dish I really don't recommend. It's purple in color, has the consistency and taste of wall-paste, although I've never eaten wall-paste, but I'm pretty sure you could substitute one for the other. We all had a good evening.

Ian and Bonnie got a lot of swim time in the pool at the condo. We went on day trips, touring the 'Big Island.' Mom and Dad loved the heat and enjoyed taking long walks on the beach. We snorkeled and saw some beautiful tropical fish, got sun burned, but it was worth it. We went on a 'Captain Cook' adventure boat with a glass bottom. When we arrived at the cove, the people, who wanted to, could snorkel. Angus and Ian did, while the rest of us watched the divers feed the fish under the boat, it was great. When Angus and Ian came back on board, Ian remarked to his Dad that he, actually saw Captain Cooks boat down there. We didn't say anything different.

We arrive back home, completely refreshed and ready to carry on. It's the spring of 1986. I just turned 37 in February and Angus is 38 in April, a few weeks from now. Ian will be ten in September and also, in September, we will be married eighteen years. Wow! And we are only starting.

Back at the shop, we are working away and gaining a reputation in the city. Now we have purchased the building from the previous owner, who leased it to us for the first five years, that being from the spring of 1980 to the spring of 1985. We are in our sixth year and doing well. We sure have a good customer base, we have met some pretty nice people along the way and I'm going to tell you all about them, as I'm sure you expected me to!

It's impossible for me to remember the dates of all the happenings, so I'll just tell you about them, as I sit here and recall some of the most memorable and funny stories.

One early morning, an elderly gentleman drives in with his car. Angus does the estimate, brings it into the office, where I calculate it and go over the procedure with him. The work will take three days. When he drops it off, I will give him a courtesy lift home. No need, he just lives at the end of the street, so he says he can walk. He books it in, we do the work and he is pleased. One day, not long after that, I take the bus downtown to make a bank deposit. When I get to the door to leave the bank, the elderly gentleman, we just did work for, is there, too. We walk to the bus stop and ride back to the shop together. He tells me a little of his past and lets me in on a little practice he has been doing for years now. He watches the gold prices and when he gets enough to buy 'an ounce,' he does just that and keeps it in a safety deposit box at the bank. His logic is this; he doesn't earn any interest on the gold tucked away, but the government doesn't know he has it either, pretty foxy, don't you think? After his wife and him passed away, his son moved into the house, a lovely spot on the inner harbor.

We had a few customers that would come in, with what we called 'whiskey' dents. Like, maybe, a fellow would drive home after having a few and hit the fence or something, causing just enough damage to be noticed, and, of course, that would never do.

One elderly man, in particular, came in one morning; actually, he was waiting for us, when we arrived at the shop to open for the day. The front end of the car had been hit hard. Angus had to take a few parts off first to give him a detailed estimate. He was fine with that, so Angus gave the old guy a ride home. Angus returns to the shop with the story of how the damage happened. Apparently, the night before, arriving home quite late and it's dark, he drives into the garage, but can't see the back wall and drives right into it. He hit the wall so hard, the garage was moved off of its foundation. Really, no kidding, Angus saw it. When the car is ready, I call and we offer to deliver it to him. When Angus arrives, the customer guides him into the garage and behold, the old guy has hung a golf ball from the rafters and it's hanging there, so when it hits the windshield, he stops. Too funny! We actually did quite a bit of work for him over the years. He moved into a big apartment complex with large brick columns that were placed on each side of the entrance. You can guess what happened; he drove in, scraped the entire passenger side of the car against the brick, and needed it fixed up. When he came to pick the car up, said he was headed up Island to see his girlfriend, she was living dangerously, don't you think. He had a very interesting past, a really hard worker and ran one of the largest electrical crews in Victoria, at one time. When he wasn't allowed to drive anymore, he was pushing ninety at that point. He called Angus and asked if he wanted to buy his car. Politely, Angus declined.

A younger lady, probably on the other side of seventy at the time, drove in. She was driving a big boat of a car, parked it fairly well and came into the office. She was petite, well dressed, sporting a head of tinted purple curly hair, a purse like the Queen would carry, and wearing white wrist gloves. I liked her right away. We chatted for a few minutes and then I called Angus on the intercom for an estimate. I was excited because I got to take her home. We talked and talked and pretty soon, we were at her apartment, where I left her, promising I would pick her up in a few days.

We hadn't seen her again for a while, but, one morning, she was on the phone with her story. She and her sister had been out late, it was dark and as she took a corner to the right, they both felt a bump of some kind. When they got to her sister's place, she couldn't get out of the car, so she slid over and got out on the driver's side. Could she come? Of course, come along. Well, she drives in and, the whole right side of the car is dented from front to rear. She told Angus where it happened, which was not too far from our house. On the way home, we drove by to see the wreckage but found, instead, a very large, trailer hitch attached to a huge bumper on a truck that was protruding out from the end of a driveway. No visible damage to the truck, lucky for him.

She was a lovely lady, she did remind me of my nanny. She, too, has passed on. I called her out of the blue, one day, just to see how she was and her son answered, so I explained who I was and he told me she had passed on. Our society will miss people like her, but, then again, maybe, they have never even met a lady like her before. She was a treat, she carried herself well, straight backed, well dressed, looked after herself, wore perfume, spoke, and laughed with life and zest. Did you know that 'zest' is one of the 24 strengths possessed by humanity. Read the definition and wholeheartedly, this woman had it, so did my nanny.

We did a lot of work for a lot of nice people, who we made feel comfortable and not the least bit embarrassed over their individual circumstance. Angus liked to chat with the fellow customers, if he had the time. It was interesting to find out what they had done during their working years and a lot were still working. Like an eye surgeon; we painted all of his filing cabinets for his office and he didn't advise anybody to become one, not even his kids. He said if he had his career to do over, he would have entered into a trade like ours or become an electrician, but not an eye surgeon.

One day, a lady drove in and Angus recognized the car from years before. After giving her an estimate, he asked if the car was from Alberta and she said yes, Edmonton. Then Angus proceeded to ask her if she had work done at Cyclone Auto-body there and yes, she had. Turns out, Angus painted that same car like some fifteen years before. Small world. I will think of some more stories later on, but, for now, it's back to the spring of 1986.

We are tickled with our motorhome; it's just the right size. A couple of years after we moved, we had a large garage built on the property. It had room for two vehicles and also a stall for a motorhome, so we can keep it inside. The fellow, who built it, was our neighbor, Phyllis, her Uncle, her mother's brother. He was a great guy, handled everything, and even got the permit. Didn't take him long either, he was very organized, knew what he was doing and we were very pleased with the building. He passed away, suddenly a few years after that, with a heart attack, if I remember correctly. Very sad, he left a wife and four young children behind.

We start BMX racing again and now, we can take our Polly with us, too! We get some camping in with Mom and Dad. They usually head out on a Wednesday and we meet up with them on the weekend. There's a place on the Island that has become a very special place for us, it's called Gordon Bay and the campground is on Lake Cowichan. We have wonderful times there, over the years, as you will find out, as we go along.

One camping trip in particular, we were in a double site, with Mom and Dad on one side and us on the other. I was in the kitchen preparing something, when Polly got up off her bed and sat at the doorway, looking out through the screened door. I didn't see her, but she pushed with her nose, opened the door, and got out. It was only seconds when I looked out, but she was gone. Now, what! Everybody on deck, Polly's gone. I grabbed her lead and we all searched and hollered and searched some more, no sign of her. It was getting late, so we decide to carry on and make supper. After supper, here she comes, right back to the campsite. We were, sure, glad to have her back. That was probably the best experience she ever had, not on a lead and sniffing her way through the bush, being a typical beagle.

We are really enjoying the freedom of the weekends, we have been campers, as far back as both of us can remember and Ian loves it, too! He rides his bike all around the campgrounds and finds trails and jumps to maneuver and has a ball. We share meals with Mom and Dad, take long walks together and laugh with each other, making the most of our time together.

Ian continues to win; his room is flooded with trophies; so many that we have to start putting them downstairs in the family room. There are a couple of Provincial races that we are registered for this summer, one in Penticton, B.C., and the other in Lethbridge, Alberta. The one in Penticton goes really well. The kids are all out practicing and Ian's just watching the older ones jump a triple; that is located at the bottom of the starting hill. The rider has a choice, jump one, two, or all three of the man-made hills. I'm in the motorhome when a rider, a friend of ours, whose family has travelled with their motorhome, too, calls in to me and says, "Mrs. MacDonald, Ian just jumped the triple." Here he comes, proud as punch, and well, he should be. Whether he will do it come race time, we will see. Yes, he does it and lands it perfect, couldn't have been better. He wins the Provincial for his class and so does the rest of the Titan Team. The trophies are almost as tall as the kids themselves.

We head home for a few weeks, now we are racing on Wednesday evenings and on weekends, too. It's a lot. I begin to have silent thoughts about maybe it's just too much now.

Over the years, at the shop, we have learned that by closing down completely for two weeks' vacation works best for everyone. As it turns out, we are usually booking our customers two weeks in advance, so all of us being away at the same time works out great. We all get a break from one another and we all come back refreshed.

After putting in a few late nights and catching up with work at the shop, we close and head off to Lethbridge, Alberta for their Provincial meet. It's a way to go, about 800 miles or 1300 km. We take two days to get there and arrive on the Friday. The track is open and busy. It's a new track and it's top dressed with shale, which is a flat rock that breaks into thin pieces with sharp edges. I don't like it. Angus doesn't like it either; it looks slippery and, probably, is. It looks nice, but that's about it. While Ian takes a few gate starts, Angus and I have a talk about BMX, in general, and decide to call Ian in for a family meeting.

The three of us have our little talk, we are tired and Ian is tired, too. We decide that we have had enough, to hell with it, we are going to go and have some family fun time. We sell Ian's bike at the track. We get in the motorhome and head to the local community swimming pool, where we have a blast. The three of us continue on with our vacation, each of us wondering what would be next.

Back home and settled in, Ian turns ten. We are happy. The BMX experience has been a good one. Ian retires in fourth place in our BMX Association. He is well respected by all the riders, and their families. The sport, the people, the whole three years has been good for Ian, in particular. He has learned a lot about himself and he has come out a winner in every way.

We take up golf. Each of us getting a starter set of Wilson Staff clubs, a golf bag, and all the accessories. It's fun Ian takes to it right away. Being September, it is kind of late in the season, but we do get a few lessons in, before they close down. We play a few rounds on a par 3 course, not too far from our house and we really enjoy it.

Once again, our rhythm is life is good. Come hockey season, Ian is signed up and ready to go. We have pretty much the same routine for a few years running, but with one major project that is totally consuming, but not for Ian, for Angus.

We have had quite a few vehicles, over the years. Let me do a quick recount and get you caught up to date. When we moved to the Island, in 1979, we were driving a 1967 Chev Malibu, parked was our 1968 Dodge Charger, and the 1964 GMC, pickup truck. We bought a 1949 Mercury Cargo-van that needed work. Angus did all the bodywork and the painting. We only used it to attend show and shines on the Island. Angus's buddy, Terry, told Angus one day, "If you ever want to sell the van, just park it in my driveway." In 1981, we ordered a Chev Elcamino and it turned into a specialty vehicle as well. In the later part of 1985, we bought a Chev Astro van, as a daily driver and sold the Malibu. Angus bought me a mint 1979 Toyota Corolla, 2dr hatchback.

One of Angus buddies had a mechanic shop at the opposite end of the block from our auto-body shop. In June of 1987, he asked Angus to go with him to Edmonton on a car rally. They would take his 1939 Ford it's black, lowered, and flamed, nice ride. So, away they go. While attending the show and shine, Angus spots a 1934 Ford, 2-door for sale. He really likes it and gets the fellow's phone number.

When he gets home, he tells me about the car and I tell him if he wants it, that's fine, but we are running out of room. He takes the Mercury van to Terry's and parks it in his driveway, just as Terry had suggested. Too funny!

Now, we have an empty stall for the Ford. Angus calls the owner and they make a deal. Then, Angus calls Terry, who is a heavy-duty mechanic and asks if he will fly with him to Edmonton, pick up the Ford and the two of them will drive it back to Victoria.

They fly out on a Friday evening, buy the car on Saturday, and start heading back the same day. One sleep over and they arrive back home on Sunday, tired but they had a good trip, no problems with the car.

Quick story, as Angus told it to me. Angus and Terry are going through the Valemount, B.C. area, driving along a fairly long straight away, when Angus hears and sees an RCMP, Royal Canadian Mounted Police, vehicle in his rear-view mirror, lights a flashing and siren going, too. He pulls over to the side of the road. Terry's reading a car magazine. The officer approaches, asks the routine questions, takes Angus' license back to the cruiser and returns with a speeding ticket. While all this is going on, Terry, never once, lifted his head, didn't show any interest at all, and said absolutely nothing, not a word. That's hilarious, when Angus told me I couldn't stop laughing, we still laugh about that.

The car is really neat. The doors are called suicide doors, because the doors open backwards, like the Bonnie and Clyde gangster car. Actually, it is the same model. Its silver in color, with a light grey interior, has a soft- top roof, and a greyhound hood ornament. The car is designed not to have a trunk, and there isn't a luggage carrier either, this could pose a problem.

In late August, we go with friends on a rod run. We caravan down to Puyallup, WA to the 'Goodguys National.' It's the biggest car show in the Northwest. We have a great time. Phyllis, Terry's wife, is pregnant, with her first child. She has about four weeks to go. She is craving ice cubes and can't get enough of them. We play Yahtzee for hours, taking breaks, now and again. We laugh and giggle and laugh some more. We really get along well. Ian has a buddy along and we hardly see them, they are busy checking everything out. There are hundreds of show cars and, it takes quite a while to see them all. We will definitely be doing this again.

Phyllis has the baby, it's a girl, they call her Christina, she's a doll, they couldn't be happier. Phyllis is relieved it's all over. She has a few months maternity leave, but there is *no* rest for a new Mom, as we know. Phyllis is a very attentive Mom. It's been eight years, since her and Terry were married, same length of time for Angus and I, before we had our Ian.

Angus starts stripping the Ford in October and I start my diet in December. By Christmas, I have lost seventeen pounds. I guess I remember that because there wasn't a turkey dinner for me that year. Marion, Dave, and their three boys, Donald, Danny, and Robbie come for a few days. They stay with Mom and Dad, who were very excited. We all had a great Christmas. I remember we all jumped in the van and we took them to Clover Point in Victoria. It's about a four- acre park that juts out into the ocean, there's a paved loop, where you drive and park, if you want to stay and fly kites or take in some fresh air. It can be extremely windy, especially, in the winter months. We get there and the kids all get out of the van. The waves are splashing against the rocks and the wind is wild. Robbie, the youngest, opens his jacket to catch the wind and can hardly stand up he is getting blown off his feet, all the while laughing like crazy. None of them had ever experienced that before, so they got a kick out of it.

New Year's comes and goes, Angus is making a lot of headway with the car and by the time he is finished, we have an entire photo album of the procedures. One night, in particular, our friend, Cliff, who has the mechanic shop, was helping Angus fit the newly chromed front grille, sounds easy. No, it wasn't. They started getting giddy about two, but being determined, they decide to keep at it and by three or four in the morning; the grille is in and fits like a glove.

A typical Saturday for us, especially, after hockey is done for the season, goes like this. We wake up early and have breakfast together. Angus heads to the shop, Ian and his buddies meet to play street hockey. Ian hauls his net on his shoulders, with his hockey gear perched on the top, across the open field next to us, and onto the tennis courts at Copley Park. I begin laundry, house cleaning, and making my diet meals for the coming week.

I'm usually finished by two and set out to see how Ian's doing. They are starving, so I take orders and make a run to McDonald's. I stop at Canadian Tire to buy a dozen hockey balls, which have been requested. I've learned not to call the shop, because Angus won't answer, anyway. Remember, its 88 and we didn't have cell phones attached to our hips. I take him lunch and try to get an ETA of when he will be home for supper. Then, I stop for groceries on the way home and check in with the boys. They usually pack it in, around five, for supper. I call Mom and we chat about the week and, *yes*, they will come for dinner tomorrow. I put supper together, Ian and I eat and I save a plate for Angus. Ian chills out for a while and plays with Polly, watches TV, and falls asleep, completely bushed. Angus might make it home by eight or nine. He fills me in on the day's progress, eats his supper, showers, and we head for bed. It's been a good day. Sundays are pretty much the same, except I stay put and *putz* around the house. The meaning of *putz* is to engage in unproductive activity, which I, whole-heartedly, do not agree with, because I get all kinds of little chores done around the house and *putz* is a good word for that, Angus uses it all the time.

Well, I've been at the diet for four months and have lost forty pounds so far. It's the end of March and I want to lose another ten pounds, before we start scheduling our summer fun.

It's pretty clear, my clothes are looking funny and my slacks are so big now that both my legs will fit into one. I start my shopping and really enjoy it. Everything from bras to having my rings sized, it's exciting for me. It doesn't take me long and I'm happy to put my old stuff downstairs in an empty closet. Most of my shoes are flopping around, too, so I need new ones.

I keep at it, but the last ten pounds is hard. Finally, towards the end of April, I'm done, fifty pounds off. One day, shortly after that, I stop at the shop and Angus sees me in a new outfit and can't believe what a change it made. He has been so busy he hasn't had any time to notice anything. The 34 is getting close to being finished. The color has been mixed; it's a beautiful burgundy, a very rich and timeless color. After painting, both, the car and the Mullins trailer look great, couldn't be any nicer. Putting the car back together will take hours and hours. I should mention that the 1934 Ford is a complete restoration, with independent suspension, a totally reworked 350 Chev motor with 400 horsepower; that means it goes damn fast, comfortably. The project will take seven and a half months to complete.

I'm going to take you back a few years and tell you a story about my quitting smoking. Ian had started Grade one, its 1983. I got sick, really sick with the flu. Angus took me to the doctor and he gave me a prescription for some cough medicine. Mom and Dad looked after Ian, because I was too weak to get out of bed. I slept for three days. I went into the shop to pay some bills, sat down at my desk, lit a cigarette, my first one in three or four days, inhaled, and started to choke. The phone rings at the same time, of course, and I can't answer it. Angus comes running into the office and picks up the phone for me. I feel bad; he has been covering for me, for a week now. I take the package of cigarettes and fire it into the garbage can. When I get home, I throw the rest of the carton, except one pack, into the garbage, too. The one pack I saved, went into the freezer, just in case.

Withdrawal comes in the form of stupid. At work, I answer the phone, but nothing comes out, there is a hesitation, where I scramble to get the words out. "Good morning, Quality Collision," easy, right? At home, I answer the phone with the same hesitation and "Hello, Quality Collision," comes out. Really. I can't look at a cup of coffee for, at least, two weeks, because I'm scared I'll want a smoke. I don't want to go out or visit anybody either, because yacking will make me want a smoke, too! I have been smoking for some twenty years, that's long enough. I find that I have a lot of time on my hands. It feels good to get some extra chores done around the house and at the shop, too, because there is no need to stop every twenty minutes for a smoke. I do succeed and haven't had a smoke since and that's almost thirty years.

OK, back to 1988. There is a rod run coming up in the later part of May. It's called the 'Blossom Run' and it's in Penticton, B.C. Angus should be finished the car by then, so that will be our first rod run with the Ford and Mullins completed.

We have booked two rooms in a motel in Okanagan Falls, which is located a few miles south of Penticton, on Skaha Lake. Ian is always allowed to bring a friend. The four or us get away from Victoria and arrive really late. Our friends Cliff, Cheryl, Gary, and Audrey are already there. We book in, get the boys settled, and join them for 'last call' in the lounge. Cliff has driven his 1939, the black one with the flames, and Gary has brought his 1957 Ranchero, we did at the shop. I remember Angus teasing Gary about putting a Chev white on the Ford Ranchero and Gary was like, "No, you didn't really put Chev paint on, did you?"

"Yes, it's a basic Chev color, with blue pearl overlay." Gary's scratching his head, not knowing whether to believe Angus or not. It was a nice effect, kind of like the oyster pearl colors of today.

We are up and at it, early the next morning, and head for the Penticton Park, where the rod run is being held. There are a lot of nice cars there, the music is playing 50 and 60s stuff, the weather is great, really a lovely setting. We spend the day looking and admiring each vehicle. Each entry is given a sheet with different categories on it, like 'Best in Show,' 'People's Choice,' 'Best Unfinished,' etc. etc. After making your decisions, you put your vote in the ballot box. We have had a great day, mixing with all the contestants and general public, answering questions about the restoration. We head back to the motel for supper and let the boys go for a swim.

In the morning, we meet Cliff and Cheryl for breakfast. Coffees are poured all around, we nitter-natter, as Cliff calls it, about yesterday's events. Cliff reaches in his pocket and pulls out a plague.

"Here," he says to Angus, "You got this last night."

It's a nice plague that says 'People's Choice' Blossom Run May 20-23, 1988. Totally unexpected, we attend, because we enjoy the whole atmosphere. We all had a good time. Polly is excited when we stop to pick her up at the kennel.

We go to Puyallup, again this year, in June. The big difference is the 34 and Mullins are done. This rod run is really big, probably 1200-1500 cars. There is a lot of tomfoolery that goes on between the guys i.e. like rubber puke that is put on a guy's car in the hot sun and once found by the owner, there's a lot of verbal abuse thrown around. Or a 'For Sale' sign that finds its way under a windshield wiper and that is not really appreciated, but done in fun. Angus finds a red dot sticker on one of the headlights. He just picks it off and throws it away. On the ferry ride home, Angus asks the guys, "Who put that sticker on my headlight?"

"What sticker?"

"The red one I found."

One of the guys says, "You were supposed to drive the car up front, to where the stage was, you probably won an award."

"Oh, really," says Angus, "Didn't know anything about that."

So, that was that, maybe next time.

We close the shop in August and we head up Island for a golfing holiday for two weeks. We stay in the motorhome and golf at different courses during the day, then head for a campground for the night. We may stay put for a couple of days and always go to Gordon Bay on Lake Cowichan. Usually, at this time of year, Mom and Dad are visiting family and friends in Alberta.

Come September, we go to a rod run in the District of Saanichton; it's between our house in Saanich and Mom and Dad's in Sydney. They really enjoy themselves. Dad gets a kick out of the old T buckets and the model T Fords. Most have been rodded out like our 34.

Ian turns twelve and he can come home after school and doesn't have to go to his after-school care home. It's different, but he likes it. He is allowed to bring a buddy home with him, if he wants to. He is into skateboarding, along with a few of his friends. On weekends, they practice on our driveway, do jumps, and have fun for hours. Hockey is upon us, once again, as time just keeps running along.

A couple of shop stories that will have you laughing:

We hired a young guy, as an auto-body prepper, by the name of Henry, who was, at the time, seventeen years old. He was with us for three or four days. I'm sitting at my desk with the office door open, when an older station wagon pulls up, alongside of the steps, leading to the office. A middle-aged man gets out of the car, sees the door open, and says to me, "Where's Henry?"

As I start to get up from my desk, Angus comes out of the shop and asks, "Can I help you?"

The man says, "Where's Henry?"

Angus takes a look down the street a block away and says, "Henry's down there."

"Well, what the heck is he doing down there?" I interrupt, "Angus, he wants to see Henry, the prepper we just hired, not Henry Street."

"Oh, that Henry, come with me, I'll show you where he is."

That was Henry's father and, boy, did we laugh about that one for a long time. I'm still laughing.

We saw Henry grow from seventeen to twenty-seven, from being a teenager to a married man. He was with us, when he and his wife decided to move up Island to be closer to family. We, also, had a body-man, Bob, who was with us for ten years, too. Bob was also a great guy. He was newly married, when he started with us and through the years, he and his wife had four children. He was a great Dad and loved being with his kids. They were excellent employees and we very much appreciated them.

We did some work for a fellow, on a few occasions, over the years. He and Angus get to know one another fairly well. The guy comes in one day, wearing a New York Yankee's ball cap. The two of them are yacking in the office, when Angus can't stand it any longer, cause the guys wearing the cap with the visor straight across, he hasn't curled it at all, so he grabs the cap off the guy's head, bends it a couple of times, and *snap*, it breaks! Angus looks up and the guy is dead serious, when he says, "Do you know whose cap this is?"

"No," Angus replies.

Well, it's so and so from 19 and something and he holds the records for; and on and on he goes. Angus is just standing there, holding the cap by the broken visor, can't believe his ears and is really feeling bad, when the guy starts laughing his head off—gotcha!

We get very exciting news, Angus's sister, Margaret, along with her husband, John and their son, Johnny, who is now sixteen years old, move from Nelson, B.C. to Nanaimo, B.C., about a two-hour drive from Victoria. It's the fall of 1988. Mom and Dad pick us up and we head for a visit to see them. It's a good time, as always there are laughs, food, and family fun. At Christmas, we have them for dinner, along with Mom and Dad. John is a chef by trade and he helps me in the kitchen and teaches me how to make a rogue for the gravy, it's fun.

In February, I turn forty. Margaret and John come for a BBQ. They have brought me a gift; it's a muffin cookbook and the cutest, little girl, birthday card. I still have both and every time I use that book, I read the birthday card again. Memories keep my memory sharp. That year, my sisters, Sandra and Vivian, each send me a jam jar, too funny, because neither of them knew it. I still have those, too!

I don't think it matters where you live, winter is winter and most often, you can't wait for spring to come again. The renewed freshness of the air, early flowers, green grass, new leaves, and hedges budding, it's refreshing. We are no different and when the signs start showing, it's exciting. It's the spring of 1989 and everything is fresh, the daffodils and tulips are in bloom, as well as the flowering plum trees, really nice.

Mom hasn't been feeling well for a while now, pretty much all winter she has had a cold that she can't seem to shake. Looking back on the calendar, I remember calling her on Tuesday, March 14th, from the shop and Dad said she was lying down. I called the following day and Dad answered again and said she can't seem to keep anything down. After work, we picked up some fresh flowers to cheer her up. She was in bed and resting, but otherwise, glad to see us. I called Dad on Thursday evening and he said she was about the same. I suggested he take her into emergency and he said yes, he would, if there was no improvement by morning. On Friday, March 17th, at about eleven in the morning, Dad called the shop from the Saanich Peninsula Hospital. Mom has had a heart attack and they are taking her to the Victoria General for assistance. Dad said he would call when he knew something. At approximately four that afternoon, Dad called and said if we wanted to see her, we should come. I immediately called Ian and filled him in and said we are on our way home to pick him up. We close the shop, speed home, pick Ian up, he is ready to go, waiting outside the house for us. He jumps in and we speed to the hospital. We are shown to the cardiology ward. A nurse takes us to Dad. He is in a room standing with a priest. When Dad sees us, he walks towards Angus and says, "She's gone." They embrace and hold on to one another. According to the doctor's, she had congestive heart failure. We are all numb can't believe she went so fast.

Mom means so much to me, to us, as a family, to Angus, this is his mother. What a wonderful Mom, a beautiful person inside and out. She has been my friend, since the first day I met her in 1965 and it's 1989. Twenty-four years and never a cross word between us. We have laughed, cried, enjoyed, and helped one another the entire time and not once, did I ever have an unpleasant thought of her. I loved, respected, and thoroughly enjoyed our time together, and we had a lot of fun. We talked together, baked and cooked together, travelled and camped together, dieted together, all as natural as breathing. I made her laugh and when I bought something from the kitchen department for myself, I always picked one up for Mom, too! She got a kick out of that and I tried to surprise her as often as I could. It's 2017 and I miss her still, as I miss my Mom.

There is a lot to do, so the next few days are a blur. We contact as many of Mom's family in Scotland as we can and ask that they relay our message to others. Dad seems to be holding up pretty good. Mom is Ian's first close-to-his-heart death and I feel so bad for him. I remember my own Nanny Foley and how I didn't think I would ever breath normal again, when she passed away. Ian and his Grandma had lots of fun, laughs, and enjoyment with each other. I know he will miss her very much.

I have to share this, it was not funny then, but now, my sister-in-laws and myself laugh every time one of us brings up the incident.

Dad needed new dress pants for the funeral, so he went to the local men's wear shop and bought a pair and told them his daughters could hem them. They chalk marked them, to where the pants should be after hemming. The girls were downstairs at Dad's, pants laid out on the rug. I have Mom's sewing scissors in hand and I cut the pants on the mark. I look up, in horror, because I just realized the chalk mark is where the pants are supposed to be 'after' hemming. Well, I'm in shock I did that. Us girls make the tiniest hem you ever did see and we pressed them good. We hung them on a hanger and hoped Dad wouldn't notice. Dad does notice, the pants are too damn short. We had to come clean. He wasn't really angry with me, but not really enthusiastic at the prospect of wearing them either. We tried to convince him that no one would notice the length of his pants. I felt really bad, because he ended up throwing them away.

Summer is here before we know it. Ian's out of school and this year, he will stay a couple of weeks with his Auntie Margaret, Uncle John, and cousin, Johnny. They all have a great time, going on bike rides, having picnics in the park, and basically, having summer time fun.

In August, we close the shop and the three of us, along with our Polly, head for the Okanagan, which is a summer vacation destination in British Columbia.

Once we arrive and set up the motorhome in the campsite, we call a local car rental agency. We rent a vehicle to drive around and see all the sites, play mini golf, go on the waterslides, take Polly for walks in the park, go swimming, pretty much play all day.

After supper one evening, we decide to go into town for ice cream. Once at the Dairy Queen, we leave the vehicle running with the air conditioning on for Polly. After the ice cream, we come out and *what*, Angus has locked the keys in the car and we haven't a spare key. It's hotter than hell outside. We go back in and call a tow truck company to come rescue us. Polly is stretched out on the back seat, completely relaxed and comfortable, while we are standing in the sweltering heat, waiting. Angus hopes the guy they send knows how to use a slim-jim, so he won't scratch the vehicle. Here he comes, middle aged fellow with salt and pepper hair, he should know what he's doing, *not*. Angus explains the situation. The guy has a slim-jim, but admits he has no idea how to use it. Angus takes control and in less than a minute, he has the vehicle open. Oh, yes, we had to pay him, too!

We get home and have a few days there, before we head for Chilliwack, B.C. We are going to a rod run called 'Family Affair.' Ian is taking a buddy with him. We pack up the 1934 and the Mullins trailer that holds the boys skate boards, suitcases, cooler, table, chairs, and any other 'stuff' that's necessary. Polly will stay at the kennels, because this motel has a no pet rule.

We meet a few couples at the motel and enjoy an evening of laughter and swimming. We all follow one another to the fair grounds. The people are great, and there are a lot of cars, and lots of people, too! One thing about driving around in one of these specialized vehicles is, you can't be in a bad mood, because everybody is waving and smiling at you, it's a good time.

On Sunday, awards are given out and Angus has won 'Mayor's Choice.' There are several hundred vehicles here and to be recognized and to be given an award is an honor. I couldn't be more proud of Angus and all of the hours and hours of work he did. Oh boy, here comes another fall, Ian is thirteen, the start of his teen years. Angus is forty-one and I'm forty, we have been married now, for twenty-one years and have had our own business for nine years. I would be very pleased if all of you are still enjoying my rhythm in life, so far.

Dad has been away visiting family and friends in Alberta. He has taken his motorhome and really enjoyed the trip. Since losing Mom, he seems to be adjusting well, although I think he puts up a good front, when we are around. I call him pretty much every morning just to see how he is and we chat about everything. He's a great guy and we get along very well. One day, we are yacking and he tells me how much he has enjoyed having a muffin with his coffee in the afternoons. I suggest he make some of his own. He laughs, when I go through the process of telling him to look up one of Mom's receipts, shop for the ingredients, and just follow the method in the book.

"How will I know which one is the best receipt?"

"Usually the receipt with the most stains on the page is probably the best one," followed by, "Then, you can throw in as many raisins as you want to," we both laugh. He did try it, but found it was just easier to pick them up at the store. I don't think he liked waiting for them to come out of the oven. Waiting for anything wasn't one of his strongest attributes.

When hockey season rolls around, Ian is more than ready. Pretty much all summer, he is either playing street hockey, on his skateboard or his roller blades, all of which, keeps him in shape. Angus and I enjoy the hockey, too. Getting together, at the rink, with the parents is good and when we travel for games, we all have a good time, win or lose, but, of course, you always want to win.

This is a funny story for parents. The three of us are sitting at the breakfast table, when Ian says, "I think my voice is changing, Dad."

"Well, usually after your nuts drop, your voice does change," Angus replies.

I'm staring at my food, not looking at either one of them. Then Ian says, "Excuse me," and goes directly into the bathroom. He comes back out and sits down again. Angus and I are pretty sure he checked himself to see if his nuts did, in fact, drop. Too funny!

At Christmas, we decide to head for Alberta. We stay with Angus's sister, Catherine, her then husband, Gary, and their two sons, Kelly, who is eight and David, who is five. They live in St. Albert, it's a city in itself, but there appears to be no real separation between Edmonton and St. Albert, one just runs into the other. Catherine is an excellent cook and what a meal she makes. The two of us start preparing food pretty much after breakfast and really don't stop till dinner is served. We laugh a lot and have a great Christmas day. Kelly and David play hockey, so we take in a couple of their games.

Our time just seems to fly by, from one season into the next. The shop keeps us going from Monday to Friday, with lots of family activity on the weekends. It's so good to stay busy. Spring has rolled around and turned into summer.

The summer, fall, and winter of 1990 pass by without incident. Ian and a buddy attend a hockey school in Penticton, B.C. Angus and I drive them there for the week's camp and pick them up the following weekend. They meet guys from all over, even some from other countries. Come the end of the week, both are ready for home. Ian turns fourteen in September and is evolving into a well-adjusted young man.

For this Christmas, we go and stay with Angus' brother, Allan, and his wife, Fritz (Theresa). They live on property not too far from Edmonton, near Gibbons. We sit down to dinner and Allan announces they are expecting their first child. Exciting news, it will be born in the summer. We go skidooing on their property, go for walks on the trails with our Polly and their dogs. We have a bonfire, roast wieners, burn marshmallows, see the northern lights, and have a great time.

It's the beginning of 1991 and my energy level is not good. I'm always tired, my weight is coming back on and I haven't enough energy to make separate meals. After I lost my weight, I complained to the doctor that I should feel like a million bucks, but I didn't. She did some routine blood work, but nothing showed. She said I was probably fatigued, because of my busy life style.

For summer vacation, we decide to stay on the Island and go camping at Gordon Bay on Lake Cowichan. We take a tent for Ian and his buddy, Rob, a cook shack that fits over the picnic table at the campsite. Angus, Polly, and I stay in the motorhome.

We have a great two weeks. A funny story, you have to picture this scene. It's a beautiful summer day at the lake. At the campground, Ian and his friend meet up with Rob's older brother and his friends, all hockey players and all put together well, nice looking group of guys. Ian lets them know he has a boat and can take them over to the nearby diving cliffs, just across the lake. Sounds great, they will meet on the dock. Ian is down there, standing in front of his Grandpa's twelve-foot aluminum boat, with a 7.5 horsepower, outboard motor attached. Moored right beside him, is a gorgeous black and gold streamline speedboat with an inboard motor that could probably run 'the mill tales of hell' out of any boat on the lake. The speedboat over shadows Grandpa's boat, so when the group of guys come walking down the dock, they see this gorgeous boat and Ian standing there. Hoots, whistles, and smiles abound, until they get closer and notice that Ian is actually standing past the speed boat and they get a look at the twelve-footer; bobbing in the water.

All six of them get in the boat, with the sides of the boat bobbing, ever so close to the water. Ian's the captain of the boat and just past a nearby island, the wind picks up and the waves start crashing over the front and sides of the boat, everyone gets wet. Too funny! They all have a great day of cliff diving and get back safe and sound.

Well, it's come to the fall of the year and I'm not getting any better. I manage to work at the shop, do the usual chores like grocery shopping, housework, and laundry. Making lunches is a chore now and after supper, I'm done; no energy at all, so I go to bed. We have a waterbed and each side has their own temperature control. I'm having night sweats every night and wake up soaked. I turn my temperature control off, but that doesn't help, I still wake up soaked. Too young for menopause, I'm only forty-two.

One night in November, I get out of bed, about one in the morning, and throw up so hard that I pass out. Angus and Ian are awakened by the crash. Angus gets me back to bed. Come morning, I don't feel sick like I have the flu or anything, so off to work we go. That evening, after a shower, I notice two lumps in my neck, on the left side. *What the hell is that?* I mumble to myself. I show Angus and he says to make an appointment, right away, to see my doctor.

After a few days, I'm in with my doctor. She feels the lumps and asks if I have a cold coming on. "No," I reply. She will set up an appointment with an ear, nose, and throat specialist, because I have said that my hearing or I should say the lack of my hearing has started to annoy my family. She advises me to tell the specialist at the time of the appointment, if the two lumps are still there.

I get in to see the specialist and he does a hearing test, which shows I have a slight hearing loss, but nothing to be concerned about, at this point.

"Oh," I say, "I almost forgot, I'm supposed to show you these two lumps in my neck," as I point to them.

"How long have they been there?" he asks, while walking towards me.

"I'm guessing it's been about a month, because I had to wait three weeks to get in to see you."

He examines the lumps and asks if I have time, he would like to extract some fluid from around the lumps and send it off to the lab.

"Yes, of course, I have time."

A few minutes later I find myself lying on a bed, while the doctor is preparing the needle. He takes a fluid sample and says the results will take a week to ten days and his office will be in touch.

On Friday, we have closed the shop for our Christmas break, which is the last two weeks in December. We are going to Alberta and the three of us are busy packing, when the phone rings.

"Hello."

"May I speak with Brenda?"

"Yes, this is Brenda."

"This is Dr. Ross calling."

"Hello, Dr. Ross, how are you?"

"I'm fine, thank you, we got your results back and we need to remove those lumps immediately."

"Oh, okay, but I'm leaving tomorrow morning for Christmas holidays in Alberta for two weeks."

"Call the office, just as soon as you return and we will book the surgery."

"Yes, I will, Dr. Ross."

"Bye for now," he says, "Have a good holiday."

"You, too," I reply and hang up.

Chapter Five: Middle Age,
1992-2005

Now, what? I ask myself. I tell Angus and Ian, but I really haven't any information, other than I need to have these two lumps removed as soon as possible.

We stay with Angus's sister, Catherine, and her family in St. Albert. We, get to see Allan's first-born daughter, Katie, who is now four months old, she was born in August. She has been named after Allan and Angus' mother, which is really nice. She is a little cutie and is such a good baby. All of us have a great time, lots of laughs, good company, and good food, a very nice Christmas. I'm very tired, not functioning normal. I accidently, put Angus's wallet that was in his jeans pocket, through the washing machine. He lost a few items, one being a gold toothpick I bought him years before, just an example of how my thinking wasn't clear at all.

We get home after New Year's, reopen the shop on the first Monday in January and call Dr. Ross's office. I speak with the receptionist and she is aware of the situation. They will be in touch regarding the surgery date. Within ten days or so, I'm booked. After the operation, the lumps will be sent to the lab and I'm advised to phone for an appointment, make it for ten days from now, he will take out the stitches, and by then, a confirmation of the results will be in. He won't discuss anything, until the results are confirmed, I was told after asking.

I have quite a slice at the base of my neck, left side, running kind of diagonally, not exactly east and west, but kind of north-east to south-west and it's about two inches long. The waiting is going to be hard, but we are always busy, so that helps.

Okay, I leave the shop for my appointment with Dr. Ross. The medical assistant takes me in to the examining room, where Dr. Ross is sitting at a desk. We say hello and he points to a chair, "Have a seat." I sit down. He crosses the room, dabs my wound with a cotton ball, soaked in hydrogen peroxide, and starts to remove stitches. He removes a couple, but the remaining ones are not ready to come out. *That's kind of odd,* I think to myself, it's been a while already. He tells me to come back in another five days. They should be ready to come out, by then. I go back in five days he takes the remaining stitches out. There is a silence in the room and I feel kind of awkward, who should talk first. I straighten the collar of my blouse, and say, "Do you have the lump results?"

"Yes," he replies, "It is Hodgkin's Disease".

My mind is going a mile a minute.

"What's that?" I ask, as he reaches past me and opens the door. I follow him through the waiting room, where he turns to me and says, "The clinic will be in touch."

"The clinic," I respond.

"Yes, the cancer clinic."

He extends his hand to me, we shake, and then he says, "All the best."

"Thank you," I answer.

I step out of the office and the door closes behind me. I start walking down the empty hallway, towards the elevator, my eyes are glassy and I'm a little shaky.

I get back to the shop, where Angus is anxiously waiting. He steps into the office and closes the door behind him, "Well, how did you make out?"

"Not good, he says it's Hodgkin's disease, and the cancer clinic will be in touch."

"What the hell is that?"

"I don't know, never heard of it before, I'll look it up in the medical book, when we get home."

The rest of the afternoon is a blur, I know we asked a couple people if they had ever heard of Hodgkin's before, but no one did.

I look it up, just as soon as we arrive at home. It read, "Hodgkin's disease is a malignant disease of the lymphatic system."

I hang up my watch, on a hook, by the kitchen sink, wash my hands, and start to make dinner. Both of us having our own private thoughts and I'm wondering how this will affect our everyday lives. Ian gets home, we sit down to dinner and I tell him what it is and I also tell him, at this point, we don't know how serious it is, but the cancer clinic will be in touch. There is really not much to say or do, we just have to wait.

We don't have to wait long. We get to the shop the next morning and about fifteen minutes later, the phone rings. It's the cancer clinic, "Could I come in for a consultation and to meet my oncologist today?"

"Yes, of course."

The appointment is that afternoon. I meet my oncologist; she is really nice, her name is Dr. Heidi Martins. We go over the results and she tells me that in order to find out what stage it's in, we have to go through some tests. After they are completed, then treatment options will be discussed.

Well, the tests start pretty quick, after that appointment, and I receive calls to go for blood tests, an ECG, chest X-rays, CT scan, a gallium scan, and two others that were necessary, but not pleasant. One is a lymphangiogram, the other is a bone marrow test.

The lymphangiogram took a couple of hours. The doctor came in after his assistants had prepped the tops of my feet with antiseptic. They explained the procedure. I would get a cut, about an inch on the top of each foot. After that, an intravenous would be set up and a radio opaque dye would be injected into the blood vessels and as they are very tiny, it's imperative not to move, until all the dye has been injected, approximately two hours. The doctor comes in, he seems grumpy, but I make light of it and smile, anyway. He doesn't stay long, he presses each foot down, so the skin is taut, and then makes a slice about an inch long on the top of each foot and inserts the intravenous needles, mumbles a few instructions to the medical couple in attendance and leaves.

"Don't mind him," one of them says, "He can be a grouch sometimes."

"That's okay," I reply, "He's probably just having a rough day." After the procedure is complete, they call him on an intercom. He comes back in, with the same mood, slaps one regular sized band aid on each foot and says, "Don't take those off for a week."

"Okay, I won't."

He leaves and the attendants help me up, as I have been lying there for a good two hours, unable to move.

It's the night before the band -aids come off I have been sponge bathing for a week. Angus and I are sitting on the love seat in the living room and he notices a smell coming from my feet. He takes a peek under the Band-Aid on my right foot and says, "You better see the doctor first thing in the morning, because I think it's infected."

I call the clinic in the morning, explain my situation, and the receptionist says my oncologist will see me right away, just come.

I'm sitting on the examining table, when Dr. Martins comes in. We pass pleasantries, while she removes both of the bandages. She gasps, puts her hand over her mouth, and says, "I'll be right back," as she backs out of the room. Out in the hallway, I hear her speaking in a hurried tone. Less than a minute later, she returns with an assistant, a bottle of hydrogen peroxide and a catch bowl. The assistant puts the bowl under my right foot, which is very infected, while Dr. Martins pours the whole bottle of liquid over my foot. She dabs some on my left foot, which appears to be okay.

The conversation begins. I tell her that the surgeon put those bandages on and said, "Don't take those off for a week."

She stood there listening to me and then she said, "Who was the surgeon?"

"I don't remember his name, but he was grumpy and his name rhymes with Grinch, like 'The Grinch Who Stole Christmas'."

"That's okay, I'll find out."

"Is he going to be in trouble?" I ask.

"Well," she replies, "I'm reporting the incident to the Medical Association."

After my feet were wrapped and as I was leaving, I said thank you to Dr. Martins, who was sitting at a small table, just a few feet away, she was writing.

I didn't want the doctor to get into trouble, but he should have known when he did the lymphangiogram, that people with Hodgkin's have no way of fighting off infection, because their immune systems have been compromised. I think he should have put in a couple of stitches in each foot I probably wouldn't have gotten the infection.

I was told to return the next day, after the lymphangiogram, and they would take x-rays. The x-rays would show where the dye travelled and where it bubbled is where the cancer is. These x-rays were different, because I didn't have to remove any clothing. It was again imperative that I not move a muscle, so I didn't. The results would be sent to my oncologist.

Now, the call comes to report for a bone marrow test. There is a saying that goes 'save the best for last,' well, in this case, it's 'save the worst for last.' The surgeon, who completes the test, is a Dr. Martins, too, no relation to my oncologist. He made the test tolerable. The skin is numbed and then the needle and syringe are inserted into the bone marrow in the hip area, where they extract enough bone marrow to send to the lab for testing. Dr. Martins says, "Okay, I'm ready to insert the needle now and I want you to think of something very pleasant for twenty to thirty seconds, because this is going to be a very sharp pain. I also need you to be still, okay?"

"Yes, I will."

I close my eyes and I see my son, Ian, on a hockey rink, in his hockey gear, skating towards me, where I am standing on the sidelines. He is skating pretty fast towards me, comes to an abrupt stop and then smiles and winks at me, before skating away.

"We're done, you did great."

That was a tough one, for anyone who has had bone marrow extracted it's a tough one. They call it a needle, but after the incision is made, the needle is actually hollow, like a straw, so the syringe can slice thin, tiny pieces of bone marrow and extract them for testing. The smile and wink got me through it and, you know, I remembered it just the way it happened, too, clear as a bell.

In between those two tests, I had a gallium injection and scan. The radioactive nuclear medicine is used to detect cancer in the body. The injection is given in the arm. You go back the next day for the scan, which shows where the gallium has collected in your organs and bones. You must lay still for about an hour and those results are sent to the oncologist.

A recap a diagnosis of Hodgkin's disease on February 4th, tests begin on February 6th, after meeting my oncologist. Throughout the month, I go for x-rays, blood work, an ECG, a CT scan, a lymphangiogram, a gallium injection and scan, and then, finally, a bone marrow test. All of these were completed by February 28th, that's it, no more tests.

It's March 3rd, as soon as we arrive at the shop, the clinic calls. Dr. Martins would like me to bring my husband in with me for a meeting. They have all the test results.

At ten o'clock, Angus and I are taken to Dr. Martin's office, where we each take a chair and wait for her to join us.

Dr. Martins comes in with my file. I introduce her to Angus we pass pleasantries. Dr. Martins sits down and opens the file.

"Well," Angus says, "What have we got?"

I'm paralyzed as Angus and I hold hands. Dr. Martins replies, "Hodgkin's Disease, Stage 4b. She had it in her neck, she has it in both sides of her diaphragm and it's highly suspicious in her bone marrow."

Angus says, "Is it curable?"

"She has a twenty percent chance of making it, fifty percent she will get it back and if caught in the early stages, it's eighty percent curable.

"4b is not an early stage," Angus says.

"No, it's not, it's the last stage."

"What about treatment?" Angus asks. Dr. Martins hands us a protocol sheet, but we can't make heads or tails of it, too technical. We both look at the paper and then look at her.

"Chemo," she answers, "Eight cycles are recommended."

Then, Dr. Martins asks, "Do you want to go have a coffee and talk about it?"

Angus and I look at each other.

"When can she start?" Angus asks.

"This afternoon around 2:00 o'clock, if that's good?"

"I'll have her back by 2:00."

We don't say too much on the way back to the shop, we are really glad there is treatment, even if it is chemo. The last stage isn't good news. Angus drives me back to the hospital at 2:00 and escorts me up to the chemo department.

"When should I come back?" Angus asks the attending nurse. It's decided around 5:00 o'clock should be fine.

I step into the chemo room, there are approximately six lounge chairs placed around the room. There are big windows on two sides of the room, making it bright, but it's far from cheery, that's for sure. The nurse directs me to a vacant chair, where she asks my name and date of birth. She then puts on a wristband and we check the info together. About fifteen minutes later, another nurse comes and puts in an IV needle, near my wrist, ouch! There is a pharmacist window, where the nurses wait, once it is open, a bag of liquid chemo drugs can be seen for pickup. The nurse checks the bag for the information label and takes it to the person, who will be the receiver. All information is matched and the IV begins.

This is kind of hard to explain, but bear with me, I think you will be able to get the gist of the procedure. It goes like this, I was given my first IV chemo treatment on a Tuesday, followed by the second treatment the following Tuesday, these two are called 'a cycle.' The following two weeks, no chemo, you take steroids and in those two weeks, your blood gets refreshed, just in time for more chemo. So, it's two weeks on and two weeks off. My treatments started on March 3rd and ended on September 30th, seven months. With the chemo, the drugs were given through an intravenous and there were four bags of different drugs for each chemo visit, so eight bags in a cycle. The steroids are taken in pill form at home.

We never have these thoughts, or at least I never did. I never even gave it a thought, let alone a second thought, that I would be sitting in a chemo room. That goes for having cancer in the fourth stage, never even crossed my mind, but here I am. I can't really say I was scared, maybe because I didn't have a guilty conscience of being at fault for getting Hodgkin's. They say it is caused by a virus, possibly because I wasn't exposed to as many childhood diseases as I should have been. Who knows?

Ian and I feel that when I lost fifty pounds in four and a half months, that I may have compromised my immune system at the time.

For the next seven months, I'm committed to chemo treatments, no radiation, as I'm too far gone for radiation. I don't have any mixed feelings about the treatment at all. I'm listening to the experienced medical field, because they know what works. My disposition has always been good, so I'm banking on that, along with keeping a positive frame of mind. I'm hoping there won't be too many days where the drugs make me sick. I'm also going to try and keep our lives as normal as possible. I will definitely stay working at the shop, because being busy is good. Angus and Ian mean everything to me, I will not die from this disease and I will not let them down either.

I was given some printed information on the signs of Hodgkin's. According to the list, I certainly had a few of those signs. One, being the swollen lymph nodes in my neck, two, the night sweats, three, the vomiting and, finally, the fourth sign was having an itchy trunk or bum. This, I did experience on our Christmas trip and I said to Angus, "My bum is itchy; it must be the dry Alberta air in winter!"

"No, it wasn't the air at all."

Fatigue was a big one, I was so tired, and that was totally out of character for me. I couldn't stay up past nine o'clock and a few times, it was even earlier than that.

I'm not going to go through the entire seven months, but I will tell you some funny stories and maybe a couple of not so funny stories that happened.

So, Angus comes back to the cancer ward at the hospital to pick me up. I'm not quite finished, so he sits beside me and we wait as the last of the liquid chemo drips from the IV bag and goes into my body. We pass pleasantries, both of us knowing this will be a long journey.

This is kind of cute. On the way home, I tell him I will lose my hair.

"All of it?" he asks.

"Every strand," I respond, "And I'm not getting a wig either."

"You're not?" he questions.

"No, I'm getting a hat, with a wire that sticks out at the front, about six inches, with a flower stuck on the end of it, and every time I move my head, the flower will bounce and make people laugh."

He looks over at me, not wanting to believe what he just heard. A few seconds pass, "Of course, I'm getting a wig," I say. I could feel his relief. We smile at one another.

I go wig shopping at 'The Bay.' I meet this really nice middle-aged woman, who has been selling wigs for quite a long time. Her experience tells me that she has come across a lot of different women with lots of different reasons for wanting to purchase a wig. I tell her why I'm there. We hit it off right away, she has me laughing, as I sit in front of a mirror and try on several different ones. I try on long, short, straight, curly, blonde, red, and brunette. Not quite decided, she says, "I know, I've got the perfect one for you."

She disappears through a door at the rear of the wig department. A couple of minutes later, she returns.

"How's this one? She is standing there wearing this bright green and black spiked 'Tina Turner' style wig. I take one look at her and we both burst out laughing. It was really funny, we both made each other's day. We found a way to turn a not so pleasant experience into a very pleasant one.

I'm finished with my first cycle. In the shower, washing and rinsing my hair, I open my eyes and the whole tub is covered with hair. OMG! Didn't think it would be coming out so fast. I call Angus into the bathroom; we decide it's time.

"Maybe you want your hairdresser to cut it," he says.

"No, I don't need a style, I just need it gone."

"Okay, let's get the scissors."

We put a towel around my shoulders and he cuts it off, all off. Actually, he did a really good job, shaved my head, and made it all even. That was kind of a tough one, a couple of tears were shed, but I kept thinking. *It's going to grow back, it's going to grow back."*

Angus was great and kept my spirits up.

I could write a few paragraphs on the side effects I got from the chemo and steroids, but there were so many and they changed all the time. I didn't miss much work, probably three or four days in total. If I got tired at the shop, I just put my head down on my desk for a while. I couldn't cook strong vegetables like cabbage, broccoli, or cauliflower, because the smell would make me sick. I didn't have to shave, that was kind of nice. My periods stopped completely and that was kind of nice, too! My body was forced into menopause, I'm forty-three.

As the months go by, I begin to feel better and my energy level is getting better. In early August, we go to Lake Cowichan for holidays. I have chemo, just before we go, and notice my right arm is puffy and red. A day or so later, it's killing me. I tell Angus just to chop it off with the axe, that's how much it hurt. Margaret and John from Nanaimo come to visit us at the campsite, she massages my arm and that makes a world of difference. The drugs slowly drain into my body and the arm does get a lot better.

I tell Dr. Martins and she says it will be a good idea for me to get a port-acath implanted, because my veins are shutting down. I guess they feel the drugs coming and say, "Oh no, you don't," and collapse. It's a simple procedure. They make an incision in the right upper chest and put the porta-cath, which is about as big as a quarter, just under the skin. The next time I have chemo, the nurse puts the chemo needle through the skin and it flows into the portacath bubble and from there, it flows through a tube and into a central vein and that vein empties into the heart. I did notice that these stitches dissolved pretty fast, so I'm thinking the chemo must be working.

It's September and Ian turns sixteen, Angus was forty-four last April and I turned forty-three last February. Our anniversary on the 28th will be our twenty -fourth. I'm excited, it's September 30th, and my last chemo treatment is finally here. I see Dr. Martins and she says they will see me in three months' time for a check-up.

It's a good feeling to be finished. The whole experience has been such a constant in our lives, it will be hard not to think of the past nine months and all that we have been through.

"Time, there is no one simple definition of time. Time is something we deal with every day and something that everyone thinks they understand. However, a compact and robust definition of time has proved to be remarkably tricky and elusive," taken from the web: Exactly What is time?

Time means everything and yet, it can be very unimportant. If you remember, the day I found out I had Hodgkin's disease, we came home, and I took my watch off at the kitchen sink, washed my hands, and started preparing dinner. Well, I never did put the watch back on my wrist and it's been 25 years now. That's how profound it was, at that particular moment, time meant nothing and yet, time meant everything.

How did I manage to get through it? The most difficult part was definitely not the hair loss or the drugs. For me, it was being in stage IV (four) that really bothered me. It made me feel as if I was neglectful, because it does take time to get to a stage four. I can honestly say I was not negligent. I went to the doctor every six months, lost weight, as was suggested by my doctor, complained about my fatigue, but until the lumps appeared in my neck, there was really nothing to test. I knew my hair would grow back and I had every reason to believe the drugs would cure me. The drugs were strong and I did feel every side effect, right down to the sores in my mouth, but the drugs have to be strong, they are killing cancer cells that have taken over. Slowly but surely, every week of every month, I did feel generally better and I kept a very positive attitude about the whole process. I was doing everything the medical profession was telling me to do.

Angus and Ian were wonderful, always asking how I was, doing chores for me, making me breakfast in bed on weekends, making me laugh, and encouraging me along the way. Family phone calls and visits were really appreciated and enjoyed. Friends, away from the shop, and friends, at the shop, were immeasurable and their caring meant the world to me.

I have to tell you about a very special person. His name is Lorne Moss. We met Lorne through a mutual friend and customer, Eric Forsberg. He and Lorne were friends, way back in high school. We had Lorne as a customer, too. It just happened that when I was diagnosed with Hodgkin's and in the fourth stage, Eric was at the shop.

Sitting at my desk, it's a Monday morning, about nine thirty, when a vehicle pulls in. I look up from my paper work and it's Lorne. We pass pleasantries and I offer to get Angus for an estimate. No, he doesn't need one. He is here to see me, after seeing Eric on the weekend.

He takes a seat across the desk from me and he is still there at noon. He tells me of his own personal experiences with Hodgkin's. He explains everything to me and lets me know what I can expect. Through his sharing, I felt even more reassured that I would be okay. I really can't thank him enough. He continues to visit through my treatment and, of course, the subject of Hodgkin's is always at the forefront of our discussions.

It is with the utmost sadness that I tell you, Lorne passed away. He was at the shop, just a few weeks before, and he didn't look good. He had undergone a bone marrow transplant and he was on some pretty powerful drugs. The last time we saw him, I knew. His wonderful wife, Kathy, had been by his side during all of his illnesses over the years, called to let us know. I have never met a stronger woman in my life and I told her so. She, with her love for Lorne, her nursing knowledge, and years of experience, had made Lorne's life the very best it could be. Together, they were a one in a million couple. To this day, we continue to exchange Christmas cards with one another and catch up with each other's news. If she called me today and needed me for anything, I would be there for her. Kathy, you are one of the best.

It's coming up to my three-month check-up. We went to Alberta for Christmas and stayed with my sister, Viv, and Wally. My hair is starting to grow back, so I ask Viv to trim it. That wasn't easy, because it's like baby duck down, all fuzzy. She does a great job with the inch or so she has to work with. I feel pretty good about the cut, so I quit wearing my wig.

We get home after New Year's and I make an appointment to see Dr. Martin's. For the last week or so, my lower back has been aching and I have a rash that has developed, it really hurts, my skin is very sensitive around my waist area and down my left leg to the knee. I will ask Dr. Martins, when I see her.

When we see each other, we pass pleasantries and she wants to see my rash. I drop my slacks and she is taken back a bit by the sight of it. There are definite red blisters that look like half raspberries to me. She tells me that I have shingles and that the chemo can trigger shingles. Apparently, there are a lot of people, who have had chemo that develop shingles. She asks me if it's okay for her to bring a medical class of students in to see the rash. I'm okay with that. An assistant comes in and gets me on the bed with my left side showing the blistered, red raspberries.

As the class enters the room, they are all smiles and thank me for the opportunity. One student has a camera and several photos are taken from different angles. Dr. Martins comes in, and reads them my history. She asks the students to guess what they are looking at. No one offers a guess, so she says, "You are looking at a full-blown case of the shingles."

The students leave and Dr. Martins wraps my leg with a special, cheesecloth like bandage. It feels really good and helps with the pain I get, when my clothes touch my skin and the open sores. I get a prescription and start taking the medication right away. After taking the meds for two weeks, the rash is pretty much gone. My results were good from my blood tests as well as the x-rays that were taken. I will need to see Dr. Martins every three months for a year, then every six months for one year, and then once a year for five years. I'm hoping there are no more surprises, it's time to carry on; we need to get our life's rhythm back.

It's the start of 1993 and I'm looking forward to being normal again. In February, Angus' brother, Allan, and his wife have their second daughter, Maggie. She is named after their sister Margaret. Maggie is the last of the nieces and nephews to be added to the family. On Angus' side of the family, from eldest to youngest, they go like this. Angus and I have one son, Ian. Marion and Dave have three sons, Donald, Danny, and Robbie. Margaret and John have one son, Johnny. Allan and Theresa have two daughters, Katie and Maggie. Catherine and Gary have two sons, Kelly and David. On my side of the family, from eldest to youngest, they go like this. Vivian has one daughter, Tamara. Carol has one daughter, Jamie. Sandra has one son, James. So, the nine of us siblings have had a total of twelve children.

Angus and I are starting to connect with friends again and are enjoying quality time together. It's not that we didn't before cancer, because we always took time for family, it's just more special now, funny how that goes. Our focus has always been on Ian, with love and our business, of course.

The next five years are kind of tough. I'm finished with treatments, but the shadow of cancer remains. You know you're scheduled appointments are waiting and tests will be taken to insure you are cancer free. The anticipation is difficult, because you are always analyzing yourself, making sure you are aware of your everyday 'being,' like how are you feeling, are you okay, not fatigued, no lumps, generally feeling good, *all* the time, it gets a bit much.

This is a cute story; it just came to me. When Ian was fifteen, we got him driving lessons. The package came with five lessons. The instructor would pick him up for each lesson and would see him through to writing the exam and then onto the actual road test for his license. After the first lesson, Ian said it went good. After the second lesson, we got a call at the shop from the instructor.

"Mrs. MacDonald," he begins, "Ian is doing so well, I don't think he needs any more lessons."

After a moment, I reply, "Oh, yes he does."

"Well, if you think so, I guess I'll see them through, for your sake," he says.

"Yes, I would appreciate that," I answer. Ian finishes the five lessons, writes the exam, and gets his license. We knew he didn't need the extra lessons and so did he, funny!

Life is moving along, I'm feeling good, no problems at all. When my six months check-up comes along, in the spring, I ask Dr. Martins if I could have a second bone marrow test and could I please have the same surgeon, Dr. Martins, no relation? Because healthy bone marrow is very important, I need to know. I also ask about my portacath, could I have it removed? She says it's a good idea to wait for a couple of years. That news didn't sit well, but I guess it does make sense.

A few weeks go by and I get my second bone marrow aspiration, where bone marrow samples are taken from the center of the bone. Dr. Martins is great, he does recognize me from a year ago and understands why I requested the second procedure. He does exactly as before, the pain is very sharp, although, another wink from Ian gets me through. The results come in and they are negative, no cancer. Yeah! I'm very happy.

Our summer comes and goes, before we know it, it's September and Ian turns seventeen. We bought him a 1984 Chev pickup he really likes it and the truck suits him. Somehow, Angus and I are spending a lot of time together. Ian is busy with school, friends, and girlfriends, just the way it should be. The shop is keeping us busy and we are enjoying each other, just the way it should be. Our rhythm in life has returned.

When my next check-up comes, I'm not concerned about the test results, as that lingering cancer shadow in my head has all, but disappeared. Results are good, no problems.

The next thing we know, it's February of 1994. Polly has had an off week, she has been off her food, not playing and generally, not feeling well. I ask Ian to take her to the vet's on his way to school and tell them to call me at the shop to discuss her symptoms.

About nine thirty, the vet calls and says he has given Polly a general examination and would like to take a couple of x-rays. He calls back and, now, wants to do an exploratory surgery to see what's going on in her stomach area. I agree and tell him to keep us posted.

Around eleven, he calls with very bad news. Polly is full of cancer. They can treat her with chemo drugs. Of course, there is no guarantee she will live three weeks or three months.

I ask, "Is she sleeping now?"

"Yes, she is."

"Hang on a minute, I'll speak with Angus."

I set the receiver down, Angus and I discuss the situation. I go back to the phone and tell the vet that we have decided to. "Just let her sleep." He completely understands and will be in touch. That was very tough. We had a lot of good times with Polly especially Ian, he will miss her. We will all miss her. She was a great beagle, full of fun. We had her for ten years, from 1984 to 1994.

This is a good one about our Polly. The four of us are out in the back yard, playing in the snow, when Polly gets a scent of something and takes off cross country, running across the street and continuing through a big open field. In a blink, she is gone. Angus and Ian jump in the car, trying to catch up with her, using every road available, while I take off on foot, calling her name as loud as I could. She is nowhere to be found. It's a long weekend, a Saturday. We have company on the Sunday it's Easter. Monday comes and goes, without a sign of her. The three of us are worried sick that she could be hurt somewhere or that it's possible someone might have picked her up. She had her collar on and a tag that had her name, the vet's name, and phone number.

First thing, Tuesday morning, I call the SPCA and inquire if anybody has called in with a lost beagle. "Yes, they have," was the answer. What a relief, they give me the ladies phone number. I call her, thank her very much, and we make arrangements for me to pick Polly up after work. I get there, ring the doorbell, and a lovely young mother answers the door, with her two children peeking around her legs at me. Polly hears the commotion and comes running, tail wagging, and jumps into my arms. The lady tells me she is a nurse. When she pulled into the parking lot on the Saturday, Polly was there and came to her for a pet. She tells Polly to "go home," and carries on into the hospital. After her shift, which was a long time, Polly was still there, sitting by her car, in the dark, and shivering, she's very cold from the wind and rain. She picked her up and took her home. They keep her for the weekend. Polly is an unexpected treat for them. They instantly fell in love with her. The kids are crying, when the Mom closed the door, but she was promising that they, too, would be getting their own puppy soon. I hope they did and I hope they settled on a beagle; they are wonderful with kids. Polly was just three or four years old at the time and cute as a button, too!

Another animal story, but this time it's about a cat that wasn't ours. I remember it was early one morning, pitch black outside and raining like the dickens. I was in the kitchen, making lunches and just happened to put on the rear deck, outside light. I saw a white cat laying on the grass in the back yard. Ian came up behind me, so I said to him, "Look out there, Ian, there's a white cat outside sleeping in the grass."

Ian looks out, turns to me, and says, "It's dead."

"Oh," I respond, as I peer out into the darkness with my hands at each side of my face and my nose pressed against the glass, trying to see any movement.

"Do you think so?" I question.

"Mom, it's raining out, do you think a cat would be out there, just lying in the grass, sleeping?"

"I guess not, it just never occurred to me that it would be dead."

Angus comes in the kitchen and sees us at the window and says, "What's up?"

Ian replies, "Oh, there's a dead cat in the back yard and Mom thinks it's just sleeping."

Now, depending on your sense of humor, this was funny, very funny and I haven't stopped laughing at that one. It was Ian's response that did it.

Angus and I are carrying on with our car events, camping in the motorhome, taking trips up Island to see Margaret and John, our friends in Cobblehill, Rae and Bernie, Cliff and Cheryl. We are enjoying getting back to normal. Ian is pretty independent now, Polly is gone, my treatments are gone and we are enjoying the freedom of it all.

We are hockey people and hockey night in Canada is pretty much a ritual with us. Angus is a Toronto Maple Leafs fan and has been since he was a young boy. Me, I'm a Detroit Red Wings fan. I remember watching games with my Dad over the years and Gordie Howe was his favorite player. Angus also likes Gordie Howe, a lot. Ian's team has always been the Chicago Blackhawks, with good reason, they are good, and when he played for the Saanich Braves in Victoria, their logo was very similar in design to the Blackhawks. I have swung over the years, as we now live back in Alberta, so the Oilers are on my list, too. I just plain like hockey very much and it's tough for Angus to change channels on me, once a game starts. He, of course, knows a good game from a bad game, but let's me watch no matter what. Can't mention hockey without mentioning Don Cherry and Ron McLean. I hope Don remains in good health and continues with the Coach's Corner for a long time, we enjoy him and his frankness, as we enjoy Ron and his polite smack.

Nothing beats a live game; we have been to several over the years. One in particular, was in May of 1992 and the Blackhawks are playing the Oilers in a conference final. We decide to fly to Edmonton to take in the game. I'm in treatment, so this weekend away will be a great diversion.

We are at the game, Chicago has won three straight so far, so a win tonight will clinch them a spot and a chance to win the Stanley Cup. The game is going good for Chicago, Ian's excited, and every time they score, we jump up and cheer. This one time, I jump straight up with my arms shooting very fast and very close to my head and I, actually, knock my wig off-kilter. I grab it before it falls off totally, and lucky for me, in all the excitement of the goal, nobody notices. Whew, too funny. Chicago wins 5 to 1, four games straight, they will go on to face the Penguins for the cup. FYI, Chicago lost to the Penguins in four games, too bad.

We head to McDonald's for a bite to eat. Walking through the parking lot, the son of friends of ours, Jackie and Rick Miller, their son, Michael, sees us and yells out, "Hey, what the hell are you guys doing here?"

We laugh and tell him we flew in to see the game, unannounced to anyone, but that I'll call Jackie tomorrow. We did see Jackie the next day and had a good unexpected visit. Rick was out of town working at the time. Reminds me of a song 'The Night has a Thousand Eyes' and it sure did that night, funny.

When Ian, at seventeen years old, got his 1984 Chev pick-up, that's exactly what I said to him, "Remember Ian, the night has a thousand eyes." Never once, did we ever have a 'problem' with our Ian, maybe the thousand eyes had something to do with that?

I have to mention our good friends Jackie and Rick Miller. We have been friends since elementary school. Angus went to school with Jackie, and I went to school with Rick. We have spent fun times with them at different occasions and also at their lake cottage. They have two children Michael and Michelle. They have four grandchildren. We have been friends for well over fifty years, probably closer to sixty years.

My rhythm in life is going along just fine. I'm happy and I'm living a life that's all good. I'm working, playing, and enjoying Angus and Ian. We have Dad over pretty much every Sunday for supper, which gives him a break from the kitchen and gives us a chance to visit with him and that's always good. I definitely have enough variety and things to do that I'm never bored. I do the same things over and over again, like everybody else and that's okay. It's like yard work for men and housework for woman, it has to be done and it never goes away. Angus and I don't need any discussions on who's doing what; we basically have followed the same pattern for years now. At home, I do the housework, laundry, cooking, dishes, grocery shopping, and Angus does all the yard work, maintains all the yard equipment, trims trees, maintains our parked vehicles, and always helps me, when I need a hand, like washing windows, etc. At the shop, I do the bookkeeping, pay bills, schedule the workload coming in and going out. Angus does everything else, which includes estimating vehicle damage, painting, over-seeing the body men, customer relations, any maintenance required, keeping the appearance up, and so many other things that it's hard to list them all. Together, we do a damn good job and there is never any arguing going on either. That arguing and fighting with each other, I have never understood. If we all do what we are supposed to do to make our lives enjoyable, then there is no reason for not getting along, there's no time. Forget about the small stuff and concentrate on being your best and doing your best, too. I'm not preaching, I'm very thankful that I have Angus. He's a great guy. He is so supportive of me all the time, just like in our wedding vows, for richer or poorer, in sickness and in health, that's the way we are with each other. We actually made a pact years ago, it went something like this, "If at any time, we find that I don't love him or he doesn't love me anymore, just say so and we will come to terms with it." Besides, we never do anything to or against one another to cause an argument. We have had our disagreements over the years, but we have always kissed good night at the end of the day.

It's the start of summer. Ian is done with school and couldn't be happier. He has a job at the driving range and is enjoying that for now. Time is marching along; one season stops and another begins. Honestly, you keep busy and pretty soon, a year goes by in no time. I go for my tests, as scheduled, and everything is good. At the end of the first five years, which is now the fall of 97, I see Dr. Heidi Martins for the last time. I don't have to go back anymore. I'm very happy, we are all glad it's over. I know as time goes by, I will only think of the good stuff that has happened. I have my life and for that, I will always be grateful. To the medical doctors, nurses, technicians, and everybody, who works in this field I have the utmost respect. A heartfelt thank you to the men and women, who develop the drugs that cure us, I wouldn't be here, without you. To my friends and family, who came visiting with love and support, you made my treatment time go faster. All the phone calls I received of good wishes were very appreciated. To Angus and to Ian, there are no words, your love, and daily emotional support you gave me, made me want to fight, and made me believe I would be cured.

It's a funny thing, if you saw me anywhere, at the shop, banking, grocery shopping, anywhere, you would never guess I had cancer, let alone a very serious stage of cancer, and there are a lot of people out there who can vouch for that, because they too, are weathering the storm. "Don't judge a book by its cover," is so true and for so many different scenarios, one never knows what another may be going through.

On Angus's side of the family, there have been a few family reunions, over the years, and they have always been lots of fun and lots of laughs. One was in Kelowna, B.C., hosted by Angus' first cousin John Dolanz and his wife, Susan. There were a lot of relatives, who showed up, some as far away as Scotland. A cousin of Angus' Dad, from Glasgow came. Morag and her Grandson, Donald. He had brought his flute on the trip. One evening, a bunch of us were sitting in the living room visiting and young Donald started playing, while Morag's daughter, Julia, sang a couple of songs for us. After they were done, Morag asked, "What can you Canadian's play?"

Silence surrounded the room, and Angus replies, "I guess the only thing we know how to play is the radio."

Over in Scotland, the people are very talented and they do put their talents to good use, when they have *Ceili's*, a Scottish party. A number of instruments are played, like the flute, bagpipes, fiddle, and a squeezebox or accordion. It does seem like if a person can play one instrument, they, usually, can play one or two more. Morag is the mother of well-known keyboard player and songwriter, Michael McNeil, from the band Simple Minds. The band was very popular in Europe in the 80s. Google them, they were very, very good. Their songs are still being played today. 'Belfast Child' is an excellent example of their talent. They were also in the Top 40, 24 times over in the UK. 'Don't You Forget About Me,' which they didn't write, but were persuaded to record is often played today. Alive and Kicking, made the top three on the USA Billboard in 1985, from their most successful album, 'Once Upon a Time.' Our son, Ian, has everything that they have produced.

There have also been family gatherings in Cadomin, Alberta. It's a small hamlet, located along the McLeod River and nestled in a valley of the Rocky Mountains. It's beautiful, but the weather can be extremely cold and the winds can do damage.

The cabin in Cadomin originally started out as a hunter's cabin, owned by Hughie, Angus' Dad's youngest brother, and his wife, Marybelle. The eldest brother, Johnny, who was the chief of police in Edson, would make the hour and a half drive to meet Hughie there, who had driven from Lacombe, Alberta, about a four-and-a-half-hour drive, to go hunting and fishing. There were times when Angus' Dad would drive from Edmonton, pick up Johnny in Edson, and head for the cabin.

This story has been told more than a few times, so I'll share it with you. A big storm is coming to Cadomin, so batten down the hatches. Hughie gets a pail full of nails and puts it in the outhouse. Weighing well over fifty pounds, he figures that will do it. Well, he leaves Cadomin and doesn't return for a few weeks. Next time he goes, he notices that something is just not right. It's the outhouse, it's gone, the whole structure has been blown to smithereens, even the pail full of nails; nothing was found! Too funny!

We have had a lot of fun at that cabin over the years. It's still in the family and is owned by Hughie and Marybelle's daughter, Heather, and her husband, Rich. As I'm writing this, it's October of 2017 and I'm sure we will all continue to gather there.

Okay, back to the fall of 1997. As the last five years have flown by, Ian is a young man of twenty-one. He is at home with us. I have to tell you about his bed. When we arrived in Victoria, he was three years old, and we ordered him a new single bed with matching dresser. Time goes by, actually, his life goes by and never once did I think to get him a new bed, wow! When he was eighteen or so, one of the cross boards broke underneath, so we just replaced the board. At the same time, we got him a new mattress, a new single mattress. Ian met me at the mattress store, because he had a truck to haul the old one there and to take the new one home. Well, Ian and I are standing with the salesman, picked out the new mattress, then the salesman looks at me and asks, "Would you like the mattress to be scotch guarded?"

I look at Ian, Ian looks at the salesman and says, "No that's okay, I quit pissin' the bed a long time ago."

That was it, after twenty-one years, a new board and a new mattress, too funny!

It's now the beginning of 1998. Actually, I'll start in the spring. It's such a lovely sunny day, so I decide to take a break and go down Esquimalt Road, about a mile, to the shopping mall. It is not a big mall there are a few shops with different merchants. There is a drycleaner with a lotto kiosk, a vision center, a bakery, a restaurant, a grocery store, and today, as I walk down the sidewalk that joins the shops, I see a 'new' storefront. There is women's wear in the window. The door is being held open by an old wooden doorstop, probably hand-made and dates back to when the first merchant occupied this space.

I walk in and start browsing. Soon a woman approaches and asks if she can be of assistance.

"May I help you?" she asks.

I turn with a smile, "Thanks, but I'm just looking."

She returns the smile and asks, "You're not pregnant, are you?" looking directly at my mid-section.

"No, I'm not, why do you ask?"

"This is a maternity shop," she responds, "But I wasn't sure if you were looking for something for yourself or for someone else."

This is my introduction to a really, really nice woman, Lois Lambert. We chat for a while and I like her. She tells me the sign for the shop named, 'Baby Thoughts,' will be ready in a couple of weeks. Right now, she is getting everything set up for her grand opening. I wish her luck and head back to the shop feeling good that I have met an achiever and a nice person to boot. I'm guessing she would be around my age, too, about forty-eight, forty-nine, somewhere in there.

I can't remember anything really significant that happened in 99', just our regular rhythm and that's just fine with us. One summer evening, I think it's a Friday, when Angus and I decide to take the 1934 out for a cruise. It's a beautiful evening. We end up driving out to the Prairie Inn for a beer and a bite to eat. They make the very best halibut and fries you have ever had. Angus parks the car in front, under the lights; it's quite visible and gets a lot of attention, too. Must have been one of the car-guys that saw the car, because the next week, when we go for a lunch, several hot rods are parked out front. The Prairie Inn becomes our favorite place to go for a Saturday lunch. The Inn is located in Saanichton, about a twenty-minute drive from Victoria.

We do continue with the rod runs, enjoying each and every one. They are pretty much always held on the weekends, so it's on the ferry Friday night and back again on the Sunday night. We have attended a lot of runs in the State of Washington, places like Puyallup, Issaquah, Yakima, Wenatchee and, Sunnyside. Each run being a bit different than the last, with one exception, the people, they are great. We have thoroughly enjoyed them at every event we have attended, as everybody is there for one reason, to have a good time. It really is a hell of a hobby, an expensive one, and lots of families sacrifice to build their car and that is why they are family friendly.

Sometimes it takes years to build the car to completion. Dad, Mom, and the kids, along with friends all pitch in. Dad might get a shifter or a new set of tires for his birthday or maybe a new carburetor for Christmas. As you have read previously, we have gone to really good rod runs in western Canada, too! Places like Calgary and Edmonton, Alberta, Chilliwack, Penticton, Kelowna, Campbell River, Courtney, Sidney, and Victoria, B.C. All with the same results, lots of fun and good times.

It's coming really close to the big change from 1999 to 2000. There is so much hype going around that when midnight strikes on December 31, 1999, all hell is supposed to be felt by everyone, with regards to anything with set calendar dates, like computer software, etc. It was known as the YK2 problem. We did not experience any problems, so life carry's on as it was yesterday.

Lois and I have been keeping in touch. I usually find the time to visit with her at her shop. She is the owner operator, so it is very difficult for her to get away. Since this past December, she has been dating an old acquaintance, a fellow she has known for years, but their paths hadn't crossed for a long time. She does appear to be very happy and I can see a twinkle in her eyes that wasn't there before.

Yes, my instincts are right, come April or May, Larry has asked Lois to move in with him. He has a condo, just up from the Gorge waterway in Victoria, a beautiful area, where taking walks is very popular. She has accepted, but she has a lot to take care of first. Her townhome, where she lives and where she raised her two kids on her own, has to be sold and she has too much stuff, all of which, has to be sorted through and dealt with, either by giving away or selling.

I go out walking around the neighborhood at our shop, to take a break and to get some fresh air. For years now, I have walked by a customer's house, they have a big Lilac bush out front. Every year, I knock on the front door and ask if I can pick a few Lilacs. Mrs. Prokopow always answers the door, we exchange pleasantries, and she says, "Yes, of course, take all you want." I thank her and leave with an arm full. I put them in the office and they smell so nice.

We have been doing work for this family, for years now. This is a good story. One afternoon, their daughter comes in with an unusual request, "Could we do a repaint on her Dad's pickup truck, while they are away on a trip?" It's her father's birthday and the repaint will be a surprise for him. Of course, we can. The daughter and her brother drop off the truck, we go over the particulars and agree on the two-week completion date. The daughter keeps in touch, making sure we are on schedule, we are. In the morning of the pick-up day, I go get some balloons, blue and white, along with some ribbon. We blow up several balloons and the guys tie them to the mirrors at each side of the truck. Angus has painted the truck white with a blue pearl in the top clear coat it looks really good. The family drives in with Mr. and Mrs. Prokopow, where they see the truck parked outside with the balloons waving in the wind. Well, you would think that Mr. Prokopow had just won the lottery he was so excited and couldn't stop walking around his truck. They were all happy and horns were honking, when they pulled away.

In June, it's a very busy time for Lois, she has now gone through all of her stuff, cleaned out the townhouse, and it's ready to show. While it is up for sale, she continues to sell items that won't be needed. This is a great idea, one that I might use in the future. Lois calls three used furniture stores, explains her situation, and could they come and give her an estimate on how much she can get for the 'to be' sold items. She arranges for each buyer to come at a pre-set appointment time and on different days. Before the first buyer shows up, she goes around the house and puts a bright yellow sticker on each of the items she wishes to sell. This will make the process a lot better for both parties, as the buyer doesn't have to continually ask what is for sale and Lois doesn't have to continually go through every room; explaining which items are for sale. All set, the first fellow shows up, they go through each room, and he looks at each item. Because he is taking notes, Lois expects him to get back to her with a price. Instead, he offers her a price for all of it. She is ecstatic, can't believe it. She immediately accepts his offer, he calls for his moving truck and within two hours, all the items are gone. Now, all she has to do is call the other two furniture stores and cancel their appointments.

The townhouse doesn't take long to sell either. By the end of August, Lois makes the move to Larry's. Larry has been a great help. They get settled into their everyday life and Lois is happy the whirlwind is over.

That same August, Angus and I take the motorhome and drive to Alberta for our two-week holiday. Catherine, Angus's youngest sister and her then husband, Gary, have purchased a really cute cabin at Alberta Beach; it's just a block away from my nanny and grandpa's cabin of old. My Dad sold the cabin a few years after my Mom was killed. We stop at Catherine's she gives us the key to the cabin. There is a storm coming, so we head out of the city right away. We make a stop for fresh groceries on route. Walking outside from the store to the motorhome, the sky surrounding us is blue black. We would really like to get to the cabin and set up before the sky opens up. We get there, pick out the spot for the motorhome, get it leveled, it is getting dark fast, and the wind has picked up. Rain like you can't believe, pouring with thunder and lightning, too! We go to sleep with the window at our heads open, just a bit so our noses can take in the beautiful aroma that has remained the same throughout the years. I have so many memories here. Tears fill my eyes, as I drift off to sleep. It feels so good just to be here again.

Angus and I spend a few days by ourselves, we take long walks around the town site, down to the big pier, the same one I wrote about in my 'early years' segment. You can Google the Big Pier it's an interesting story. As we walk on the pier now, it doesn't seem as large as it once was, funny, I guess, because we have grown. We have a wonderful few days together, reminiscing about the past, our families, our parents, my Grandparents and friends, days and times gone by. I'm so glad Angus was a part of all that, he knows, only, too well what this place means to me, it gets to him, too!

So, fall and winter come again. We are busy in our everyday. I turned fifty-one this past February, Angus turned fifty-two in April and our Ian is, twenty-four. He is out on his own now and doing well. He is always busy doing something and that's a good thing. Ian is always welcome to stop by for a home cooked meal. Remember; there are no cell phones, there might be, but we don't have them. I'm pretty sure, this Christmas, we go up to Margaret and John's in Nanaimo. Ian drives to be with us; always good company, good fun, and good food.

So, the New Year is here, always looking for spring. Once the tulips and iris break through, the tree blossoms are not far behind. We plant our annual flowers in the beds around the house, we like pansies, as they seem to last better and longer, for some reason.

Sandra is planning a trip to visit us this summer, in late June. Dad is planning a trip to Alberta with a friend that he has gotten to know over the last couple of years. Her name is Joan and they met while out walking in the neighborhood. One thing has led to another and they have been seeing each other to share a dinner or to take a walk. They seem to have a lot in common, they enjoy each other's company, they are both widows, and they both come from farming backgrounds. Joan has family in a region near Westlock, Alberta and Dad knows some folks there, too.

Sandra comes for her visit, it's good and the weather is good. Dad's cherry tree is loaded. We take Sandra out for a drive and stop to see Dad. He is leaving on his trip with Joan, in the morning. While we are all outside picking as many cherries as we can, Ian stops by to see his Grandpa. The motorhome is all packed and ready to go.

We say our goodbyes and wish them a safe and enjoyable trip.

Arriving in Alberta, Dad drops Joan off at her relatives' place, just outside of Westlock. He carries on to Allan's, Angus' brother's acreage, near Gibbons, where he will stay for a few weeks and will visit friends and family. He really enjoys his Granddaughters, Katie and Maggie. Its summer holidays for them, so they are enjoying time together.

The phone rings at the shop it is Allan with very bad news. Dad has passed away.

He left Allan's that morning and headed to Westlock to pick Joan up. They were outside picking rhubarb for making rhubarb wine. They came inside and while Joan was putting some last-minute things together, her sister made Dad a cup of tea. All of a sudden, Dad didn't feel so good, he slumped over, the sister called for Joan, she came running, someone called 911, but he couldn't be saved, a massive heart attack.

We are stunned, he was doing so well or so we thought. The three of us fly to Edmonton and stay with Angus' sister, Catherine. The next week is a blur. We all manage to pull ourselves together, make arrangements for the service, call as many of our family members and friends as possible in Alberta, British Columbia and over in Scotland. The service is packed. A lunch follows with a lot of family and friends in attendance. There are funny stories, laughs, and regrets that we only see everybody at weddings or funerals. That's just the way it is, we are all young enough that between working full time, involvement with our kids' activities, busy with our everyday lives, that time goes by way too fast. I remember making comments over the years like, time waits for no man, neither do airplanes or ferries, so lets get going.

Dad MacDonald, Donald Alexander MacDonald, what a great guy—he was always up for anything. He laughed from his boots and died with his boots on. I can still see him standing tall, hands in his pockets, and giggling car keys and loose change, as he rocked back on his heels and forward on the balls of his feet, then his head would go back in laughter. Dad will be missed very much by all who knew him.

He had a habit of stirring his tea loudly, *clink, clink, clink*, as the spoon hit the sides of the cup, then he would drop the spoon on the table, it would literally bounce a couple of times, before it came to rest. When Ian would stay with Grandma and Grandpa, that racket was Ian's alarm clock! At our house, I bought some plastic coffee spoons that ended the *clink, clink, clink*, too funny. I still have those spoons; they are brightly colored, red, yellow, green, and orange. They stand in a clear drinking glass next to the coffee maker and remind me of Dad and also, the painted rocks my Nanny and Grandpa had around their flowerbeds at the cabin.

Dad came from a family of five, four boys and a girl. The only sibling remaining is his brother Hughie. The family lost a baby girl, Jessie, while on route to Canada from Scotland, when they immigrated in 1923. She was buried at sea.

Dad met Mom over in Scotland, while on leave during the Second World War. They both were born on the Island of South Uist. Dad knew of Mom's family before his family immigrated many years before. I believe Kate was at home, looking after her aged mother, when she and Dad met, fell in love, and were married. Mom came to Canada shortly after the war, as many war brides did. Kate came from a family of twelve and of those twelve, I only had the opportunity to meet one of her sisters, Maggie, a lovely lady, she had a quiet disposition, like Mom.

This is a cute story. One of Kate's siblings had a daughter named Jean, she was always known as Jeannie. Kate and Jeannie were very close. As a small child and feeling sad about her Auntie being taken away by Donald, she scratched his eyes out of a picture that the family had of the two of them. Jeannie was always a warm and welcoming person, she never married, and she lived in a well-kept house in Kilbride, South Uist. She went about her business on a gas-powered scooter, too cute. She sadly passed away in 2017. Angus met her once, when he went to Scotland to surprise his Dad, while he was visiting. Ian also met her, when he travelled with his Grandpa to Scotland on a holiday. Ian said she cried, when they arrived, and pretty much cried the whole time they were visiting her. Very sentimental she was, kind of like me.

When Angus and Dad were driving around Uist, they decided to stop at the local museum. Effie, the curator, was in the middle of giving the visitors a tour. The museum had received some old photographs for display, so when she saw Dad come through the door, she, immediately left the tour and came to Dad. "Donald, come see these old pictures I have here. Anybody, who has looked at them so far, can't identify any of them".

Dad walks over, has a look, "Well, this is so and so and he's related to this so and so," as he points out to her, who they are. Now, Dad left for Canada, when he was four years old, went back during the Second World War, took Mom for a holiday, after he retired, and went back a few times after Mom passed in 1989. His memory was something else.

Dad, Donald Alexander MacDonald, he meant the world to me. He was always in a good mood, and he had a great disposition, loved life, really enjoyed his life and he was quite a teaser. His ability to remember people was uncanny, really a special gift. He would get annoyed if you didn't remember a person that he spoke of, recent or not. He would say "Don't you remember me telling you about him or her?" Frowning the whole time, expecting you to have the same memory recall as he had.

He was a teaser like I said. While I was working for the Provincial Government, we had a city bus that would come and park just in front of our building, after work. The bus was a special connector that took us to the main route on Jasper Avenue. One day, I get on and who's driving, it's my father-in-law.

"Well, hello," he said, "How's my favorite daughter-in-law today?"

Dad was not a quiet guy, so the whole busload would hear him. "I'm fine," I would reply, beaming from ear to ear. You know, I never did catch on for a long time, but I was his only daughter-in-law, at the time, so, of course, I would be his favorite, too funny! I rode on his bus many, many times and he was always the same good-natured guy, full of life.

On his right hand, Dad only had half of his index finger and I'll tell you how that happened. Dad was raised on a farm, near a small town, named Stony Plain, Alberta. When the family immigrated, in 1923, his Dad, Allan, and his wife, Marion, along with his brothers and sister were sold a section of land, organized through the church, and it was basically in the middle of nowhere.

There was an old house on the land, no electricity, no running water, and no toilet in the house, nothing of convenience at all. They all worked very hard through the years, as you can imagine. Over in Scotland, Allan was a sailor in sail and steam, quite an accomplishment at the time. He didn't want his boys to have to go to sea like he did, so he brought them to Canada to start a new life, he was fifty-three years old. Gutsy, they all were. No experience at being a farmer, he had a lot to learn and learn he did. He went to the University of Alberta and took agriculture, so he would know what crops would grow in the area, etc., etc. His farming neighbors were very helpful. Pretty much self-sufficient, everything was homemade. Marion was shown which berries were good to eat and she would make jams and pies. Making bread daily, milking cows, churning butter, growing and harvesting a vegetable garden, keeping house, and making meals to feed five growing children every day and the laundry. I can't even list all that she and they had to do on a daily basis to survive. The tasks were arduous, to say the least.

Back to how Dad lost his finger. One day, while the boys were outside chopping wood, they stopped for a break. They were sitting on tree stumps, when Dad said to Rod, "Here, Rod, chop this off," and placed his index finger on top of a stump. Well, Rod swung that axe around so fast, the half index finger was chopped off, before Dad had a chance to pull his hand away. They put Dad in the back of a horse drawn wagon and clip-clopped to Edmonton, which took hours. By the time they got there, the finger couldn't be saved. When the war came, three of the boys, Rod, Johnny, and Dad went. Hughie was too young, so he and Maryann stayed on the farm. Dad wanted to join the Navy, but they wouldn't take him, because of the lost finger, so he joined the Army instead. FYI, the three boys came back safe and sound.

I have so many stories to tell of my father-in-law, who turned out to be so much more to me. I was fortunate to have him in my life from 1965, when I met Angus, until he passed in 2001, some thirty-six years. We never had a bad word between us, ever.

Dad was a good husband, a good father, and a good grandfather. He was an excellent provider; he drove a city transit bus for some thirty-four years. He worked the early shift and he was one of the first buses to leave the transit barns in the morning. After his eight-hour shift, he would go home, where Mom would make him a bite to eat. After a twenty-minute nap, he would go to his part-time job, which was driving a truck for a depot that delivered general merchandise, along with food items to local businesses. Lots and lots of nights, he would get home late. Mom would stay up, feed him a late supper, and together, they would sit at the kitchen table and have a cup of tea, while discussing their day. After some sixteen, seventeen hours, his head would hit the pillow for a few hours rest, only to get up and do it all over again the next day. He did that for years, to provide for his family, talk about an inspiration.

At their home in Sydney, where they retired, they had a neighbor, Jack Calmer, was his name. He was definitely a city man, in the newspaper business, and knew nothing about growing a vegetable garden. He and his wife, Veronica, only took up gardening, when they retired and became Mom and Dad's neighbors. From Dad's deck, he could look down and see Jack's back yard, in plain view. So, one morning, Jack's outside, working in the garden, when Dad notices that he's planting potatoes.

"Hey, Jack," Dad hollers from the deck, "You planting potatoes over there?"

"Yes, I am," responds Jack.

"Well, let me give you a pointer," Dad calls back.

"What's that, Don?" Jack asks.

"If you want those potatoes to grow, you have to put them in with the eye of the potato facing up,"

"Oh, is that so?" Jack queries.

"You bet," Dad reassures him.

So, Jack placed the potatoes very carefully in the holes with the eyes facing up. I can't honestly say that Dad ever told Jack any different, funny.

Eggs, being a city girl, I always thought a chicken had to be with a male, in order to lay edible eggs, not. I always thought a brown chicken laid brown eggs and a white chicken laid white eggs, not. Dad straightened me out; apparently, it's the color of the chicken's ear lobes that determine the color of the egg. White ear lobes, produce white eggs, and brown lobes, have brown eggs. Now, you know, and hens don't need a rooster to lay eggs either.

I will probably get to a few more stories about Dad, but for now, its back to August 2001.

Ian approaches Angus and says he would like to try working at the shop, become a painter, like Angus. Well, that sounds great. It happens to be vacation time for us.

Ian will stay at the shop and take care of any bookings for when we get back. Remember, no cell phones attached to our hips. We give Ian a call, every once in a while, from pay phones, to see how he's doing, everything is fine.

This year, we decide to take a three-week vacation. It's our first three-week vacation since we both starting working in the 1960s, some thirty-six years ago. We pull out in the motorhome and head for the interior of British Columbia. We just lost Dad and feel that he would want us to carry on. It will be good for us to get away and relax for a while.

We have a great holiday, the weather is really nice and warm, a perfect summer. We came across a campground, called Kettle River Provincial Park; so, we pull in. Angus drives around it's really big; the sites are large with lots of trees and greenery between each one. On our second trip around, we spot a nice secluded site that's vacant. We drive in, get the motorhome set up, then register, and pay for three nights. Well, after three days of excellent weather, swimming in one of the biggest swimming holes in the beautiful, crystal clear waters of the Kettle Valley River, taking long walks along the river's edge, having camp fires at night, and sleeping like babies, we are not leaving. We register for four more nights.

This is so funny, bear with me, it's good. During the day, we discuss our supper plans. I tell Angus I would like to make some pan-fried potato rounds, where you cut the 'skin on' potatoes into slices about a quarter inch thick, then fry them to golden brown. We have a flat grill that will fit perfect on the barbeque. Sounds good! Angus will cook the potatoes, while I complete the rest of the meal inside the motorhome. I'm prepping the potatoes, while Angus starts the barbeque. After the potatoes have been sliced and spiced up, then tossed in a bowl with some oil, I lay them out on the flat grill, making sure the entire surface is covered with the sliced potato rounds. I throw out the few slices that don't fit then I put them back in the bowl. I call Angus and tell him the spuds are ready. He takes the bowl and the flat grill over to the barbeque. I'm looking out the kitchen window and see him taking one slice at a time, out of the bowl, and arranging it on the flat grill. I get his attention and tell him to just pour the whole bowl full onto the pan. He does and as he maneuvers them around the pan, he notices that they fit perfectly. Well, I can't tell you the struggle I have with myself at that moment. You can see he's thinking. *How the hell did she do that?* Now, should I fess up and tell him that I premeasured the potatoes to fit the pan *or* should I just let him go on thinking that I'm good, really good? His head turns towards the motorhome in wonder. I start laughing and tell him that I 'pre-measured' the potatoes to fit the pan. It takes a second for that to register, then he cracks up…boy, have we laughed and repeated that story many times over the years, I'm laughing now.

The days and nights go by in a flash. We are on the seventh night and we are out of everything fresh. I manage to put something together for supper. I make a platter of cheese, crackers, pickles, and open up a tin of brown beans. We talk about asking the young man who comes around with the firewood, if he could run us into Rock Creek, some ten kilometers away, for groceries in the morning. We sleep on the thought of staying, but in the morning, we decide to move on. We really had a good, fun, totally relaxing time here, so we will definitely be back.

Back at the shop, it feels good to be home and it feels good to have Ian at the shop with us, too. Fall turns to winter and winter to spring with the flowering plum, cherry, and magnolia trees, it's beautiful.

I'm visiting Lois. She is sitting on her stool, behind the counter, going through the mail.

I walk in, "Hi, how's it going?" I ask.

"Good," she replies. I notice a really large container of pink colored liquid, sitting beside the cash register.

"Are you going to drink all that?" I ask.

"I'm going to give it a go," she says.

"That's a lot of liquid, you doing a cleanse or something?"

"Not really, my legs and ankles are swollen quite a bit and Larry thinks I'm not drinking enough water during the day."

"I can't stand water by itself, so I made this raspberry drink for myself."

"Let's see your ankles," as I walk around the counter, while she swings around on the stool and pulls her slacks up to show me. They look terrible, very swollen. I bend down and press my thumb into her leg, just above the anklebone, and hold it there for a few seconds. Once I take my thumb away, the imprint is very visible.

"I remember when I was pregnant with Ian, the doctor did that to me and said I was toxic."

"How long have you been swollen like that?"

"Oh, I guess the last couple of weeks or so, and I don't have any energy either."

"I think you should see your doctor right away," I suggest.
"Yes, I think I better do that". I try not to let on, but I'm worried.

I wait for a full week, before I go to see how she is. There is a woman behind the counter, who I have seen at the shop before. We pass pleasantries and I introduce myself to her. She tells me that she will be filling in for Lois, because she is going through some tests ordered by her doctor. I was relieved to hear that Lois didn't waste any time in contacting her doctor.

It's another couple of weeks, before I get back and this time, Lois is there. She fills me in on the tests she has had already and lets me know she will be going for a colonoscopy and how she is dreading it. After that's over, she will be finished with all the tests and will wait for the results.

I'm at the shop, it's a beautiful day, and when I look up from my desk, I see Lois has pulled in. She comes in and sits across from me. She has just come from the doctor's office with very bad news she is terminal. After tears are shed, we gather ourselves and she says, "They have offered me a clinical trial, no guarantees, of course."

"Are you going for it?" I ask.

"I don't know, would you?"

Without hesitation, I say, "Yes, I would, you never know, it just might work."

"I'll have to talk to Larry tonight, when he gets home from work."

I walk her out to her car and she will let me know what she decides.

I purposely stay away, because I don't want her to feel like I'm pressuring her in any way. It has been awhile and I'm getting anxious to hear from her. She finally calls the shop and I'm holding my breath, as she tells me she will start the trial soon. It will run from mid-October until mid-April, six months. Another very important decision, she will close her maternity shop. She wants to spend time with Larry and during the treatment she doesn't want to worry about her shop. I know she is heart-broken about that. There will be a lot to organize and to take care of, but with Larry's help, they will get it done.

At the shop, Ian has settled in really well, he is a very quick learner and he is doing a great job. Before we can blink, he has completed his written exams, has won an award for being the top in his class, and has earned his journeyman's ticket.

Summer rolls around again. We drive to Edmonton with the motorhome, where we park at Allan's acreage for a week or so. We visit family and friends, we go see my Dad, he is not doing very well and has been in the veteran's ward, Colonel Newburn Division at the University of Alberta Hospital.

Dad has been through a lot. It's 2002 he has been without Mom for twenty-four years. He was widowed at fifty-six, when Mom was killed and she was fifty-eight. I don't really know when he started drinking again, but it definitely took a toll on him. He lost the lower half of his right leg a few years ago and the recovery process and getting used to the prosthetic was difficult. On holidays, we always go for a visit for a few hours, usually take him out for a lunch or a supper. After seeing him now, in the hospital, he isn't good, he is pale, he has lost weight, he tells me he is very short of breath, and what a terrible feeling it is to take a breath and there's no air. Angus and I say our goodbyes, we can only hope he makes it for our next visit at Christmas. Sandra goes to visit him at least once a week or more, trying to keep his spirits up.

Back at the shop and working away, fall comes fast. Lois is gearing things down at her maternity shop and she really is looking forward to relaxing during her treatment and spending time with Larry. She sees her son often, as he lives in Victoria. Her daughter travels from Kelowna, British Columbia, as often as she can. She is busy raising a son on her own, while attending nursing school. The clinical trial is on schedule it will start soon.

Sandra calls one evening, it's Dad, is failing fast. I know it's very hard for her to go see him and I'm very thankful she does. A few days later, she calls. I pick up the receiver, all is quiet, and then she says, "He's gone." It is October 10th and Dad just turned eighty on September 7th. Charles Cecil McQuade; known to all as 'Cec.'

My Dad was a great guy he put up with a lot in our house, nine kids, four of his own and usually, four or five orphans, too! He was a very hard worker, being a caretaker for the Public-School Board. His schools were always kept very clean. My Dad liked to go camping, he was a very good bowler, and he liked playing crib, darts, and shuffleboard. There are some people who can tell a joke and make people laugh, Dad was one of those. When we were young, Mom and Dad would have the occasional house party, us kids would be woken by the music and dancing, so we were allowed to go into the living room and say, "Hi," to everybody, possibly have a treat, then back to bed, we would go. I remember dancing with my Dad, putting my feet on top of his feet, as he would lead me around the room. Good times, they always go too fast, don't they? My Dad taught me how to skate he was very good. Dad was very strong, if anybody needed anything moved, they would call Cec. Mom and Dad were quite social, they were very active with mixed, five-pin bowling twice a week and they had a dart club with four or five couples that got together once a month. Each month they would take turns hosting the evening, usually on a Saturday evening and the dart games could go on, until the wee hours of the morning.

My Dad was a sailor, a submarine detector during World War II. I have a picture of him in uniform with a cast on each wrist. He fell off of the crow's nest during a storm at sea. He has a beard in that picture and when asked about it, he would say he didn't trust anybody with a razor to shave him and then he would laugh, so I know that wasn't true. It was probably too painful to shave with his broken wrists, so he just let the beard grow. It wasn't a long scraggly beard; it was a neat and full beard. After the wrists healed, he didn't wear a beard, but much later, he had a very thick full mustache. It was like Tom Selleck's 'Chevron' mustache, the American actor, who starred in Magnum P.I. Dad served on the HMCS Prince Henry, one of the three Prince's war ships, the others were Prince David and Prince Robert. He came home safe and sound.

Dad came from a family with five siblings, one brother, Jim, and four sisters, Alice, Gert, Gene, and Gwen. I'm pretty sure that when Dad passed, Gwen was the only one still living and she was in British Columbia at the time. She had taken ill and couldn't attend the service.

I remember, as a small child of elementary school age, maybe five or six, if my Dad was getting ready to go out, us kids would ask him, "Where are you going, Dad?"

He would answer, "I'm going to the moon, want to come?"

Of course, we would say, "Yes," he would just laugh.

Cribbage (Crib) is a good card game and my Dad taught me how to play. I learned pretty fast, because after my second practice game, he actually took my points, if I missed counting them. Years ago, if a person got a twenty-nine-point hand, they would call it into the newspaper and your name would appear, along with the actual cards you held in that hand to count the twenty-nine points, which is the highest points you can get in Crib. My Dad got two of them.

You can't really take 'anything back' in life. I haven't any answers, as to why my Dad became an alcoholic. Why does anybody, because they can, I suppose. I know my Dad would have had a better quality of life, that's for sure. After Mom was killed, he never met anybody else. I wrote him a letter once and told him that none of us kids expected him to accept being alone, if he chose not to be, so I guess, he was a one-woman man.

The three of us fly to Edmonton for the service and arrive a few hours, before the service is to start. At Catherine's, we change our clothes, grab a bite to eat, and head over to the funeral home. I get to see Dad, before the service, and I made a comment to my sister, Sandra, as we stood looking down on the open casket, "He looks good," I say.

"Yes, he does" Sandra replies. Sounds kind of 'off,' but in a good way, he did look good. He was finally, at peace. I loved my Dad and I always tried to be the daughter he wanted me to be.

Back in Victoria, at the shop, there is a message from Lois, her treatment starts in a couple of days and she will keep in touch. October runs into November and before we can blink, it's Christmas. We don't go to Alberta this year we have just been there. With Maggie and John in Nanaimo, we either went to their house or they came to ours, in any case, we were with family, all is good.

2003, and Lois finishes her colon cancer clinical trial, it's April. She is not driving, because the drugs have affected her feet and they are numb. Larry has been great, after he gets home from work, they make supper together, and then he takes her out for an evening drive and possibly, an ice-cream cone. After being so independent for so long, it's hard on Lois to have to rely on Larry, but he doesn't seem to mind.

One morning in June, Larry is getting ready for work. He comes out of the bedroom and as he is walking towards Lois, who is sitting in the living room sipping her morning coffee, she looks up, and says, "Larry, you look yellow."

"Yes, I know, it's been coming on the last couple of days."

"Well, that's not good."

"I really think you should go to the hospital."

"I can't drive, so call your brother over, he can take you." Well, Larry's brother comes, takes Larry to the hospital, he calls Lois, and says they are doing some blood tests. Larry stays that night and the next morning, he is flown to the Vancouver General Hospital. With Larry's permission, the Victoria hospital calls and let's Lois know that Larry has leukemia and that he will be going through further testing in Vancouver. She manages to get things organized at the condo, packs a bag, and heads for Vancouver, on the bus.

At this point, I have no idea of anything that has taken place. It isn't until four, maybe, five days later, I get a call. It's Lois, she is very upset, Larry has a rare form of leukemia and it's highly probable that he won't make it. She fills me in on the past few days. Larry has been advised to get in touch with his family members, to make his will out, and to get any loose ends attended to. I know she is devastated, she sounds so weak that I can hardly hear her speak on the phone. She is by his side night and day. They have moved a bed into Larry's room for her. She will call again, when she can.

Larry passed eighteen days later he was fifty-one years old. A friend of Lois' called to let me know when and where the service would be held. I did go to the service, and it was so full, that people were standing. After, I made my way to see if I could speak with Lois. I got a glimpse of her through the crowd and she looked awful. Finally, I did get to her, there were no words spoken, we just clung to one another.

Also, in June, Angus' youngest sister, Catherine, after her divorce, has come to live on the Island. She is a lab technician and has applied for and has received a position at the Nanaimo Hospital. For now, she will live with Maggie and John. After looking for a few months, she buys a really nice home, just on the outskirts of Nanaimo, south end. Her sons, Kelly and David, are grown, Kelly is twenty-two and David is nineteen. I do believe, at that time, Kelly was working in Northern Alberta and David stayed in St. Albert with a friend to finish an educational course he was taking.

While on vacation one summer, can't put a date on this one, but we go and stay a few days with my sister, Sandra, and her then partner, Scott. They have property just outside of Fort Assiniboine, located approximately an hour and half drive north of Edmonton. Remember, no cell phones. Sandra has drawn and mailed me a very good map of the area, with colored houses, barns, animals, and anything else that would guide us to their place. It worked great, no problems at all. We had a good spot for the motorhome, really a nice acreage with lots of room, a vegetable garden and a clean outhouse to boot. We all had a great visit, good food, and tons of laughs.

This is a good one. One evening at home, in Victoria, can't put my finger on the date, but Angus and I are watching the evening news. A story comes on about a guy in the Fort Assiniboine area with a ham radio, who had been able to reach and speak with the astronauts on board one of the space shuttles that was up there on a mission of some sort. The camera crew and news reporters show up, they showed the property, and gave an interview with Scott. During the interview, Scott told them of the apparatus he uses for the ham-radio, and outside there is not much more than a pie plate on top of a pole for reception. He became known as the 'hillbilly from Tiger Lily.' Tiger Lily, named after the flower, is a small hamlet, not too far from Fort Assiniboine. I looked up the meaning of the ham radio, it goes like this, from Wiki; the use of radio frequency spectrum for purposes of non-commercial exchange of messages, wireless experimentation, self-training, private recreation, and emergency communication, etc. etc.

This is what was *not* in the news. After a few days pass a *knock, knock, knock,* Scott opens the door and to his surprise, there is a team of people from NASA standing there. The 'Visit' wasn't meant to be pleasant, badges were flashed and their intent to check out Scott's equipment was foremost on their minds. They wanted to know how this Canadian, in the middle of nowhere, was able to reach and speak to the astronauts. They went through all the gauges and apparatus used by Scott and left shaking their heads. A few weeks later, Scott received a parcel from NASA. Inside were hats, mugs, and memorabilia, autographed by the astronauts he had spoken with, very nice.

Scott Smith or Scottie, as people called him, his name was actually Angus Smith, from the same Island my Angus' Mom and Dad were from, South Uist, Scotland. He was a one-man band, played the bagpipes, guitar, and was a singer of any type of song you requested, he was a very talented man, and he was funny, too. He was an entertainer in and around the Edmonton area for years. Scott passed away in 2017 of ALS. Really sad, he will surely be missed.

We must have taken our vacation earlier this year, because it's the last week in July, when another 'event' takes place. Angus and I are driving home from the shop, after work. We stop behind a station wagon on Esquimalt Road, two beagles pop-up in the back window, "Oh, look at the beagles, they are so cute." The traffic light turns green, we continue behind the station wagon, and then, the right signal light flashes.

"I'm going to ask to see them," says Angus. We pull up behind and a lady gets out from the driver's side and notices us right away. Angus opens his door and approaches the lady, "Honestly, I'm not following you, I'd just like to see your beagles."

"Oh, of course, you can," as she opens the tailgate. We stay for a few minutes, explaining that we, too, had a beagle. We inquire where she got them and she responded by giving us the breeders name and number. The breeders are on the Island, near Cobblehill, close to where we got our Polly. It's been almost ten years, since we lost Polly. Angus and I yack about the pros and cons, sleep on the idea of having a beagle puppy, and decide to give the breeder a call.

Well, our timing couldn't be better. The breeders, Laura, and her husband, Dennis, have a female ready to give birth in a few days. We make a quick trip up Island to meet with them. It's a nice family atmosphere, the breeders have four children and they all love their beagles. Angus and I request a female and we can tell they are not too fussy on selling females, but after a lengthy interview, it is decided that if there is a female born in this litter, we will have her. We are happy. Laura says, before she gives us a call, she will wait a couple of days after the birth just to be sure the puppy is okay.

We get the call, the litter is born on August 10th; there are four males and one female. There is Charlie, Lincoln, Buddy, and Molly the fourth male has yet to be named. We go visit and hold our tiny little puppy, she smells wonderful, like a newborn baby. We go visiting once a week, Molly grows into her name very quickly. All the puppies are doing really well. Comes our anniversary, the weekend of September 28th. Angus and I decide to take the weekend and go up to Tofino, on the northwest side of the Island, where we have a really nice thirty-fifth anniversary.

We have arranged to pick Molly up on our way back home. We are in the car driving home with her, Molly is in my arms and I say to her, "Well, Molly, we might be older, but we will make sure you have a fun life."

Angus is fifty-five and I'm fifty-four.

A friend of Lois's telephones one evening, she is in the hospital, not doing well. They try her on a schedule of chemo drugs, but they are just making her too sick. She goes into surgery and now has a colostomy bag. I go see her a few days after surgery, she seems to be doing as well as can be expected, although, I know she is very disappointed about the bag, not so much that she has to have it, but because she knows her condition is not improving. How bloody hard is that to go through, she has been through so much already. She is a strong woman.

154

The caregivers are wonderful, always asking if she wants anything, can they do anything for her. One day, she surprises them and asks if there is any way they can give her a bath. Well, they will see, if that can be arranged. Yes, early one evening, after supper, her two favorite nurses come, get her in a wheelchair, and take her for a bath. She repeats the procedure to me. They get her undressed wrap her in a towel, and maneuver her onto a sling. There is a fairly large machine that lifts Lois up, swings her slowly, and then lowers her into a bubbling whirlpool of warm water, lovely. The nurses are great, they let her soak for as long as she likes, and it feels wonderful. Lois sleeps like a baby that night.

Molly has been home for about eight weeks. She is adorable. Angus and I decide we will take her to the shop with us, no staying at home like Polly did. She has everything she needs and is quite content to be with us. I walk her a few times a day she is a typical beagle, nose to the ground.

I go to the hospital, once a week, to see Lois, she is waiting for a bed in the palliative care unit, but for now, she shares a room with three women. Lois seems to have a lot of visitors, whenever I go, so it's hard to get into a conversation. One night I go late, hoping I will be the only one there, as I would like to have a few minutes alone with her. As I enter the room, Lois is sound asleep. I write her a note because she looks so peaceful I don't want to wake her. I acknowledge the woman directly across from Lois. We know each other. She and I were on our son's hockey team executive, for a couple of years. She is recovering from breast cancer surgery, a mastectomy. Turns out, she was at home after surgery and wasn't feeling well, so they put her in the hospital for closer observation. We have a good visit and catch up with our son's news. Lois and Cathy have had a few conversations, she tells me that Lois spends quite a bit of time sleeping these days, which isn't good. I say my goodbyes and tell her I might see her the next time I come.

There is no next time, Lois passed away on December 10th. Her daughter called and explained there would be a service in the near future. Angus and I really liked Lois, she was a very intelligent, nice to be around kind of gal. She had a good business head on her shoulders and always so easy to laugh. A very strong disposition, while facing adversity, wasn't afraid to ask for advice and not afraid to give it either. She was loved and respected and you earn that in life, we will miss her.

At Christmas time this year, we take our Molly and head to Alberta, we will stay with Allan on his acreage. Ian is busy with his girlfriend and her family and that's okay, too. Molly has a soft-sided kennel on the back seat, the flap is open, so she can go in or stay out and lay on her blanket. She loves to sit and look out the window. This is our first long road trip with Molly. She is such a good traveler, we stop, every once in a while, to get the three of us out of the car to stretch, no problems at all, she is four and a half months old. Once at Allan's, Molly has a great time with the other dogs, we all go for winter trail walks and visit with family and friends. It's a good Christmas, we take Molly wherever we go and everyone enjoys her.

After New Years', we get back to the shop. Ian is doing a great job. Angus is overseeing everything and I'm doing the paper work. As the year runs along, Angus is first to realize that the shop is adequate for us, but Ian needs to be able to make his own personal progress. Angus and I are not ready to retire, and Ian is just beginning. The auto insurance company, being run by the Provincial Government, is very dictatorial and you end up being a bobble-head, of course, in the government's favor.

All repair, replace, and refinish times are quoted from the government's own estimating system. Private insurance companies have their own estimating system, too, and if there is a difference, the Provincial Government system is always used.

The shop ends up fighting for any additional time required to bring the repaired vehicle to completion. It's a system, where you are told from start to finish with very little room for compromise. It's too detailed to explain, so let me just say, even when you are fully qualified and have many, many years' experience, your expertise goes nowhere. If you even try to bill the Provincial Government for anything that has not been approved by them, they deduct that amount from the balance they owe the shop. It's an unsettling year.

Due to the situation at hand, in the spring, we decide to move back to Edmonton, Alberta, where we will open an auto-body shop in our own name. Oh, boy!

Chapter Six: Middle to Old Age, 2005-2018

We have a lot to do, three properties need to be sold and two new properties need to be found and purchased. It's April, we have completed twenty-five years at Quality Collision Repairs Ltd.

First things first, as I draw up an outline of what we need to accomplish. Everything goes well, according to 'Hoyle,' that's Edmond Hoyle. The closing date for the shop is set for May 31st It is listed and is sold within a week, with the agreed possession date. The house and rental property next-door are listed and sold to the first fellow that looked at the properties. After negotiations that had more to do with the possession date than price, the acreage and rental sell in two weeks, with the possession date of June 15th. All the while this was happening, Angus found a house for us, near Fort Saskatchewan, Alberta, about a twenty-minute drive northeast of Edmonton. He always said if he found a house with an indoor pool, I would have it and he did. Angus flew to Edmonton to see the house and to look at a building for the new shop. Negotiations followed and we bought the house, which sits on an acreage and we also bought the building for our auto-body shop. The possession date for the house is June 15th and the shop is July 1st. All five properties were signed and sealed, whew!

We are now left with organizing the actual move itself. Through a fellow for whom we did work for at the shop, we find out he is a long-distance mover, we negotiate. He and his team will move the house furniture, etc., and the vehicles, too. We hire a smaller moving company to move the contents at Quality Collision, equipment, and stuff. Ian and his buddy, Rori, who have been friends since elementary school, and still are today, moved our everyday driver on a flat deck trailer. Ian towed it with his Chev pickup and parked it at the new house. The two of them met the moving company at the new shop, unloaded the contents and then, returned to Victoria.

We sold the El-Camino, the Chev Impala, and the Astro Van. We had just bought a Cavalier, the one Ian towed to the new house and we also bought a Chev Silverado pick-up truck. Angus towed our utility trailer, full of our garage stuff, behind the pick-up and left both at the new house. As the new house was empty, there are no problems bringing 'stuff' and leaving it. Angus met the moving team with the first load, the house furniture and the Mullins trailer. After putting things in their appropriate rooms in the house, Allan drove Angus to the airport and he flew back to Victoria. I had a rental, so I picked Angus up upon his arrival.

The moving team returns to Victoria. Angus and the mover, Adam, will handle the second and final load. They load up the 1934 Ford, the 1964 GMC pickup, and the 1968 Dodge Charger. Angus hops in the moving van with Adam and away they go. Arriving at the new house, a neighbor spots the vehicles and offers to put them at his storage company. He also offers Angus a good price. The neighbor calls Angus, 'Big Shot,' where there is no end to Adam teasing Angus on their drive back to Victoria. Every once in a while, on the road, Adam looks over at Angus and says, "Big Shot, eh," and they laugh. Adam drops Angus off at home they have had a good trip.

Angus and I are now left with a few odds and sods. We put them in our enclosed aluminum trailer, mount our bicycles on the lid, and then hook it up to the motorhome. That morning, the real estate agent meets us at the house and we hand over the keys. We gather up our Molly and head for the ferry. Not knowing how long it will be, before we return. Friends and family will bring us back, but for now, looking forward is all we can think about. It's June 13th, 2005.

Talk about a whirlwind, but you know, Angus and I enjoyed all the excitement and when you are doing it for your family, it feels really good.

Angus and I, along with our Molly, take a few days for ourselves, just to relax and get some rest, because we still have a hell of a lot to do. Ian will join us in a couple of weeks. He will be bringing his girlfriend with him. She has family in Edmonton and has spent a few years in Edmonton herself. I don't recall exactly, but they have been going together for a while now. She will work with us at the shop, as our receptionist.

I forgot to mention that months before we decided to move back to Alberta, before any properties were listed and sold, I had booked a flight to Edmonton, to see my sister, Sandra, for her birthday. It turned out that by the time I was to fly out, Angus had already been to Edmonton and bought the new body shop and our new house. When I arrive, Sandra and Bill drive me out to see the house. The real estate agent is already there, when we drive up. I open the front door, took one look around, and immediately said out loud, "Who the hell is going to clean this!"

After a few days on the road, we pull onto the acreage and set up the motorhome on the south side of the property. There will be so much going on that we will stay in the motorhome for probably a couple of weeks, anyway. We have a ton of work that needs to be done. Contractors need to be found to build onto an existing double garage, which is a separate building away from the house. All new windows and doors have been on order, they will be arriving any day to be installed.

This is a brief description of the property, Angus describes it 'as a high-end fixer upper,' and it really is. Our brother-in-law, Bill, who ends up doing a lot of electrical work for us, says that the house has been built very well and he has built a few houses himself. The house is a two story with a finished basement, seven bedrooms; five on the top floor and two in the basement. The main floor has a large front foyer with a fifteen-step staircase to the upper level, a large living room, dining room, large kitchen, and family room. Off of the kitchen, is a bathroom and sauna that lead to the indoor swimming pool, the pool is sixteen feet by thirty-two feet and goes from three feet to over nine feet deep. There is a landing with two steps, down to the pool. The west side is all windows, with garden doors going out to a forty-foot-long deck, that's ten feet wide. Four skylights, along with all the windows, keep the room very bright. The east wall is all glass that looks into the front foyer. There are two wood burning fireplaces, one in the living room, the other in the family room. Both have been converted to natural gas. An oversized, double garage is attached at the side of the house, so when looking from the front, the garage doors are not prominent. There isn't one thing in the house that can be left untouched. All of it needs to be repaired, replaced, or shown some TLC and lots of elbow grease. I could go through the whole house with all of you, but believe me, when I tell you, I have seven, type written pages of improvements we have completed, since moving in, in 2005. From replacing hardwood flooring to replacing every door hinge, nothing has been left undone. The deck, at the rear of the house, needed to be safe for our Molly. We chose white railings with two gates, one opening towards the back and the other opens at the side of the deck. Molly will now be safe, with a doggie door installed in the back door of the house, she can go out and come in, at will, and she loves it.

This is one of her experiences. One day, in the early fall, three moose came onto the acreage. With no fencing, animals frequent the property. Molly got a whiff of them and she ran, like hell, through the doggie door, barking her little heart out. Molly has never even seen a moose. There was a female and her two calves. Well, Molly barked and barked and barked some more, she just would not settle down, so after an hour and a half, I picked her up, took her to the car in the garage, and put her in her kennel. Her heart was just pounding, so I was hoping that would calm her down. It did work and we were very relieved, because she was so upset. Molly turned two in August and I believe this happened, sometime, in late September. She is a real sweetheart, just guarding her ground from threats.

Angus spent days and days clearing over grown bushes from around the house, that were unsightly and were covering windows, trimming, and shaping those worth saving. Cutting down and removing roots from a couple of spruce trees that would be in the way of the newly modeled double garage. Besides, they were ugly, ugly trees, so getting rid of them was a good thing.

The exterior of the house is red brick with white siding. There are six dormers, at the front of the house, a real classic look. We asphalted the semi-circled driveway at the front and carried on with asphalt for the whole driveway area that runs along the side of the house and ends at the end of the newly constructed large triple garage, a big area. We put in sidewalks, along the north side of the house, the west side, and also, a sidewalk from the rear of the house to the triple garage, so much cleaner than dirt. The new triple garage is big enough to put the motorhome inside with two high doors, one at each end of the building, so Angus can drive in and continue out the other end, no need to backup. We also put together three large sheds with flooring and electricity. One is used as a pump shed and it houses the filtration system for the irrigation. The second shed houses the lawn tractor and accessories, while the third shed is a catch all for the small maintenance equipment, like the leaf blower, the weed whacker, rakes, shovels, a work bench, wheel barrel, spray washer, gardening tools, stuff like that. The property still has plenty of room and I call it, 'the back forty.' It's a grassed area and the rear property line is covered with natural, scrub brush and mature, leafed trees. Beyond that, is a cliff that drops down to a creek bed, very quiet, so quiet your ears ring. We have neighbors on both sides, but the distance between is far enough away to be comfortable.

At the front, we went with a white railing fence with two electric gates, one at each end of the semi-circled driveway. Nice, white lantern-styled lights illuminate each side of the gates. There are perennial flowers and trimmed cedar bushes on both sides of the front door. We have permanent flowers in clay pots, dotting the property at door entrances, which look good. We are not running around watering flowers, worrying about the wind or rain destroying them and they don't die, when we go away for a month at a time. Of course, they need to be replaced every couple of seasons, but well worth it, summers are short, where we live, so we are into enjoying our time as much as possible.

Angus spends a lot of time maintaining the property on a daily basis, so when it's time to get away for a golf game, a getaway 'down south,' or a getaway in the motorhome, we thoroughly enjoy it.

One evening, shortly after we moved in, I was outside at the front of the house, near the road, when a woman approaches. We smile at one another, say hello and immediately, I like her. Lucky for me, she lives next door. We chat for a while. I learn that she has two daughters and that she has been recently widowed with her husband passing away, just six months before. I can see his death is still very raw for her, as her eyes well up at mentioning him. She is young to be widowed so early in life. I'm guessing she is around my age. The eldest daughter is Amber and she is twenty-four, the youngest is Ashley and she is twenty-two. I do believe that both were attending university, at the time I met their mom, Grace. That night I mentioned to Angus that I met the neighbor and that it will be nice to have a woman my age to possibly visit and have over for tea and we do.

So, here we are, it's nearing late fall, the triple garage is finished, the back yard is totally dug up, and a new septic tank is being installed. We are working away at the shop. Ian and his girlfriend are staying with us. Everything is running along fine. The new signs for the shop have been made and installed, it's 'MacDonald's Collision Center' and it feels good. The shop is very busy, we have us four and a couple of body-men. The shop is a controllable size, just like Quality Collision in Victoria, only bigger. Larger in square feet with two spray booths, a lunchroom, two bathrooms, a reception area, and a separate office upstairs, which, is where I do the accounting and data entries. I call it 'the penthouse.'

There was a lot of work to get the shop into the condition we wanted it. We pretty much refurbished it, painted the interior and exterior, had the lot totally paved and fenced, bought new equipment, and had signage made.

Once news in the trade gets out that Angus is back in Edmonton, he gets quite a few fellows dropping by to reconnect and that's great. Angus is not painting anymore, as Ian has taken over and he does an excellent job, all of us do. There are no 'come-backs,' as we call them, and in our business, that's huge. You always want to see the rear end of the car, leaving the shop.

We are now six months into the move. Ian and Karli have moved out, purchased a condo in Fort Saskatchewan, about a ten-minute drive from us. We will continue renovations and upgrading the house and property for, at least, the first five years, as there is always something to do, organize, and get done.

I was thinking the other day about the door hinges I mentioned earlier, so I decided to count them. This total includes exterior man doors, interior man doors, and closet doors. There is a total of forty-four doors. Four double garage doors, and two fourteen-foot garage doors. I guess that's why I mentioned them there is a lot of door hinges and pins to replace.

Over the next couple of years, we reconnect with friends and family. We love hosting the special times during the year, like Easter, summer BBQ's, birthdays, Thanksgiving, and, of course, Christmas. Each dinner is different, as well as who can make it at the time. We always have lots of fun with everyone who joins us.

We have reconnected with our friend of over thirty-some years, Art Broos. His wife, Cathy, and their first-born son, Lawrence, are the ones who came to Hawaii with us in 1979. They had three more children, a girl, Jennifer, and two more boys, Ryan, and Bobby. Cathy passed away in October of 1996. Art called the shop in November to let us know. What a tragedy. Cathy was a great gal. We really liked her and her gentle way. When we would go to Edmonton from Victoria, we would see them for a visit.

Art was working in Hinton, Alberta for a while, so one summer vacation, the three of us stopped with the motorhome. I hadn't been in such an active house atmosphere for a long time and I enjoyed every minute. The adults decided to take the kids with a picnic lunch and head for Jasper National Park for the day. It's a beautiful day; we go to a glacier-fed lake, just off the Yellowhead Highway. The view is spectacular, the water is a gorgeous turquoise and the lakefront we have to ourselves. Molly's tail never stops. The kids really enjoy her and take her for long walks. We all have a great day. Ian and Lawrence go swimming in that frigid water and I'm pretty sure the rest of us just waded, *brrr*! We got back in time to put a BBQ together, visit a bit more, then off to bed, tuckered out from all that mountain fresh air, Molly, too!

That visit was a few years before Cathy passed away, but that's how we remember her, smiling, happy, and busy with her family, and truly loving every minute. Cancer; the cure will never come fast enough.

It's February, my fifty-eighth birthday. My sister, Sandra, and her husband, Bill, join Ian, Karli, Angus, and I for a dinner out. We all come back to our house for coffee and dessert. Ian hands me my birthday card, I open it, read it, and at the bottom, it is signed, "With Love," from Ian, Karli, and baby! OMG! I'm going to be a Grandma. We are going to be Grandparents. It's really early, they haven't told anybody yet, but everything seems fine. The baby is due in September, same month as our Ian and our anniversary, too! We are all very excited for the months to go by quickly. Yes, the months seem to fly by and before we know it, our granddaughter is here. Quinn Theresa MacDonald is born on September 5th, 2007. Mom and baby are doing fine. It's a very exciting day, we are Grandparents to a beautiful baby girl and she is gorgeous, of course.

Karli is now a stay-at-home mom, so I'm in the shop a couple of days a week, which is just fine with me. I usually go in on Tuesdays and Thursdays, but I have the option of switching my days around to suit myself, which is really nice.

I can't really remember what day it was that Ian said to his Dad, "You really don't have to come in anymore Dad, you've done your time."

Well, that didn't sink in, so the next day or so went by and Ian says, "Well Dad, if you're coming in, then I'll go home."

After that, Angus retired. He has a lot to keep him busy at the acreage, so Molly and Angus are at home, now. With me gone two days a week, it seems to be working out well.

Ian is the shop manager, estimator, prep-technician, and painter. The shop is too busy, so he hires a painter and gets some relief, although his days are still long and hard. As time goes by, everything is running along fine. Ian, Karli, and Quinn have their own home. We try to see them on the weekends. I stop at their house, probably once a week to take Quinn for a walk in the park.

Angus' sixtieth birthday is here, it's April 17th of 2008. I plan a party. The day of the party arrives and we get a snowstorm, a really bad one. Most of the people make it. The highway conditions are less than desirable, let's put it that way, and we sure didn't want anybody getting into an accident. Ian comes in by way of the double garage attached to the house. He gets Angus' attention and says, "Come see what I got, Dad." Angus follows him outside, where he sees a Yamaha Rhino, sitting in the box of Ian's pick-up truck.

"Oh," Angus says, "What are you going to do with that?"

"Nothing," Ian replies, "It's yours."

Well, what a nice surprise. For those of you who don't know what a Yamaha Rhino is, I'll explain.

It's a four by four, all-terrain vehicle, an ATV. This one seats two, side by side, and has a box in the back for stuff. The color is camo, short for camouflage. Angus added a cab, a heater, a windshield, and a blade for pushing snow. We haul it on a flat deck aluminum trailer and have taken it on camping trips; it's a fun off-road vehicle. I bought Angus a nice watch with an inscription on the back to celebrate his sixtieth birthday. It was a fun day and everybody arrived safe and returned home safe.

Down the road from the shop, there is a Triple E dealer, where they sell motorhomes. They are made really well and made in Canada. We stop to take a look and end up buying one. We buy a '32-footer,' a Commander, Class A with two slide outs; one for the bedroom and one for the living room. We sell our Travel Aire, which we have had since 1985, some twenty-three years. It was always kept inside and was always looked after, inside and out. We got top dollar for it, when we sold it. The salesman actually told Angus that he restored his faith in humanity after seeing that it was really in the shape Angus told him it was in, before the fellow saw it.

We have the new motorhome for just a few weeks before we take our maiden trip to B.C. In 2007, we bought a 2007 Chev, model HHR, a cute, retro-styled station wagon with a high roof and five doors, which seats five passengers. Its design was inspired by the '49 Suburban,' referring to the 'Heritage High Roof.' We have the appropriate hitch installed, hook up the HHR to the motorhome, and away we go.

In August of 2008, we head for British Columbia. Angus's nephew, Danny, has property approximately thirty minutes from Nelson, where Danny's parents, Marion and Dave live. I'm pretty sure it took us a few days to get there, camping along the way, and getting to know and enjoy the new motorhome. We stay in a lovely Provincial Park named 'Blanket Creek.' The vegetation is really different in that area, very lush. It's a few miles south of Revelstoke. Molly loves it. We take her off leash and let her chase gofers from one hole to the next. The gofers tease her, one will stick his head out of a hole, so Molly runs towards him and as soon as she gets close, he retreats down the hole and another pops his head out of another hole, so Molly runs to catch that one. She has a great time, so do we. Making our way to Danny's, we go through a small village named 'Nakusp.' It's a cute little place, located on the shores of the Upper Arrow Lakes in the West Kootenay area. We stop for lunch at a very popular fried chicken drive-in called 'The Hut.' We make a point of going there every time we are anywhere near Nakusp, the food is that good.

Once we get to Danny's, we set up the motorhome and start exploring the area. We have fun filled days. Marion and Dave come to spend time and we go golfing, have BBQ's, relax, and have bon fires in the evenings, it's a great holiday. We go shopping in the 'Historic' Nelson, where they have restored and preserved over 350 heritage buildings. Nelson is known as the 'Queen City' and has been for over hundred years.

As I sit and write, I'm going to carry on with our summer vacations from that first trip in 2008 to now, 2018. I'll do them all for you. I can't remember what events took place, as they happened each and every year, but I'll do a summary. All of our vacations have been so much fun and as the years go by, each vacation has become even more special that the last.

Every year in August, for three weeks, we go and play with everybody who shows up. Marion and Dave from Nelson, Maggie and John from Nanaimo,

Allan and his daughter Maggie came, when, Rob, Marion, and Dave's youngest son got married in the area in 2012. The week of the wedding, everybody met at Danny's. We had big outside breakfasts, BBQ's in the evenings, some of us went golfing, others went for rides on *floaties* down the river, some went into Nelson shopping, and we always took a drive to Nakusp for the day. We would wonder through the town's street market and pick up fresh vegetables and of course, we always stop at 'The Hut.' We have been on the beautiful Kootenay Lake with Marion, Dave, their dog, Bubbles, and our Molly, from morning till night. They have an inboard motorboat that's lots of fun. We pull over at secluded beaches to have our picnic lunch, to hunt for treasured rocks, go for a swim, and to let the dogs run.

In the past four years, we have caravanned from Nelson to northern Washington, USA. There have been four units, Marion and Dave, Maggie and John, Allan and us. We start booking the trip in April, so we can get close to one another in the campsites. We all have a ball, swimming in either a lake, river, or in the pool at the RV park. At the river, we go after lunch and end up staying all day, playing like kids, in and out of the water, keeping cool, and taking the dogs for a swim, too. Around seven in the evening, we walk back to camp to make supper and usually by ten, we are dead to the world and call it a day.

This summer's trip, 2018 is all booked. Angus and I get really excited, because it's so much fun. I really can't thank Marion and Dave enough for all the hospitality and fun times they have shared with us. It has been wonderful. We will all camp until we can't and I'm hoping that time will be a long time from now.

Back to 2008 a few weeks after we get home from summer vacation, Ian surprises us with a trip to Las Vegas for our 40th anniversary, all expenses paid. He has also gotten us tickets to take a helicopter ride through the Grand Canyon, where we will have a champagne lunch to celebrate.

We fly into Vegas and get a shuttle bus to the Hotel, which is located on the strip, no need to rent a car, we can walk to wherever we want to go or get a taxi. The weather is really nice, hot, actually, and we are excited to be here. The next week is full of fun, as we enjoy each day from morning till night. We order in breakfast at the hotel and enjoy, as we watch people walking the strip. We go see the show 'Love,' by Cirque du Soleil. The show is about the Beatles and couldn't have been any nicer. Thoroughly enjoyed the show, so much so that I would probably fly to Vegas and back again, just to see the show, it was that good. We do a little gambling in the hotel's casino, slot machines, it's fun and we both end up losing our twenty dollars' worth of nickels. The helicopter tour of the Grand Canyon was wonderful, a beautiful day, not a cloud in sight.

As we are walking towards the helicopter with our group of six, I notice that the number on the helicopter is 68, the year we married, kind of funny. The pilot was great. We were gone all day. Flying into Vegas, it was just past dusk and he asked if anyone would like to fly over the strip. Of course, we all clapped and yahooed that yes we all would. So, he flew the helicopter from one end of the strip to the other. It was quite the experience, we were flying low, all the lights were flashing, as we flew past all the hotels, we could see the people on the roller coaster on top of one of the hotels, plain as day, it was a great time. Angus and I booked a table at the Paris Hotel, which is a half-scaled replica of the Eiffel Tower that's in France. It has a roof top restaurant. We get a taxi and arrive on time. The food is really good, almost the best we have ever had and the champagne we ordered to celebrate was delicious, although we had to leave the remainder of the bottle there, we had our fill. What a day, what a week, thank you, Ian, we will never forget this anniversary, truly a wonderful experience.

Fall turns to winter and we are approaching our second Christmas with Quinn, she is now fifteen months old. Quinn usually, comes to Grandma and Grandpa's on Friday evenings and has a sleep over. We have a swim in the pool and she loves it. We laugh and giggle and sing songs. After that, it's bath time. Grandpa and Molly play with Quinn, while I make supper, I can hear them giggling in the family room, it does my heart good. I sleep with Quinn and we love that. It's a very special time for me. We laugh, sing nursery songs, and before we know it, we are cuddled up and fast asleep till morning. Molly, who has slept with Grandpa, comes to our bedroom door and nudges it open with her nose, we awake with big smiles on our faces. Ian comes to pick her up on Saturday, around lunchtime. Quinn is such a good baby, she is on the go, from morning till night and she doesn't nap. Very, very, occasionally, she will fall asleep during quiet time, sitting with me on the love seat. I'll read her a story and I can see her eyes getting heavy, so I keep reading and very slowly her eyelids close and she is so calm, I love watching her fall asleep. I did the same with our Ian, wonderful.

This past winter has been a long one with the cold and snow. We decide to take a couple of weeks and head for Phoenix, Arizona. Angus' cousin, John Dolanz, and his wife, Susan, have been going down for six months, at a time, for years now. It is mid-February; we leave a day before my sixtieth birthday. We rent a vehicle, because there are mountain passes to drive through and we don't want to drive our own vehicle through all the muck.

Our neighbor, four properties down from us, has offered to mind our Molly, while we are away. Devika, well into her 70s, is an animal lover and we couldn't possibly have a better Molly-watcher than her. She knows beagles, as her father had one for years. Devika loves to hear Molly, when she is baying on our back deck, usually when she has caught a scent of either deer or coyotes that frequent our area.

We leave early in the morning and pull up to the USA border, around eleven, after stopping for breakfast and to gas up, along the way. The line-up is not too long, we inch closer, the light turns green, and it's our turn. Angus rolls the window down, good mornings are exchanged, and then Angus hands the officer our passports. The officer begins by asking the usual questions, like;

"Where are you headed?"

"Phoenix, Arizona."

"How long are you going to be in the US?" "Two weeks"

"Where will you be staying?"

"Hotel in Mesa."

"What's your license plate number?"

"I don't know off hand, it's a rental."

"Why are you driving a rental?"

"Because I don't want to drive my own vehicle through the mountain passes."

And it went on from there, the officer must have asked Angus another three or four questions about what kind of car did we drive at home, was it not suitable for the trip, and why was it we didn't want to drive it now? Really!

Okay, pull up to the side of this building on the left, leave everything in the vehicle, including the ladies purse and give the keys to the officer that will be there waiting for you.

"What the hell is this all about?" We question ourselves, as we do as he instructed. The officer takes the keys and tells us to go inside and take instructions from officers at the counter. We walk in, it's pretty quiet, we walk up to the counter, and the officer points to a door on our right. We walk towards the door and another officer opens it, then after going through that solid door, we hear a click, the door appears to be locked behind us. There is another counter where two officers are waiting for us to approach. Once there, we are each handed a declaration form, declaring all items we have in our vehicle. We finish the forms and hand them in. We take a seat, I'm fuming, but Angus is not. We are speaking low, we are confused and feel like criminals and have done nothing wrong, absolutely nothing. I'm not impressed by the way we have been treated, the locked door did it for me. We are kept there for well over an hour, closer to an hour and a half, when a female officer comes to the counter carrying my purse and two apples we had in the car. She tells us they have to keep the apples, because there isn't a sticker on them. I tell her that I had washed them at home and took the stickers off. I suggested they eat them,

167

rather than through them away, she just smiled. A male officer comes with our passports in hand and says we are free to go. Angus was curious, "What was it that caused the red flag?" he asks.

"The rental," replies the officer, "We have had people use rental vehicles for smuggling drugs and others that drive rental vehicles down here only to sell them, so we have to be careful."

We leave, I'm still very upset and I really resent being treated like we had done something wrong. Angus settles me down. They were only doing their jobs.

"Right," I'm not convinced.

Despite the incident, we carry on and have a great time. We visit John and Susan at the RV Park, where they have been staying for years. They know quite a few couples and some come from where they, too, call home, in Edson, Alberta. We have a good visit with lots of laughs, reminiscing about old times, and family events gone by.

While there, we also visit a long-time family friend, Sandy and Marlene McLaren, who have recently purchased a home in Mesa, just a short distance from where we are staying. Sandy's family, were neighbors of Angus' family growing up. The four of us go out for a good meal and also reminisce about days gone by. I never had the opportunity to meet Sandy's Mom, Jeanne, but all say she was a lovely woman. She had passed away, before I started dating Angus. Angus told me all about Jeanne, he thought the world of her. I did, however, meet Sandy's Dad, Alexander Sandy McLaren on several occasions. As I'm writing this, Sandy Sr. passed in May of 2018. He was 98 years young. He was a great guy, good husband and a good Dad to his kids. He will be missed, but not far from our thoughts. He served in the army during World War II and was awarded the Four-Star Military Medal of Bravery and France's highest Medal of Honor. When discharged, he was a Sargent Major, now that's a huge accomplishment in itself.

Arriving back home, without an incident at the border, we are greeted with snow that has not melted yet. Next year, we may leave a little later.

I have to take you back just a bit, because I forgot to tell you about a trip my sister Sandra and I took. We flew in 2006 to see our eldest sister, Vivian. At that time, she was living in Oshawa, Ontario, retired, on her own now, having spent over thirty years with Wally. Wally is a nice guy and they had many happy years together, but it just came to an end. The three of us gals have a wonderful week together. Viv takes us everywhere. We go shopping, take drives in the countryside, and stop for fresh fruit at a market, eat toasted, coconut marshmallows and giggle like kids. We have a nice sunny day at home, swimming in her pool, just relaxing and enjoying each other's company. It was really good for the three of us to get together and have fun.

Okay, now back to the spring of 2009. The snow, eventually, goes and the green appears once more. The smells of spring are great, so fresh, and so clean, somehow. Leaving the windows open on a cool fresh spring morning, lovely. There is so much to do on the acreage in the spring, especially for Angus. He makes a 'To Do' list every day. I put a stop to him about 4:00 in the afternoon, that's enough, he goes outside around 9:00, after breakfast and a swim, so that's seven hours and he doesn't stop. There have been lots of days, when he has spent more than twelve hours doing chores. Yes, our acreage and home are gorgeous, so you can see the time he spends on it, but I tell him his body needs to rest, too! He comes in, we discuss the day, have dinner, relax with some TV shows, and then it's off to bed.

During May through July, we do get in a few games of golf. We love playing with Ian, he is our instructor, too, and after the game, we go for a bite to eat, it's a great day. We always have our Quinn on Fridays for a sleep over, she is now creeping up to two years old and we enjoy her so much. She loves our Molly and can do anything to her. There is a lot of kisses and hugs. Quinn gets a treat for Molly and gets Molly to run after her through the kitchen, dining room, and living room, giggling all the while, then, finally, Quinn will give her the treat, but first it's "sit," and "shake a paw."

Quinn told me, when she was about five or six, that Molly was right-handed.

"How do you know that?" I ask.

"I ask her to "shake a paw," she always shakes with her right paw."

I must say, after she leaves on Saturday, you will find me on the couch in the family room, having a nap. You would think that after breakfast, a swim, a bath, playing with us, and our Molly, she would nap, but she doesn't. Sometimes, if she appears grumpy, I'll suggest a quiet time. We will sit and I will read to her, she will almost fall asleep, then her Dad will come, and she runs like the dickens, yelling "Daddy, Daddy," so cute. He picks her up into his arms and there is lots of hugs and kisses.

By the time August rolls around, we are ready to play. Our three weeks has been booked and we are off. On our second trip out with the motorhome, we start by spending a few days at Danny's, near Nelson. We have BBQs with Marion and Dave, go for a river run with our *floaties*, take a drive up to Nakusp, and have a lunch at 'The Hut.' We branch out a bit this year and head south, all the way to Northern California. We have a ball, finding different RV parks, golf courses, and parks to take our Molly for walks. When we golf, we play nine holes, because we don't want to leave Molly alone for too long. She is great, she usually jumps up and sits on my seat in the motorhome, just keeping an eye out, for when we might return.

During that summer, my sister, Viv, moves back to Edmonton, for good this time, or, at least, I'm hoping for good. For many years, she worked for the GWG Company, out of Edmonton. Over those years, she was transferred back and forth, I think, two more times, between Edmonton and Ontario, before retiring. Viv's only daughter, Tamara, her husband, and their four daughters live in Edmonton, so that will be nice for Viv.

Come September, we have a lot of flagged family dates. Quinn's Birthday on September 5th, Viv's on September 20th, Ian's on September 23rd, and our anniversary is on September 28th, which is now, our forty-first. Our Ian is thirty-three, Quinn is two, and Viv is sixty-three. Just keeping myself on track.

Here comes Christmas, again. We host Christmas and have Angus' brother, Allan, his then wife, Fritz, and their two daughters, Katie and Maggie, over. Every other year, Ian goes to Victoria, because Quinn's other Grandma and Grandpa live there. I cook the turkey on the BBQ and it's really good. Angus got me four pieces of muffler pipe, cut in widths of the grill, so the roasting pan doesn't touch the grill and when the lid is closed, the BBQ acts just like an oven. The oven in the house is free to be used for other food items, good idea. If it's -20 below zero, the trips out to the back deck, to check the turkey, are quick ones. We always have a good time.

Angus and I plan another trip 'down south,' as we say. This year we will go to Palm Springs, California. Angus has another cousin, Bill, and his wife, Maureen, who have been going to their second home in Indian Wells, for some fifteen years or so. They go down in November and come back in May, to their first home near Calgary, Alberta. Bill worked for Shaw Cable for years, as one of their top executives and is now retired.

I ask Viv if she would mind looking after our Molly, while we are away. No problem, she will. Viv is an animal lover from way back. I don't think she has ever been without a dog or a cat. She usually has both. Right now, in 2010, she has Dozer, who is a really nice gentle Staffordshire Bull-Terrier a rescue dog he is a good one.

We leave a little later, around mid-March; hoping spring will be earlier on our return home. We drive our own vehicle on this trip and we know our license number at the border crossing, and, of course, they don't ask that this time around, LOL! The drive is good, we like our road trips, it's the only time we buy gummy worms and thoroughly enjoy them, too. After two and a half days, we arrive in Palm Springs. The weather is really nice, the flowers are in bloom, and the golf courses are busy with Canadians. We Canadians are known as 'Snow Birds' down south, but in some areas, they call us 'The Golden

Geese,' because their economy perks up considerably, while we are down there. Palm Springs is so easy to get around, it has a ring road that circles around seven different Cities, they are small and one city runs into the other. The only way you can tell that you have crossed into a different City, is the signage.

We book into our hotel; we are in a suite with lots of room for the two of us. We leave a message with Bill and tell them we are here and would they like to get together. After a wee while, Bill calls and invites us for an evening at their house. He will call down to the gateman and let him know who we are and what time we will be arriving. Oh my, what a beautiful area. Once inside the gate, the houses and their yards are kept very nice, lots of flowers, and not a shred of anything lying around. Bill and Maureen have a beautiful open-plan home, it's gorgeous, and they are right on the golf course. We have brought a photo album or two and the four of us have a nice evening, reminiscing, and enjoying a home cooked meal, delicious. First time Angus and I meet Maureen, she's a great gal and funny, too!

Bill and Maureen, golf and we have been invited to play a round of golf with them the next day. The course is beautiful. There is one hole where you get to the green, turn around, and there are twenty-six sand traps that you can only see from that direction, amazing. I'm not sure if it's this trip or the one following, but we are invited to have lunch at the country club restaurant, of course, we will. Oh, man, everything is just as good as it can be; the food, the service, the view, breathtaking. When we get home, I send a Thank You card and tell Bill and Maureen that after leaving them, I said to Angus, "That's as close to heaven as I'm ever going to get."

When we pull up to the house after our trip, the snow is so high, that before we can get in, Angus has to dig the snow away from the gates, so much for thinking spring would, actually, be arriving soon. In the morning, we drive to Viv's and pick up our Molly. Viv has enjoyed her company and absolutely no problems between the two dogs.

During a regular week, I try to see Viv and Sandra for coffee. We pretty much always meet at Viv's. After texting, we decide on the day and time, which is usually on a Tuesday or a Thursday, because I'm in Edmonton on those days at the shop. It's a chance for us to go over what we've been up to and we always have a good laugh, and there usually are some goodies to go along with our coffee.

Come August, we jump in the motorhome and enjoy another holiday in British Columbia, taking in all the days and nights with family, it just doesn't get any better.

Ian and Karli have signed Quinn up for pre-school, she is three on September 5th. The school is in Edmonton and driving from Fort Saskatchewan to the school, drive over to the shop to put in a few hours, and then back to the school and out to Fort Saskatchewan at the end of the day gets to be a bit much. So, the kids sell the house and move really close to the school, a really good idea. Karli is back at the shop now, learning my position. I still go in two days a week and that works out well.

As always, time goes by like a flash and before we know it, fall and winter have come and gone.

It's now the spring of 2011. Viv and I start golfing together on Wednesday mornings. She is an excellent golfer; I can only hope to be half as good. May, June, and July, I have been stopping at a golf range on the way home from the shop and I think it's helping. Viv and I enjoy our golfing. We go to the clubhouse for a lunch, nice to be with her. I really enjoy her company, she never runs out of things to talk about and always keeps up with what's going on in the world around us, she's very intelligent, likes to laugh, likes to shop, she is generous, she is always up for anything, and has a bright outlook on 'things,' in general. We golf for three to four years running, until her hip gives her too much trouble and she has to hang up her clubs. I really miss those days with her and haven't found another partner since. I still golf with Angus and Ian and on holidays, we golf a lot, so I'm feeding my fix for golf, every chance I get.

In July, Angus takes the Ford and the Mullins trailer to the Fort Saskatchewan car show that is held annually on the Canada Day weekend. Molly and I drive over a little later and meet up with Angus. The car gets a lot of attention and so does Molly. We have a really nice day, the weather is beautiful, there are a lot of cars on show and we visit with car guys and the general public. Around 3:30 or 4:00, we decide to head home. I take our Molly with me and we drive home. About a half hour later, Angus drives in. He gets out of the car with a trophy in hand. After I left, Angus was leaving, when a car guy asks, "Where are you going?"

"I'm heading home," Angus replies.

"Well hold on, we got something for you."

The fellow gets Angus to drive the car up to the front, where they presented him with a trophy for 'Best in Show.' 'Best in Show' is really a nice one to win, because it's the general public that votes for the car they like best. What a nice way to end a great day.

After our summer vacation this year, we decide to go away for our anniversary. We go to the rocky-mountains and decide on a very scenic spot called Pocahontis Bungalows. These bungalows sit at the base of the rocky-mountains, just inside the Jasper National Park's east gate. The bungalows have been there for a very long time. They have been renovated over the years and new ones have been built. Our family would pass them on our way to Miette Hot Springs. There is a public swimming pool located at the end of a fifteen-kilometer drive up the mountain, breathtaking view, once you arrive on top.

We have a wonderful few days there with our Molly. She loves going for long walks in the crisp, clean air. There are remnants of an old town site, where you can walk through and see old, old housing foundations. A plaque is posted outside of a very large vault that was once used as a 'pay-day' vault for all of the coal miners. As you drive by on Highway 16, you see nothing and that's a real shame, because there are thousands of visitors to Jasper National Park every year and our Federal Government has done nothing to educate or to show people a large part of our history in that area.

This September, Quinn is four, can't believe how time has passed. We keep busy, always enjoying our home and always planning ahead, so we have 'things' to look forward to. My Mom was always like that; she organized and planned events months before they happened. I guess that's where I learned it from. Simple enough to do, if there is a birthday coming up, why wait for the day before to get the card or the gift purchased. When you do it a while before, there is no pressure to get it done and it works out better for you, in the long run. Same as Christmas, I usually start in October, carrying a list with me of what I think I would like to get. When I see something, I pick it up, pretty soon the list is finished, and I have time to breath, before Christmas day arrives. Make things easier for yourself. I'm not the only one who writes lists for what they need to pick up, I see women all the time with lists in their hands, while shopping, especially, for groceries. Hosting a big dinner for any occasion can be a lot easier, if you go through your menu and make a list of the items you need to get ahead of time.

This Christmas, we have Quinn. Christmas is for children and what better way to celebrate. We have a house full this year, including a young couple and their first-born son, who is about a year and a half. The house is alive and it's great.

We set up two Christmas trees, one in the family room, a traditional green spruce and a white spruce in the living room. The green one is decorated with a very wide variety of ornaments. There are some decorations that we have had for years and years. Some are handmade and have been given to us by friends and family. Ian has made a few, a long time ago, in elementary school and they are hung very carefully at the front of the tree. Quinn, also, has made a couple at school and we have them hung at the front for all to see. We enjoy setting up this tree. The process starts with a pot of coffee and Bailey's. Angus and I reminisce about Christmas's gone by, of course, all of our loved ones are mentioned and stories are re-told again. Before we know it, the bags of decorations are empty and the tree is finished.

Angus sets up the white tree. It came complete with tiny colored lights. We have a train that he mounts near the top. There are three cars that go around and around the tree. It's kind of cute, the conductor shouts out, "All aboard," the headlight lights the way and it's off, chugging along, while the whistle toots and the wheels *clickety clack* their way around the track.

Our rhythm in life is good. Life is kind of funny, some weeks, months, and even, some years just run along with no hic-cups and nothing really, really good or really, really bad happens. There are also times, when your gut tells you something's going on; something's just not right. And so, it was with Ian and Karli. Their split finally happened in 2012. At first you are sad, especially for Quinn, but as time goes on, you realize it's going to be just fine. The really good that has been constant, is their love for Quinn and if that's the only thing they agree on, that's good with me. Ian is a terrific father, he and Quinn do everything together, it's been six years now and Ian hasn't missed a beat with her. He continues to give her every opportunity to experience life to its fullest.

They go camping in their fifth wheel and meet up with good friends and their kids, ages ranging from three to sixteen, seventeen years old. Quinn has been riding her own quad and dirt bike, since she was four. Ian has a dirt bike and side-by-side quad and they ride for hours and I mean hours, sometimes, six-hour rides and Quinn loves it. We have gone on camping trips with them, too, and it has been nothing short of a good time, a hell of a good time. The parents are totally involved with the kids and keep them busy from morning till night and beyond. We loved it. There was the chili cook off and the deep fry night. Everything you can imagine was deep-fried, everybody gets involved and it's so much fun. They, also, had a boat race down the river, but not in a real boat, in a homemade toy boat that was put together with anything you could find that would float. There was a table with some supplies. Quinn and Grandpa made one and painted it. I think they had a mast on it. All the boat-maker teams were called to the edge of the river. On your mark, get set, and go… you would give your boat a push to send it into the current. The river had a big U and the boats were put in at one end and then we all ran to the other end, to see them come around the bend, funny, it was hilarious. Quinn and Grandpa came in second and won $20.00.

Ian told me about a chili cook-off, but didn't have any details, just make a pot of chili, so I did. The morning of the cook-off, I put together my homemade chili it's good. Quinn comes knocking on the motorhome door, "Grandma, I need to have your money."

"What do you need money for," I ask.

"The chili cook off," she replies.

"Oh, and how much money do you want?"

"I don't know," she says, "I'll go find out."

She comes back in a few minutes and says, "Fifty bucks."

"Fifty bucks," I exclaim, "I'll have to see if I have fifty bucks, let me look."

I look and between Angus and I, we get the fifty bucks together. A while later, she comes and says in kind of a panic, "Grandma, come on, you have to bring your chili now."

"Okay, I'm ready," I respond.

I take the big pot of chili and set it on the table they have set up, along with a soup ladle, some bowls, and spoons. There is a commotion behind me, I turn around and there's this cute little kid carrying a volcano of chili, with sparklers all around it.

I just forget what the rest of the contestants were set up like, but there was no way in hell I was going to beat that kid. Of course, I did not win, I lost in my presentation, no wonder; I thought I was just supposed to make chili. Next time and there will be a next time, I know a little bit more about this fun-loving group. Oh, for your information, there were four who entered and the winner took the $200.00 dollar prize. I'll have to kick it up a notch next time.

Ian and Quinn go for bicycle rides in Ian's neighborhood and play in the park. On rainy days, they build Lego and play games on their X-box 360. When they go to the water park, it's for the entire day, mid-morning till closing; they get their money's worth, that's for sure. Golf is another fun thing to do. Ian is an excellent golfer and instructs Quinn, she really enjoys it, too. Because of her age, they play alternate shots, so slow play is not a problem on the course. One of their best games so far is an eighty-four, that's pretty damn good in my eyes. Come winter, they go skiing in the mountains and have such a good time. They head out after breakfast and stay till the last horn is heard, signaling the end of the ski day. Recently, they have taken up squash. Quinn is getting pretty good at it, too, she has beaten Ian a few times. Skating, Quinn has learned on straight blade skates and continues to use them. They take their pucks and hockey sticks over to the local rink, sometimes, they have the rink to themselves, if not, they will join in with others, such fun. They also shoot pool together, I'm not sure which game they play the most, snooker or 8 ball, but it doesn't matter, they are together enjoying each other's company, that's the important thing.

Every second Friday, I pick Quinn up from school and she comes for a sleep over. On Saturday, Ian comes, we all have a lunch together, and then the two of them head off to enjoy the rest of the weekend. Angus and I are very thankful that Ian shares his Quinn time with us.

Dozer, Viv's dog, hasn't been feeling well for a few months now. In March of 2012, after Viv has exhausted all treatments offered to Dozer, she has no alternative but to put him down, he is suffering. Sandra and I go with her and Dozer to the vets. As you can imagine, it's very sad. Dozer has meant a lot to Viv, he has been a beloved companion for years and she will miss him dearly.

As I mentioned earlier, in August of 2012, Marion and Dave's youngest son, Rob, gets married. We have our motorhome at Danny's. Maggie and John have their trailer there, too, along with Allan and his daughter, Maggie. It's a great week the weather is hot, really hot. The day of the wedding, all went well. There was a good turnout of both friends and family. We always have lots of laughs, good food, and fun for all. It was a very nice time.

This winter is kind of strange, we get cold, cold days and freezing rains, and when the snow falls, it covers the ice underneath, very slippery conditions. Angus is outside, when he slips and falls, bangs his head really hard on the cement, and for two weeks or so, he doesn't feel quite right. We figure he had a concussion.

Come June, he is again working outside, and at the end of the day, he mentions to me that he must have gotten something in his eye. He washes his eye out using an eyewash cup, but come morning, its worse. There seems to be a curtain in the eye that is blocking his vision. We phone the optometrist and they take him right away. He needs immediate surgery it's a detached retina. "What," never heard of that. Off to the hospital and after a three-and-a-half-hour surgery, he is left with an implant in his right eye. We will have to wait and see how he does. We are hoping the eye-site will be restored, although we have been told and understand that it will take time. He has to return to the hospital early the next morning. After that examination, it is explained to us that the surgery went well, so now comes the healing. Well, who has time to sit around and wait for that to happen, we have places to go and people to see.

It's a difficult summer, because Angus works with so much equipment outside, like hedge trimmers, leaf blowers, grass tractor and a weed wacker, to mention a few, he climbs ladders and is always doing something, like working on one of our parked vehicles, checking things over, changing oil etc. etc. and your eye site is extremely important.

A simple thing like filling the bird feeders, you have to be able to judge where the hook is, so you can hang it back up in the tree, depth perception, and it is frustrating, of course, he gets it, but it takes him longer and you don't get used to doing things slower than you did before. We do manage to get in a few golf games, before we head out on holidays. Angus wants me to stand behind the hole on the green that we are aiming at, because, sometimes, he sees two of them. He will bring me a coffee, set it down, and half the cup will be on the coaster, while the other half of the cup will be on the table. After looking up the detached retina, we are pretty sure that the fall Angus had on the ice, when he banged his head really hard, probably had some bearing on the detached retina.

We leave on holidays, as planned. Angus drives really well, although his eyes are very tired at the end of the day. As time goes on, his eye site does improve a lot. He goes for three-month check-ups and on one of them, the surgeon, who did his surgery, did a laser treatment that helped quite a bit. It's been five years and there is no sign of any further damage and his check-ups are good. Whew!

Also, in August, Sandra and Bill's dog, Aerio, had a massive seizure and because there is no way of telling when the next one will occur or how many she will have to endure, the decision is made to put her down, she is fourteen years old. Aerio was a mix of Jack Russell and Terrier. A smart dog, always up for playing catch with a Frisbee and, boy, could she jump, again and again and again, she loved it. If your hand was hanging over a lawn chair arm she would duck her head, under your hand, and wait for you to pet her, all the while sitting and looking up at you with those eyes. They will surely miss Aerio and her energy. Sandra and Bill still have Sheba she is a mix of American Eskimo and Corgi. She looks like an American Eskimo, white in color, same coat, same face and ears, but she is short with those Corgi legs. She is a very good dog and loves going for a car rides. She and Aerio are about the same age. Our Molly turns ten on August 10th, so far, she is doing great.

Come September of 2013, our Quinn starts grade one. Ian turns thirty-seven and we celebrate our forty-fifth anniversary. I swear, the older you get, the faster the time goes. Quinn likes her school, she has been going to the same one since she was three, so this won't be much of a transition for her and that's a good thing.

Winter is upon us, once again. In February 2014, for my sixty-fifth birthday, we go to Jasper National Park and stay in their 'Athabasca' cottage, on the grounds of Jasper Park Lodge. The cottage is named, 'the honeymoon cottage' and it should be. It's a really cozy cabin. It's private and perfect for relaxing and spending quality time together. Of course, we take Molly and the three of us have a lot of fun. There is a lake on the property that freezes during the winter months, so we take our skates and enjoy. They have fire pits, benches, and hot chocolate, really nice and Molly gets to meet and greet, which is one of her favorite things to do.

This is a good one. The three of us arrive; we unload our 'stuff' and get settled. The bedroom is separate and there is a kitchen/living room area, complete with a wood -burning fireplace. The bathroom has a Jacuzzi tub. Angus goes in to use the toilet, the water in the bowl is frozen solid, rock hard. I call the front desk; they will send someone right away. A fellow comes, "Yup, it's frozen, alright." He gets to work. There is a crawl space under the cottage, where they can access 'the workings' of the bathroom. We have to go, so we take Molly for a walk to the main lodge and use their facility. We check in between three and four that afternoon, so by the time we get back to the cottage and the fellows have everything up and running, it's dark. A knock comes at the door, we are handed an envelope from the messenger, who rode over to the cottage on a bicycle. We open it and there is a note saying we are invited to a complimentary dinner for two for our inconvenience. The messenger tells us to just call the front desk, when we are ready, and they will send a car to pick us up. Well, sure didn't expect that. We get ready to go out for a free dinner at the world-famous Jasper Park Lodge, how nice is that, and all because our toilet was frozen. Well, the meal was great and we really did enjoy every bite and it set us up for a very enjoyable week. We had fires every day, the wood being delivered to our door every morning, along with the newspaper. We ordered in our breakfasts, made our own fresh coffee and lollygagged, until we felt like getting dressed and then we would head out for a short drive to the town site of Jasper. We found a local pub that made craft beer on the premises. The food is good and the beer is excellent. After window shopping, taking pictures of the mountains, and walking Molly, we head back to the cottage to enjoy a totally relaxing evening. Google this, you will find everything I mentioned and maybe you, will experience this one day.

It is now the spring of 2015. Angus and I drive from our house, through a residential area that brings you into the center of Fort Saskatchewan, and for ten years now, we have noticed a house and yard that really are well kept. A couple live there and usually it's the fellow we see outside, doing the yard work. Angus says, "One of these days, I'm going to stop and tell that guy how much I appreciate what he does." One day, in April, Angus is driving home and spots the fellow, so he pulls over. He approaches, introduces himself, and they get into a good conversation. Angus does tell him how much his efforts are seen and appreciated.

Come May, Angus takes me out for a Mother's Day breakfast. We happen to sit down at a table, directly across from 'the couple' with the nice place. We introduce ourselves to one another, we like them right away. Another time, we see them again, while having a coffee at McDonald's. They have been in Fort Saskatchewan since 1970 and they sure know a lot of people, people are always saying hello to them, it's great.

After our summer vacation this year, we start planning our fall getaway. We decide to change it up this year and head for Vancouver Island. There are friends to see and Angus' two sisters live there, Maggie and Catherine. We go for a week and take Molly. On this trip, we leave the motorhome at home; we take the car and stay in places where Molly can stay, too. Once on the Island, there is a lot to do. We go to our favorite place on the Island and that's Gordon Bay on Lake Cowichan. We have spent a lot of time here, over the years. As we drive closer to the entrance of the campgrounds, Molly is at the window, even before we roll the window down for her, she knows exactly where she is. There are only a couple of places we let her go off lead and this is one of them. There is a trail that ends at the water, so she has nowhere to go, so it's perfect. She is so happy here, she runs ahead of us. If she goes too far and can't see us, she doubles back, tail just a going. The fall smells and clean fresh air are wonderful, not to mention the eye candy of the surrounding tree covered hills, the colors, and the sparkling water. When we get back to the car, we take out our camping chairs and just sit and relax on the beach area, taking it all in and yacking about our many camping trips we have had here with Ian and Grandpa and Grandma.

We stay with Maggie and her husband, John, in Nanaimo. The four of us have a really good visit. We go see friends and reminisce about times gone by and laugh at ourselves. Everybody is doing well and the visits are very enjoyable, lots of laughs, too much food, but what the heck, we are on vacation. Of course, a week goes by in a flash and doesn't seem long enough, but, sometimes, the shortest visits turn out to be the best.

There is a special place that Angus and I would go for lunch on a Saturday, when we lived in Victoria, 'The Prairie Inn.' The Inn is a neighborhood, pub-style restaurant that's in Saanichton, a district outside of Victoria, about a fifteen-minute drive. The Inn has a very long history and goes back well over a hundred years, really a good spot. Whenever we go to the Island, we always stop for halibut and chips, accompanied with a beer, a full-flavored beer, like Richard's Red, yum!

We haven't been down south for a couple of years now, so we start talking about taking a trip in April this year, 2016. We go back to Palm Springs, and have a great time, golfing and meeting some nice folks. We took a day trip to Huntington Beach, the original 'surf city.' You know the song and the lyrics by the 'Beach Boys.' FYI, Surf City was written by Brian Wilson from the Beach Boys, and Jan Berry from Jan & Dean. It was first recorded and made popular by the duo, Jan and Dean, in 1963. It took several years for city officials to officially get Huntington Beach to be known and nicknamed 'Surf City.' The final decision was made in 2008, after a long dispute with Santa Cruz. Google this, it is very interesting. We enjoyed Huntington Beach so much that we are going to make it our destination next year.

When we get home from Huntington Beach, we are busy, right up until we leave again for a ten-day trip to Chinook Cove Golf and RV, just outside of a small town in British Columbia called Barriere. The weather is so nice, it's the end of May and the temperature is 25 Celsius or 80 Fahrenheit, the golf course is in excellent condition. We have a fun filled week with Molly. We schedule our tee off times for nine holes in the mornings, it's cooler and that leaves the rest of the day to go exploring the area with Molly.

I guess it was early in June, when I went to my doctor to get my medications renewed. While there, she tells me it's time for a mammogram. I get the letter and go for the appointment in mid-June, around the sixteenth. They call me in, do the mammogram, and ask me to wait while they check it. The nurse comes back and asks if I have time, they would like to do a biopsy, the surgeon just happens to be here that morning, so I say yes, I have time. It's a pretty easy procedure where they insert a needle into the concerned area and take a tissue sample that is sent to the lab for examination.

A few days go by and I receive a phone call from my doctor's office, she wants to see me. I go and she lets me know the results from the biopsy are in, it's cancer. She explains that it's in an early stage, 1 or 2 and says the Cross Cancer Hospital will be in touch. She says with confidence that I will be fine and I know she means it.

I get out to the car and just sit for a few minutes. I'm thinking, *Here, I go again*.

I honestly thought, that after my stage four Hodgkin's in 1992, that I was finished with cancer. *Think again*, I say to myself.

I walk in the door at home, where Angus is anxiously waiting. I go over what the doctor has just told me. First there will be surgery, followed by radiation treatments. We are, once again, faced with adversity, but at the same time, we are grateful that there are treatments.

Within two weeks, I'm notified of my surgery date, it will be July seventh of 2016. Perfect timing, we will be leaving on our annual vacation come August. I may not be able to golf, but that's okay. Angus takes me to the hospital the surgery goes well. After a couple of weeks, I meet my oncologist. I let her know that we will be away for the month of August and I will start my radiation treatments in September. She doesn't seem to like that very much, but informs me, as long as I start before or around the three- month mark from when I was diagnosed, that will be fine.

We go on vacation, meet up with Maggie and John and Allan at Danny's. We have a good few days there. We meet Marion and Dave from Nelson, then we all head for Sullivan Lake in Washington State. The previous year, we had lots of fun swimming in the lake every day. This year, it's raining, drizzling, cloudy, and generally, not nice weather to be down at the lake. We do other things, like visit quite a bit around the campfire. Us gals go walking with the dogs and we make time for me to read my book to them. They really enjoy it, so that's encouraging. I have read that it's a good idea to share your work with others to get some feedback. The feedback I have received has been positive, but I wonder if that's because they know me and might not want to hurt my feelings, if they say something that's not complimentary? Time will tell, because I do want to have my book published. For now, there is still a lot to do, so I'll just keep on writing.

Molly, she gets sick, so after we leave Sullivan Lake and arrive at Deer Park, Washington, we go shopping. Marion advises with an upset tummy, Molly would probably do well on boiled chicken, organic rice, and organic pumpkin. Molly seems to like her new menu and her tummy seems to be settling down. Our stay in Deer Park is really enjoyable. I feel good golfing, after my surgery, no problems. The golf course is right next to the RV Park where we have full hook-ups and that is very much appreciated in the hot weather it's around 33 Celsius or 96 Fahrenheit. After seven nights, we say our good byes and that's tough. As always, I'm consumed with emotions and it gets contagious.

Angus and I have a week to ourselves and have made reservations at Chinook, where we stayed in May to June. Molly isn't feeling well again, her tummy isn't holding anything down and she's running from the back-end. Angus and I are on guard through the nights, we will take her in, when we get home.

Oh, boy, we arrive home and Molly is whining, she needs to go bad. I open the door and she runs through to her doggy door, with me right behind her to open it. She just gets onto the back deck and her tummy let's go. Poor Molly, she feels awful making a mess, but we keep telling her it's okay. On the Sunday, we decide to take her into the hospital. We find a vet hospital that is open, so we call and explain Molly's symptoms and they say to bring her in right away. The staff couldn't have been nicer and they loved Molly, too. The vet examines her and advises that she should stay overnight; they will hydrate her with an intravenous and they will call sometime tomorrow.

It's a strange feeling not to have our Molly at home. She turned thirteen on August 10th. After supper, Angus and I discuss the possibility that Molly might not come home. If she doesn't make it, we decide to take her ashes to Lake Cowichan on Vancouver Island, a place she loves.

I go to the shop on Monday, hoping to go visit Molly in the hospital. Late afternoon, I get a call saying she is ready to be picked up. I'm very excited and call Angus to give him the good news. When I get there, here she comes, tail just a going, as she crosses the floor and we greet each other. The receptionist goes over the procedures they performed on Molly and it sure seemed to work really well. We are so excited to have her home.

Going through the mail, when we get home from vacation, I find a letter from the Cross Cancer Radiation Unit, with my impending radiation schedule. I begin on August 30th and the treatments run for sixteen days in a row, minus weekends. The staff is so nice, always respectful, and they make you feel comfortable. I don't seem to have any side effects, other than I get tired easily. I do go to the shop all through the treatments and feel fine.

After my treatments are finished, we decide to take Molly for a trip to Lake Cowichan. We were going to take her ashes, so why not take her, while she is still with us. At the end of September, the three of us head to the Island. It's a beautiful fall trip, the colors and fresh clean air, wonderful. This is Molly's trip and we stop a lot to take her for refreshing walks and she loves every minute. We arrive at Maggie and John's after the two-day trip. We celebrate our forty-eighth anniversary. Ian just turned forty and Quinn is nine.

It's a nice Christmas, but Angus and I notice Molly just doesn't have the usual energy that she once had. Opening her Christmas gifts by herself were always met with a lot of enthusiasm, tackling each gift with zest, shaking the package while gripped strongly in her jaws, and playing with them for quite a while after opening them. This year she had to be coaxed by Quinn to open them and she lost interest soon after.

Over the last year or so, Molly hasn't been sleeping well. She gets up around four in the morning. Angus and I take turns getting up with her, Angus, most times. It's a very quiet time and I get a lot of writing done. When Angus gets up with her, he feeds her and they sit together on Angus's recliner, where Molly promptly falls asleep between his legs and Angus can't go back to sleep, once he is awake.

We take Molly to the vet she has been going to since we moved in 2005. They love her there and always announce to everyone when she comes in. "Molly's here, hello Molly," and that makes her tail wag. The vet does a few tests and Molly is put on, yet, another mediation. Age is catching up to her and the vet says she probably won't get better and that it's up to us to decide when it's time, 'to let her go.'

It's January 2017 and Molly is still on the chicken, rice, and pumpkin for her tummy. She is losing control of her bowels quite frequently and she hates it and of course, she is confused to what is wrong. I'm having a heck of a time trying to give her the medications. I try fooling her and stick a pill in a piece of meat and that works a couple of times. I also try peanut butter and she just licks the peanut butter off the pill. I try mixing them up with her food, but when she's finished eating, the pills are at the bottom of the bowl, not good.

Quinn was with Molly on Friday and I did explain to her that Molly isn't well. On Saturday, before Quinn left with Ian, she gave Molly a lot of hugs and kisses. The two of them have a very special bond and this will be hard for Quinn. Later that same day, we decide it's time. I call the vet and we make the arrangements for Monday, February 6th. Angus stays with her on Saturday night and then, on the Sunday night, I sleep on the couch and keep her company. She is very restless, off and on her bed, she goes outside and gets turned around. Since she was a pup, she has slept with us, in between the two of us. For the last month, she has been too restless and prefers sleeping downstairs on her day bed.

I had cooked a pork roast and had left overs in the fridge. I sliced off a pretty big piece, cut it into bite size pieces, and called Molly. I fed her one piece, at a time, until it was all gone and she loved it, no hidden pills to work around.

At nine o'clock the next morning, Angus carried Molly to the car wrapped in her favorite blanket. I drove to the vets. We had made arrangements ahead of time, so we didn't have to stop at the front desk to do any paperwork. That worked out great, we walked in and the vet directed us to a room, already set up. I'm very proud of Angus and I, because Angus held her in his arms, while the injection was going in and I held her little face in my hands, whispering, "It's okay sweetheart, it's okay," and as her little head slowly rested in my hands, she was gone, so peaceful, so final. As long as I live, I will never forget that moment. We did it, we held ourselves together for Molly; she was relaxed and left this world in such a calm state.

On the same day we said goodbye to Molly, we received a message from Angus' cousin, Heather, informing us that her Dad, being Angus' Uncle Hughie, had passed away the previous evening, he was ninety years young. She will call again, when the family has more information on the service.

Uncle Hughie, the youngest brother in Angus' Dad's family. Everybody loved Uncle Hughie, he had a great sense of humor, loved the outdoors, and fishing. He was a real teaser, too, like his brother, Don, Angus' Dad. He was quick witted and enjoyed a good laugh.

This is funny; Hughie flew to Victoria to visit Dad from Lacombe, Alberta, where he and Marybelle raised their five children, Heather, Shannon, Rod, Keltie, and Casey. Dad loaded up his motorhome and the two of them drove up island to do some camping and fishing.

On the way, Hughie offers to 'gas up' the motorhome. Dad pulls over at a gas station and Hughie insists, "He's got this." Dad neglected to tell Hughie that the motorhome had two tanks. "Yikes," That was quite the bill Hughie paid and Dad just laughed.

Another time; the two of them were driving in the motorhome and Dad got tired of having to repeat himself, so he says to Hughie, "For God's sake, Hughie, you can't hear a blessed thing I'm saying to you."

"No, I can't, Don". "How about lending me one of those hearing aids you got?"

Dad takes the left hearing aid out and hands it over. Hughie sticks it in his left ear, "Fits pretty good," he says. So, Dad's driving with the right one and Hughie's the passenger wearing the left one, too funny.

On that same fishing trip, Hughie puts on the waterproof fishing pants and heads into the river. He's got a great spot out there, catching one fish after the other, Jack Salmon. He doesn't have anywhere to put the fish, so he sticks them in the fishing pants. A wildlife officer comes along and checks for their licenses. The officer checks Dad's license, all in order. Dad tells him that he and Hughie bought them at the same time, so the officer just yells out to Hughie over the sound of the rushing water, "How's the fishing going?"

"Not worth a damn," Hughie replies, all the while the fishing pants are dancing with live fish and of course, he has over the limit to boot. Whew!

Angus and I just heard this one from Allan on our summer vacation 2018. It goes like this; Uncle Hughie walks up to Allan after Dad's service. "Ya," he says, "I was just wondering what you guys did with your Dad's teeth?"

"What was that Uncle?" Allan says.

"Well, you never know, might just come in handy, if a guy had a spare set."

What a guy, full of it and that will be sorely missed by everyone who knew him.

Oh, have to tell you this one, too! Long time ago, when Hughie and another brother, Rod, were still bachelors, they lived together in downtown Edmonton. They went halfers on a vehicle. Hughie had taken it out one evening and smashed it up. When he walked in the door, Rod says, "Where's the car, Hughie, I didn't hear you pull up?"

"Oh," Hughie answers, "Your half is wrapped around a pole down the street."

And that's the way they were with each other.

While still bachelors, it was Hughie's turn to make supper, so he did and called Rod to the table. Hughie begins scooping out the grub and slaps a spoon full onto Rod's plate.

"What the hell is that?" Rod exclaims.

"Its sardines and beans," was the answer. I tell you, you had to be quick to be around these characters. I looked up a description just to make sure I'm using the right word. Character: the mental and moral qualities distinctive to an individual. Yes, got the right word.

In the early spring, Angus and I drive to Vancouver Island and spread our Molly's ashes on the beach at Lake Cowichan, the place she loved so much.

We leave for Huntington Beach, California. It's April and the weather is wonderful. We stay at a hotel, just across the street from the ocean. The beach is so much fun, lots of activity and we like that. We love to see everybody out and enjoying, it does your heart good. We take our folding chairs, a cooler with a few beers and head over for a relaxing afternoon. Couldn't have been nicer; watching kids running in and out of the water, trying to make sand castles, while their parents relax. Some couples cuddling together and giggling with each other, while others play beach volleyball or fly kites, it's pretty busy. Angus and I are taking it all in. We have made dinner reservations for Angus' birthday at 'Duke's,' a famous seafood restaurant, a few blocks from the hotel, so we better get going.

Once away from the sea breeze, we are feeling very warm, hot, actually. We get back in our room, put our stuff down and I take a look in the mirror, "Yikes, I'm burnt. I take my bathing suit off and I'm as red as a cooked lobster." Angus comes to the mirror, has a look at himself, he is also red, really red. I don't have anything on hand for a burn, so we shower in tepid water and head out, walking to the restaurant for dinner. We stop at a drug store and pick up a can of Solarcaine for the burns. Walking down the street, holding hands, like we always do, when a foursome approaches on the opposite side of the sidewalk. We smile as they pass by and one young fellow says, "You guys look great," with a big engaging smile on his face

"Yes, I bet we do." Giggling as we walk on.

We are seated at a window table overlooking the sea view and the iconic Huntington Beach Pier. It's a beautiful view and we stay until the sunsets on the horizon, lovely.

We return from our evening out, strip off, and spray each other down with the Solarcaine. Our skin is actually hissing and tiny bubbles appear everywhere. We are so burnt it's been a fun-filled day. We lay on the bed stretched out and moaning, can't even stand the sheet touching our bodies. We say good night and drift off to sleep. That was Angus's sixty-ninth birthday and one he won't forget any time soon.

The next day, we take a walk on the pier. It's huge, there are fishermen that line both sides of the pier all the way down and you don't need a fishing license. The pier is 1850 feet in length. At the end of the pier is an all-American diner called Ruby's, the food is delicious and there's plenty of it, too. This is a perfect spot to watch the surfers and the young men and women play volleyball. Sure doesn't take long for an afternoon to fly by.

When we return home from Huntington Beach, I have a mammogram it's the end of April. Same routine, a few days go by and they want to do a biopsy on my left breast. The previous biopsy was on my right breast. Okay, I go, this one is at the Cross Cancer Clinic. Simple enough procedure, but these boobs are starting to bug me, just a little. My regular doctor's office calls, she would like to see me. I go in to her office and Dr. Carter is great. I'm sitting on the chair in the examining room. She comes in and we exchange pleasantries. She brings up the information onto her computer screen, looks over at me, and says in kind of a whispered voice, "Its cancer."

"I kind of thought it might be," I reply.

"It's a stage 1/2 like the last one."

"Says here that the Cross will get you in for surgery as soon as possible."

"If you have any questions or concerns before that, just give me a call, you should hear from them in a couple of weeks for sure."

That was it… here I go again. All I can think of is, it's a damn good thing I don't have three or four of them, wouldn't that be a bitch.

Surgery date is set for May 16th, which would have been my Moms 97th birthday. Angus takes me to the hospital, everything is the same as the first surgery; it feels kind of funny, because in July it will be a year since the right breast surgery, but it feels like yesterday. Everything goes well. I'm to see the surgeon in two weeks for a general checkup. All is well… I'll be fit as a fiddle for our August vacation.

My sister, Sandra, is having a milestone birthday, her sixty-fifth on May 31st. Viv, Sandra, and myself meet for our birthdays every year and have a lunch together. We also get together in December around Christmas, too. We really like this Italian restaurant, not only do they have good food and good service, they let the three of us sit and chat with one another until we are ready to leave, it's nice.

This is a good time to tell you a little bit about my youngest sister. Sandra is a real cutie; she has a big heart and feels good when she is helping others.

186

She is very creative and she makes things that you would get at a craft fair. She is a good decorator and knows what looks good with what. She enjoys shopping, she is an animal lover like Viv and she loves the heat, hotter the better. She has been a hard worker. She worked in a meat packing plant and that was hard, heavy and extremely cold work. Trained in dog grooming, she had her own grooming business for ten years. She is retired now, but with her and Bill renovating their house, there is always a lot to do.

Angus and I go away in the motorhome for a few days at the beginning of June. We have a good time. I'm not golfing yet, too soon after my surgery, so I rest quite a bit, which is good for me. I notice a kind of bubble developing on my left breast, where the incision was. What the hell is this?" I ask myself.

I go see Dr. Carter and she says that the bubble is known as a Seroma. It's not cancer it's not a threat and may take up to a year to go away. Now that I know what it is, I'll look it up. Google says, the formation of a Seroma is the body's response to dead space within tissue that was attached to something before surgery and that they are quite common. It is a buildup of fluid and can become a discomfort.

My radiation treatments are the same, sixteen days straight, minus weekends. By the end of June, I'm finished and ready to carry on.

Sometime in July, Angus and I start going for coffee at McDonald's in the afternoons a couple times a week, depending on how busy we are. We meet up with Russ and Dianne, the couple with the nice place. We really enjoy their company and we have lots of laughs. Sometimes, there are eight of us sitting at the same table; we are the loudest group in there. We have a good time, laughing, joking, and telling stories, it's fun and the people we have met are great. It's a really good way to spend part of your afternoon. This is a social for us, that all started when Angus stopped and met Russ out in his front yard. It does take a while to memorize all of their names and to get to know who belongs with whom, etc. We enjoy the getting together.

One of the first times we go, Angus and I are introduced to everyone who joins the round table. In conversation, reading comes up and I mention that I'm writing my autobiography. Dianne is an avid reader and seems interested, so I ask her if she would like to read what I've done so far. She says yes. It's July 2017 and I started writing January 1st, 2016. After I hand write about ten to fifteen pages, I type the material onto my computer and print out the pages. Angus is my editor; he proof reads to find any typing errors, and generally, tells me if he likes it. I give Dianne a copy of what I have written so far and after a while she gives it back. She finds it very interesting, likes the easy read, and says I have a way with telling a good story and that she laughed a lot. I really appreciate feedback and I have told her to be honest with me, if she falls asleep while reading, she can tell me. She has read pretty much all of it to date and says she hasn't fallen asleep once. Now, that's encouraging, don't you think?

It all starts in January each year, I text Marion and Dave to give them our itinerary. They respond that everything is good on their end. Maggie and John won't be joining us this year; they will spend time with their grandchildren on Vancouver Island. Allan's not sure yet. Come March, I start booking the campsites and pretty soon, it's all done. Marion and Dave do the same.

This August vacation is very different, for the first time in fourteen years Molly is not here with us. About a week before we go, I start the usual routine, making lists of things we need to bring, along with items we just can't forget, like our passports. Angus is very busy getting his stuff done, too. All packed and ready to go. Come morning, we are excited to get down the road. After a couple of days on the road, we get a call from Marion. She explains that Sullivan Lake campground is covered in smoke, too close to a forest fire. They are trying to relocate us to another campground in the general area. Great, I tell Marion whatever is good with them will be fine with us, too. She texts just a little while later and says they have found us a spot in a campground called 'Edge Water,' it's not too far from Sullivan Lake. It is located on a river and that it looks good. I look it up on Google and it really does look good. So, we have a place to camp, that's a relief.

I can't put my finger on this vacation being extra, extra enjoyable with Marion and Dave, but it was one of the best, if not the best vacation so far. The four of us pull into the new assigned campground and love it, absolutely love it. The camping spots are roomy there is a lot of trees in between sites and a very short walk to the river. Marion and Dave have two small dogs, Bella and Pepper. Bella is the eldest at seven and Pepper is six. Bella looks like a Princess all decked out in white thick fur, with a tiny face and pointed ears. She has some black on her head and ears. Bella is a Pom Papillon cross. Pepper is patched with black and white, shorter fur, and floppy ears. Pepper is a Maltese Shih Tzu cross. Both are rascals in a good way, they give lots of love and joy. They love camping. Pepper is a squirrel watcher, she will sit forever and wait at the base of a tree and wait for a squirrel to come down, but most times, the squirrel just jumps to another tree and gets away.

The river is wonderful, it's wide, and long enough to look like a lake and the current is perfect. There isn't a smell to this water, absolutely pristine, you come out after a swim and can't smell or feel anything on your skin. We stay at the river pretty much all day. The guys go down to the beach area and start clearing away debris, rearranging rocks, and basically making us a beach area. We start hauling 'stuff' around eleven thirty in the morning. After the chairs, umbrellas, coolers, towels, munchies, and beer are at the beach, we hit the water. The dogs love it, too, and they go in for a swim to get cooled off, each being held by Marion and Dave. The weather is around 30 degrees Celsius, which is 90 degrees Fahrenheit it's perfect for playing in the water. Around six thirty or seven in the early evening, we head back to camp. Now that it's cooler, we make our suppers and get together after to visit, have a drink or two, and talk about the day. Sometimes, we take turns in hosting a supper, not anything too fussy, but food always seems to taste better when someone else prepares it. I wonder why that is? We pretty much have the same routine for seven nights and we agree that the time has gone by too fast and we could actually stay longer.

We pull out and head for Deer Park, WA, a small town about a twenty-minute drive from Spokane, WA. The town is nice, it's clean, has everything you need, and still has that small town feel to it. The RV/Golf Resort is not too big, clean, has full hookups, laundry facility, a swimming pool, hot tub, and a recreation building open to all.

Have to tell you this story from one of our previous vacation stops here at Deer Park. Through texting, we decide to bring some games to play. We brought a bingo game, with a rotary cage, and an automatic random ball selector, numbered balls from 1-75, along with bingo cards and bingo chips or tokens. We choose a bingo night and we all head to the recreation building to play. There is Allan, Marion, Dave, Maggie, John, and Angus. I'm the caller. Well, we have so much fun, laughing and joking around and you can hear us outside the building. A guy pops in, soaking wet and wearing nothing but his swim trunks with a towel wrapped around his neck. In a very enthusiastic voice, he says, "I didn't know there was bingo here, is there bingo here every Tuesday night?"

"No, no, this is just a family bingo night," was the response.

"Oh, too bad," he says, "Sounds like you're having a great time. I'll leave you to it." We say good night to him and carry on. That was so funny, the expression on the guys face when he first opened the door, was priceless, he was so excited and then we had to let him down. Dave said maybe next year we should post a bingo night and open it up for all to come. Haven't done that yet, but maybe, some time we will, good idea.

Right next to the RV Park is a lovely golf course with a driving range. We do some golfing there. While Angus and Dave are away golfing, Marion and I have a reading session with my book, we laugh and we cry. We have known each other, since we were teenagers. I was born at the beginning of 1949, in February and Marion was born at the end of 1949, in December. We get along really well I wish we lived closer to one another. I love her company, her enthusiasm for life, her smile, her laughter, and she has a nice voice, too. She is also kind, generous, and has a loving heart. When we are together, we are natural with one another and that is wonderful.

We take Marion and Dave out for dinner to celebrate their 50th wedding anniversary. The next day, the four of us say our good byes; we really don't want this vacation to end.

Angus and I head north to Barriere in British Columbia to Chinook Cove, where we will spend a week before leaving for home. We meet a nice couple there, Kathleen and Larry. We have a few happy hours together and we really enjoy their company. They have a cute older dog, named Tippsie, I believe she was about twelve at that time. Larry golfs while Kathleen likes to read. The three of us golf a few times together and it's fun. We do keep in touch.

Getting home towards the end of August is always busy. Angus has lots to do outside and I have catching up to do at the shop. September is here, Quinn turns ten on the fifth, Ian turns forty-one on the twenty-third, and we are married forty-nine years on the twenty-eighth.

Don't you just hate it when the telephone rings either too early in the morning *or* too late at night? Something's not right. This phone call comes in the morning, around eight-thirty, and it's Maggie, Angus's sister from Nanaimo. I feel it before I answer it's not good. Maggie lets us know that Dave has had a very serious emergency surgery for an abdominal aortic aneurysm, known as an AAA. He is alive, but the surgeon can't believe it, almost no one survives, especially in the condition Dave arrived at the hospital. His aorta had been leaking for at least a couple of days before the condition was diagnosed. Because of the weather, he couldn't be flown, so they drove him by ambulance from Castlegar to Kelowna, British Columbia, about a three-and-a-half-hour trip. Very dangerous ride, because the aorta could have ruptured at any time along the way.

It was touch and go for days after the surgery. Marion didn't leave his side. She and a very close friend, who happens to be in the medical field, went with her from Nelson to Kelowna. She was a great help, because she explained all the medical terms to Marion, so she could make sense of it all. As the days and nights passed, we were all so worried. He did gradually get better and better and he made it home for Christmas. After having such a great time in August, it just seemed unbelievable. Just goes to show you how fast these hic-cups can happen to anyone, at any time. Dave has made a full recovery; we all couldn't be happier for them.

Winter sees us through to another year 2018. My Seroma hasn't gotten any smaller in fact it's bigger now. I see my oncologist at the end of March. She doesn't like it and suggests I make an appointment to see the surgeon and have it drained. Well, I tell her that's a good idea, because it is uncomfortable, but I'm going away in April, so I'll have to do that when Angus and I get back.

We leave for California in April, before Angus' birthday. We head straight to Huntington Beach. This trip, we spend a lot more time there and we are busy doing something different every day.

We go to the beach, it's the same as last year, lots of fun, lots of activity and it's hot, too. We don't get burnt this time; lesson learned. Some of our memorable moments are going to Chip Foose Auto Design shop and taking a tour, meeting Chip, and buying some souvenirs to take home. Foose Designs have won so many awards over the years, you will have to Google, it's fascinating.

Going to the 'Sugar Shack' café on Main Street. What an experience, best breakfast in town. The café is open seven days a week from 5:30 am to 3:00pm. While waiting for our breakfast, a couple came in and sat at the table next to ours. We pass pleasantries and the fellow says he has been coming to the Sugar Shack for breakfast every day for over thirty years. He tells us the history.

The café opened in 1967 and at that time, the area was booming. There were a lot of workers looking for a place for breakfast, so Sugar Shack opened their doors at 5:30 each morning to serve them. Even today, the café is open for breakfast and lunch only. As the story goes, the original owner was a single mom, raising five girls on her own. She worked and worked and eventually, was able to send all five girls to College. I tried every site available and I could not find the history, so I'm very thankful to that fellow. He himself grew up in the neighborhood and still lives in the same house that belonged to his parents. I'm guessing this fellow was our age, sixty-five or so, he said he was retired from a career in construction and house building. I bet we will see him next year at the Sugar Shack.

Going to In and Out Burgers for lunch is always busy, busy and we enjoy that. All the servers are young, dressed in red and white, they are eager, they smile at you, and that does your heart good. The whole place is red and white, refreshing, the music's playing, it's a very UP experience. So, if you're grumpy and are having a bad day, stay home, until you feel better.

While there an older couple sit down next to us. The woman is a small petite lady of Cuban decent and she was very interesting. Her partner was a very pleasant, soft-spoken gentleman, and hard of hearing. I said something to him and she answered for him and said he was hard of hearing. I told her that I wear hearing aids and she points to me and indicates to him by sticking her fingers in her own ears that I wear hearing aids, he just smiled at me and shrugged. She says he is too damn vain and it's driving her crazy. She asked where we were staying and said she lives just a few blocks from our hotel. She gave us her address *and* invited us over for a visit. She was very friendly, keeping herself fit, looking after her grandchildren after school each day; a real whirlwind and full of energy. She is very thankful to be in America. Together with her husband, they fled Cuba in the sixties, landed in California and before the day was done, he had a job washing dishes. They went on with their lives and always stayed in California. Sadly, he passed away. I do remember her address, so maybe we will visit on our next trip.

Going to Sancho's Tacos a small eatery, just down from our hotel, with very good food, is an experience. They have tables outside where six or eight people can sit and enjoy. Just across the street, you have a beautiful view of the sea and beach. Again, you see people coming and going, walking in swimsuits, carrying coolers, Frisbees, and Surf Boards, enjoying everything around them, it's great.

There is a bench, where maybe three people can sit at one time. We pass this bench on our way to and from the hotel. One day, we stop for a coffee and a sweet at a coffee shop that's located right beside Sancho's. We take our eats outside and sit across from the bench. Three fellows are engaged in conversation, they node and we say hello. Soon, Angus joins in with their conversation, laughing and joking is definitely a priority. The next day, we go back for lunch and the same three fellows are on the bench. We didn't stop, but pleasantries were passed back and forth. Angus told them they were just as ugly today as they were yesterday and that got them laughing. Next visit, we will definitely be checking out Sancho's and the bench.

Before we leave on our trip, Angus searches the web and finds out that a car club known as the Donut Derelicts meet at Adams Avenue Donut Shop in Huntington Beach, every Saturday morning from six thirty to eight thirty. They started meeting in 1986 for a coffee and a donut, while taking their cars out for a cruise. Soon, the gathering caught on and now, there are lots of car enthusiasts that come out to enjoy the cars, talk with the owners, have a coffee and let's not forget the donuts. I had a Cronut the last time we were in HB, so while we are taking in the car show, we go into the coffee shop and our mouths drop open. You just can't imagine how much pastry there is in that shop. Tons of it, Cronuts, too, and it's going out the doors as fast as they can serve it up. This is a favorite spot; we will definitely be making another stop here. The car show is just an excuse for the guys to get together and the donuts well… they are the icing on the cake.

While in HB, you will find there is no shortage of diverse foods. There are lots and lots of places with lots and lots of choices. It's a fun, fun place to visit, it feels safe, people are friendly, traffic is not too busy any time of the day, and the air is so fresh. You can park at your hotel and walk to so many venues, it's great.

After celebrating Angus' seventieth birthday at 'Dukes,' we head for home. We have had a very satisfying week. We did a lot, found a really nice golf-course for next year in Costa Mesa, had a great breakfast there, went shopping, enjoyed the beach, went to a Seadoo competition, went to a car show, met the famous Chip Foose, met some interesting people, and ate some good grub. We laughed and laughed and are still talking about our stay. Next year, we will go to Catalina Island, looking forward to that, because we will be back.

While driving through Idaho Falls, we decide to stay, the weather is perfect and we haven't had enough vacation yet. We stay at a hotel with nice rooms, friendly staff, and an American Diner next door. The locals are telling us that the falls this year are running extremely fast and they are something to see. We go take a look, it's not Niagara Falls, by any means, but there is a hell of a lot of water. It's a very pretty setting and well worth the stop. Originally, the water was known as 'The Rapids,' below the town's bridge. Some years later, a retaining wall was constructed for a hydroelectric power plant, which enhanced the rapids into falls.

Dixie's Diner is a must. This place has a very good selection of sixties comfort food, as well as the whole diner is retro, back to the 50s and 60s style. The music is great, the staff wants to be there, the place is cozy, and welcoming, especially at night, with their neon lighting. They serve up a tasty, satisfying breakfast, lunch, and dinner. We will definitely spend a few days in Idaho Falls again. Sounds like we eat a lot, well, not a lot, just often! LOL! Isn't that a big part of any holiday, getting away and doing things you don't normally do at home?

We arrive home and spring has sprung. I contact my surgeon's office, as suggested by my oncologist, for an appointment. It has been a year since my left breast surgery was done, I see the surgeon on May 8th and she drains the Seroma and extracts 200cc's, that's approximately seven ounces of fluid. I'm concerned about infection, but she says not to worry, "I won't get infection."

Famous last words, I do 'get infection.' At the end of May, the breast is drained again. I'm put on five days of antibiotics and I have to go to the hospital every two days for the surgeon to drain the breast of accumulating infected fluid. Another five days of antibiotics and it's under control. A couple of weeks go by, I have a very sensitive area where the surgeon had to drain the same area over and over again. That procedure has left the skin almost transparent, because, now, the original incision has split. There is a small bubble and I'm scared it will get bigger, just like the Seroma did. On June 27th, I'm booked for surgery. The surgeon explains to me that the skin will never heal, so she will open up the original incision that has split, then she will clean it up and pull the two sides of the incision together, stitch the area and that will be it. Okay, let's do it.

This is not good. After the surgery, I go back as instructed after a two-week period to have the stitches removed. A few of the stitches have 'over grown,' and because of that, she has to pull so hard that two of the stitches are ripped out. That leaves an opening, it's bleeding, but she puts a bandage over it and says, "It will stop bleeding."

Yes, it did stop bleeding, but it was very annoying because after a few days, that opening and a couple more started to leak this clear, yellow liquid and it was sticky. I can't go in the pool for fear of another infection, so July goes by with me wearing bandages during the day and airing the area overnight, hoping it will form a crust and heal up. Now, it's close to holiday time and eighty percent of it is spent in and around the water. I'm concerned, actually panic is a better word, so I go see my regular physician. She ensures me that the sticky residue is a normal healing process and gives me a prescription for antibiotics, in case I get into trouble, while away on vacation.

We leave on July 30th and the damn thing weeps the whole time. I wear waterproof bandages in the river, but I just can't take a chance on the swimming pool at Deer Park, I've had enough.

We do have a good time. Allan joins us this year. It was so good to see Dave doing so well after his near-death experience last December with his AAA. Marion and I get our annual read time in with my book and that's always good, she enjoys it and so do I. The two of us go out for a day of shopping and of course, we stop for lunch. Angus and I are taken out for dinner to celebrate our 50th anniversary coming up and that was very nice.

We arrive home on August 25th, after twenty-seven days on the road and the left breast finally stopped weeping on August 23rd. Wow!

Quinn turns eleven on September 5th and she finally gets a puppy of her own. 'Honey' is a Havanese, a really cute ball of fluff. After she gets her shots, Quinn will bring her for a visit. We are so excited for Quinn and for us, too. A lively puppy around the house again will be welcoming for sure.

It's September 21st, Angus is busy getting the fall chores done. I go pick Quinn up from school. When Angus comes in from a day outside, he complains of really sharp pains in his mid-section. Angus has a little dinner with us, but can't stay up sitting, so he goes to bed early. This is the first time Quinn has experienced Grandpa not feeling well. Ian comes on Saturday; Angus comes downstairs and has a very light lunch with us and then heads back to bed. It's Ian's birthday on Sunday and we have planned a nice supper for him and

Quinn. Ian says if I don't want to make dinner, it's okay, but I've already purchased everything fresh, so I'll go ahead and make his birthday dinner.

Quinn and Ian return on Sunday, we have our dinner but without Grandpa, he can't even stand the smell of the roast cooking. A short while after they leave, Angus comes downstairs fully dressed and ready to go to the hospital. I know this is serious. I have known Angus for fifty-three years and never once has he been in bed, ill.

The pain is escalating, so by the time we get him checked in and they start taking a blood sample, his pain level has gone from a six to a ten. They take X-rays and do a CT scan. Everything goes pretty fast, the results are in, it's a twisted bowel and emergency surgery is strongly recommended, we can't wait. The surgeon comes in and explains the procedure, Angus says, "Let's do it, the sooner the better."

Within forty minutes, the surgeon has gathered an operating team. Angus is being prepped. A nurse comes in and inserts a long tube into Angus' nose that travels down to the bowel. When a small amount of air is pumped into the tube, this green, yucky stuff comes up through the tube and empties into a container behind his head. I'm watching this and the container fills to the 500 cc's, that's about seventeen ounces, before it starts to slow down.

At ten to one in the morning, they take Angus into surgery. The surgeon suggests I go home, because he doesn't know how long the surgery will be. He will call me later.

Well, I get home, of course, I can't sleep, so I start writing and pretty soon, I flop over on the couch and fall asleep. I'm woken by the telephone, it's the surgeon, everything went well and he will explain when he sees me. I can see Angus any time it's three-thirty in the morning.

Sometimes in life, you don't have time to consider, to analyze, to prepare, to get educated, to get scared, to even get your thoughts together, and maybe, just sometimes, that's a good thing. Another hic-cup in life, I'm scared now that the surgery is over, I know it went well, but how is he going to be?

I get myself ready and head over to the hospital. A ten-minute drive from the house and today, I'm thankful for that. I walk in and the room is dark and quiet, the curtains are pulled closed all around him. I take a deep breath and peek around to see him. He is resting, the tube is still up his nose and this time, the yucky stuff is brown and you can hear gurgling noises coming from the tube. I touch his leg and his eyes open. He is still very sleepy. After just a few minutes, the surgeon comes, we shake hands, and I thank him very much for everything. He goes over the operation with both of us. Angus is very fortunate, because the surgeon was able to untwist the bowel it then began to regain its 'pinkish' color the surgeon's job was done. It will be a four to six-week recovery relaxing and not lifting any weight is an essential part of healing. Angus goes into the hospital on Ian's forty-second birthday and returns homes on our fiftieth anniversary, September 28th.

Angus is home we are so pleased they were able to fix him up, because according to the web, it could have been a lot worse. I tend to his blisters that he got from the tape that was holding on his bandages. Every day they get a little better, but it does take a few weeks before they clear up. We go to Angus' regular doctor to have his staples removed. Ouch, the doctor pulls most out, but it's another week before they are all out. Angus has started his fifth week of recovery it's October twenty-first. He is now doing a few light chores around the acreage and he did vacuum for me today, so he is definitely coming along.

We were planning a trip to Vancouver Island before this happened. We were to leave the morning of September 27th I had made hotel reservations for along the way and even had the suitcases upstairs, ready to fill. Oh well, we will have to go next year. I'm very thankful that the surgery happened, while we were still at home.

This weekend, on October 19th, we have Quinn for a sleepover. She brings Honey with her. An adorable little puppy, so much fun we have with her. We let Quinn know that she can bring Honey anytime she likes. It was so nice to have a lively puppy in the house again. She will bring Quinn lots of love, just like our first beagle, Polly, brought to Ian. It's Sunday, October 21st, we are meeting Russ and Dianne for coffee this afternoon.

I have always said that it has been my intention to stop writing 'when my book catches up with my life' and it has.

I will end my book, as I have ended everyday now for so many years. Angus and I get into bed. The lights are all off. I lean over to Angus and say, "Goodnight, Hon, I love you."

"Goodnight, Hon, love you, too," he responds.

We kiss. I lie down and get settled.

"Goodnight, Ian's Dad."

"Goodnight, Ian's Mom."

JUST A FEW THINGS I'D LIKE TO SAY:

I have a few regrets, because I wasn't strong or I was embarrassed or the timing wasn't right. I really regret not going with Angus and my sister Vivian, when they identified my Mom's body. I can't honestly say I would have looked at her, but I would have put my hand under the blanket to just touch her hair for the last time and to say goodbye.

I regret not speaking at a few funeral services I have attended. When they ask if anyone would like to share a story with those gathered to celebrate the life. After all, that's why we are all gathered, to share stories.

I regret not telling my Mom and Dad that I loved them, and that really bothers me. I know they knew, but not to tell them occasionally was wrong. I'm making up for that now, as I never leave our son, Ian, without giving him a hug and a kiss *and* telling him, "I love you."

That goes the same with Angus, too.

I regret not asking questions about my Mom and Dad's earlier lives. Of course, over the years growing up, you find out the 'basics' of their lives, but I mean the real close to their heart stuff. My Dad was a submarine detector for the Navy during the Second World War, so handsome in his uniform and my Mom worked for Northwest Industries, making airplane parts, so cute in her white coveralls with her hair tucked in a scarf and knotted at the front. They are gone now and I will never know.

I regret not taking the time, out of my own busy life, to keep in touch with close friends and now, I only see them at the occasional wedding or funeral, so sad. They may feel exactly as I do. There are a couple that we see three or four times a year, to share a laugh about old times, have a meal, and enjoy each other's company and to catch up on their kids and grandkids now! How time goes by. I'm sure there are a few more regrets, but those are the ones that mean the most to me.

HIC-CUPS: I put 'hic-cups' in the title of my book, because, to me, it means a break in your life's rhythm, it's something that catches you off guard, an interruption. You hold your breath. A hic-cup is usually something that is negative; it knocks you down, makes you struggle to get up, but doesn't totally destroy you. A devastating fire destroying everything you hold dear. Any number of national disasters like, floods, tornados, hurricanes, there is so much that can happen to and in one's life. It could be an unsuspecting death, a life-threatening disease, and unwanted pregnancy, a divorce. Spiritually and emotionally, you are tested, but not ruined. You pull yourself together, gain strength in thought, and succeed in dealing with the situation at hand. That ability to respond to our hic-cups in life is harbored in each and every one of us.

THE NEXT CHAPTER: You won't read in detail. This chapter will come soon enough. Angus and I have spoken at length concerning our next move in life. We know we will not stay on the acreage, for many reasons. We know we will have to be in a secure and safe environment for our well -being. At this time, I can't say we are looking forward to the challenge, as our wants and needs, will be hic-cups that will have to be ironed out. As a couple, we have always worked issues and situations out, and have come to very positive results. I'm not worried, together Angus and I will be fine. It has been said, "Once one door closes, another will open," and this next chapter will be exciting for both of us.

POST-SCRIPT: I would be amiss without telling you about the area that Angus and I live in now and have been since 2005. It's a really lovely setting with 22 acreages, and each one is over an acre in size and there is plenty of space between them. We have had thirteen years of pretty much, dead quiet here. There is a ball park at the end of the road from us, but we never hear anything from there and if we did, it would be people having a good time and that's an okay noise. Our neighbors have been friendly and we have gotten to know a few, over the years. Our closest neighbor to the north of us is Grace and her daughter, Ashley, her sister, Amber, is living in New York City with her partner, Nick, they are architects. Over the years Grace and I and Angus have had many visits back and forth for tea, to share a meal, or to spend the afternoon during the Christmas holiday season, lovely. We have also been invited to other neighbors and have enjoyed them very much. George and Lila, a really nice couple that we have gotten to know. George is in his ninety-third year and Lila is in her eighty-sixth year. They have been married for sixty-nine years, as long as I have been alive. They are great people, always welcoming you for a visit, sometimes for coffee, along with homemade baked goods, and other times, to share a meal. Usually, when we stop at George and Lila's for a visit, it can be from three to five hours and it never seems that long until you leave and wonder where the time went. Both are doing well and they are truly an inspiration. Angus and I have hosted a few meals too, as well as having a few in for tea in the afternoon. We had quite a few neighbors over for a bonfire, one evening, and we devoured a lot of chili that night, along with a few spirits to keep us warm in the cool autumn air.

We have walked our Molly down the road that passes in front of the acreages for years, and there were lots of waves and neighbors pulling over for a pet and to say hello. Quinn loves it here; she is so comfortable when she comes. We have been here for all of her life she really enjoys it. Stability is a very good thing. This home has been a very good one for Angus and I.

Summary of 'My Rhythm in Life with Hic-Cups'

I started writing my autobiography on January 1, 2016 and finished on October 21, 2018, that's approximately 2 years and 9 months. The purpose of writing my story, as I said in the introduction, is because I have wanted to write about my life for a long time now, call it an 'itch.' Over the years, I have read quite a few autobiographies and biographies, mostly about famous people. I have enjoyed the autobiographies the best, because they are written by the person and not by somebody else. The autobiographies are told in truth and for me, a story that is real, that has real characters, and tells of real emotions, and happenings in their lives, is not only touching but you can learn so much from them.

In my story, I take you from my birth in February 1949 to now, October 2018. When you read in detail, my experiences in life, you will laugh out loud, you will cry, and you hopefully, will be amazed at how much I remember. I do say, "It's the memories that have kept my memory sharp," and there have been so many. I start with the love of family, my maternal Grandparents, and how I cried when my Nanny left the room, because as a small child, I thought she was leaving and she was only going to the bathroom. I tell of my unusual family upbringing and of our generous and giving parents, who share their home with so many children over the years and how emotional it is when tragedy strikes without warning. The strength we must find within ourselves to make it through and how profound it has been over the years.

I'm sixty-nine years old and in that time, I have lost too many people that have meant so much and yet, I have gained so much in knowing them. You will learn of them. You will read some really funny stories about Angus and I. One where we get stuck on our wedding night, when the neon light flashing 'Open,' was our only option, six bucks for room number six. I tell of stories that will have you laughing out loud and you will want to tell them to your friends. There is one when a father comes looking for his son, who is employed by us, and Angus tells him he's down the street. The father becomes confused, scratching his head, and wanders what the kids doing down there.

I give you an insight into our son's upbringing and how busy our lives were then with his hockey and BMX years, and the fun we had. For twenty-six years, we lived on Vancouver Island, and you will read of our camping adventures, that we all enjoyed so much.

You will read of a personal, life-threatening disease, a battle that had to be won, because there was no alternative. You will read that the battle had to be fought not only once, but three times. Hopefully, you will gain knowledge and find strength in how I handled the dreaded 'C' word.

In our family business, you will read about some of our customers that had some awkward moments and how we managed to get them through. Funny accidents, is there such a thing? Yes, there is. Like the time an elderly gentleman struck his garage so hard it came off its foundation and how a sweet little old lady and her sister felt a tap of some kind and when they got home, they couldn't get out of the car.

You will learn a thing or two about how to organize a move. There were five properties involved, at one time; it's a piece of cake, right?

In writing my life's story, I really want the reader to become inspired. I hope my stories will encourage the reader to start thinking about their own life and how much life means. All of us are in this life together, we truly mean something We don't have to be famous, we don't have to be rich and powerful in the world, we just have to be the best we can be for our families and the people we choose to be with, while we are in this world. Yes?

Finally, I must tell you that from day one of writing, it has always been my intention to stop when my book caught up to my life and it did. It just happened to be perfect timing because I'm healed, Angus is healing, and we have been married for fifty years, a milestone. Our son, Ian, at forty-two, has married Claire, a lovely gal from England. All of our family members are in good health and all of our friends are in good health, so cheers to everyone and I wish you all the very best...that life has to offer.

My Rhythm in Life Is Good ... Really Good!

THE ETERNAL RHYTHM OF LIFE SYMBOL